# NEVER
# LAURA

### EWGENIYA
### LYRAS

HAY PRESS

## HAY PRESS

*an imprint of*
## RENARD PRESS LTD

124 City Road
London EC1V 2NX
United Kingdom
info@renardpress.com
020 8050 2928

www.haypress.co.uk

*Never Laura* first published by Hay Press in 2023

Text © Ewgeniya Lyras, 2023

Cover design by Will Dady

Printed in the United Kingdom by Severn

ISBN: 978-1-80447-038-1

9 8 7 6 5 4 3 2 1

# NEVER
## LAURA

# 1

---

Nobody told me why I should live; I would have to find out on my own.

I had no idea what killed those three billion people – made them jump from skyscrapers and bridges, hang or drown themselves, take pills, cut veins, put plastic bags over their heads. Whatever made them do it spared me. I tried to die – it didn't let me. What a waste. I didn't need to live; I had no friends, and my parents didn't love me enough to stay alive. I hated them; I hated this world.

The third wave of the suicide pandemic was over, but even now, years later, there were still plenty of cases and no official explanation. The Church blamed people and machines; people blamed machines and the Government; and after a few sloppy statements, the Government refrained from blaming anyone – they didn't know what was going on. People took their own lives without a reason. Theories proliferated, involving aliens, viruses, AI, parallel worlds, autocrats and other antagonists, keeping people entertained but on edge.

I was on edge because every day I woke up in the world I hated, and every day I had to find something, usually a new fixation – a new source of mayhem to help me push through the existing pain.

\* \* \*

Black night primed the canvas of the city and neon lights painted the portrait of its drunken soul. The pinks and purples bled through my windows, filling the apartment with rich magenta. Looking at my reflection in the floor-length mirror, I thought about the hidden ad for *Dirty Castle* and the experience of *ultimate freedom* they sold there.

*Transcend the limitations of your body. Free yourself from the boundaries of your mind.*

The delayed targeted ad, which probably came with drugs I'd taken yesterday, played in my head. It showed a woman lying on a bed, eyes closed. Euphoria parted her full lips – and they were the most delicious lips I'd ever seen. I wanted whatever she was experiencing, whatever made these lips so hypnotic. A wreath of energy hovered over her, illuminating her amber skin with turquoise and purple light. Her freckled face zoomed into the forefront of my field of vision as the voice continued.

*Discover your true nature. Find out who you really are.*

The visual was fading. Like any other hidden ad, it felt like a dream that I would forget – unless I thought about it long enough to let it convince me I needed what it offered.

I thought about it.

I'd try anything that promised to free me from the prison of my body and its memories – although, of course, none of these promises were ever fulfilled. My purpose in life was to find one that eventually would. It was my entertainment, it kept me busy. I didn't have the slightest idea what the experience in this particular ad was – a drug, some new tech, or a mix of both – but in my mind I had already created an image of how something would shift in my brain, a secret door would open, and I would see in myself something very different to what I saw in the mirror. I was such an easy target for scammers, but I didn't mind. Death never scared me – it didn't want me – and the lack of fear took me out to the streets, which grew darker and more dangerous with each new attempt to liberate myself from myself. At this point, I didn't necessarily want to die, but to see where my exploration would lead. And in this city there were no limits.

I put on a strappy silk dress, red lipstick and a black woollen coat, and walked out of my building. A police bot stopped in front of me. Green laser beams fanned out from a rectangular glass surface where human eyes would have been and swept across my features – a random check. It thanked me for my cooperation and rolled off down the street on its single wheel, its head rotating from side to side, the web of green light catching the identities of strangers.

More and more police robots guarded this for-ever-lost place, and as theories about machines stealing our souls spread, more and more people resisted them. I didn't mind the bots – they were just heaps of metal, and besides, they were everywhere now. A third of the world's population had killed themselves; the other two thirds were either suicidal or permanently high, scared out of their minds. Someone had to feed those still living, cut our hair, serve us drinks, synthesise our drugs, maintain our roads and build our cars, fix our teeth and replace valves in our hearts, write poetry and music for our souls and make all sorts of executive decisions. These robots probably didn't like being here either, watching us, their creators, excel in self-destruction – that sight would depress anyone, even a thing with no heart.

Under my feet wet asphalt glittered. It was autumn. It always drizzled at night at this time of year. A group of young people – two girls and three boys – passed by me, juggling chatter and giggles. Their eyes had barely dried from daytime tears, but their minds were already rescued from reality by their drug of choice. One of the boys turned around, called me beautiful and sent me an air kiss. No, nothing could mask the lack of life in human eyes, not laughter or air kisses, not sequin dresses or red leather trousers and all the rebellious sex drive bursting from underneath them. Not even skin screens, which were supposed to make you feel more alive in a body that was less your own. Like animals in the zoo, we all looked the same – different faces, different expressions, extravagant clothes and otherworldly prosthetics, but always the same lifeless substance animated for the night with alcohol or drugs.

'Come with us!' yelled the boy. Snake scales glistened on his face.

For a moment I considered it. Habit, I suppose. But tonight I was going to find out how to *free myself from the boundaries of my mind* – sex and alcohol would have to wait. I kept my hopes high. *Ultimate freedom* was what every fraud promised, and I had met many, tried what they offered, and always remained disappointed – and yet, I hoped that this one would deliver. Then again, I had hoped that all of them would; I was addicted to this state of anticipation. The interval between the expectation and disappointment was where I lived. It wasn't a bad place to be, I thought, considering the alternative was a continuous homogenous numbness.

I turned the corner into a side street. It was narrow and dark – no neon signs, no holo-banners; only a few old-fashioned wall-mounted yellow lights. In a noodle shop across the road, a bot in a white chef's bandana spun a thick snake of dough. The storage room in the back probably led to a themed bar that led to a VR sex club that was connected to another spot, and another and another. The whole city was a web of clubs within clubs within clubs – a subway system of its own. Once you started down this road, you'd be lucky to get out within a few days. This rich nightlife infrastructure catered to the recently developed segment of orphans, both the young and the grown-up like me – although I didn't feel like an adult. I was twenty-six, but mentally I was stuck in an indefinite ageless state. What did it even mean to grow up when there was no childhood to begin with?

I kept walking.

And there it was – *Dirty Castle* – a small, distressed sign, barely readable, on a rusty metal door. You didn't knock on these kinds of doors, you waited. You stood there, acting cool and feeling lucky to have found a gem like this, and waited for as long as it took. It was a place that offered something you hadn't yet dreamed of. And whatever it was, it wasn't cheap.

After waiting for fifteen minutes – a critical point when they'd had time to scan my retina, get information on my bank accounts and find out that I lived on a humble monthly allowance paid out of my trust fund – I faced one of the cameras on the right above the door and sucked my middle finger: a gesture that said I didn't give a damn what happened to me and was ready to strike any bargain.

In a few moments the door opened.

A bouncer dressed in a black suit gestured me in. At the end of a corridor, another guard eyed me up and down and pointed at a full-body scanner. I stepped inside. The machine checked me for everything from knives to bioweapons hidden in my intestine or woven into my flesh. The man glanced at a tablet in his hand, nodded and opened a door, which revealed the main hall. The place looked like an enchanted theatre, with a stage at one end, and it was filled with small tables, around which chairs were gathered. The scent of tobacco, leather and vanilla compounded into a powerful spell. The room was dark, and a heavy mist of amber light seeped out from somewhere. There was no music, only muffled voices and the occasional trickle of liquor. Almost all of the chairs were occupied, although many of the guests wore robes or dark clothes, with hoods and masks. Some were modified so much they likely wouldn't recognise themselves in the mirror.

The spectators sat still, facing the stage. A girl moved between tables, placing something into their open mouths – drugs or mind links. The guests didn't look at the girl, didn't speak to each other; their eyes were glued to the stage, as if afraid to miss a single beat of what was going to unfold before them. Although I couldn't see their faces, I could see the tension in their erect postures, could read impatience in their outstretched necks, and I could picture animal hunger in their eyes. The anticipation made me curious — but not enough to wait for the show to begin; I came here for the experience offered in secret rooms, and my desire to buy into it had already grown into an obsession.

After I was security-screened by another guard, I entered what looked like a laboratory — a big space divided into glass cubicles. Inside, people were smoking, getting injections. Some lay dead still, deep in illusions; others were sleepwalking.

I had seen many of these before — drug hotels — only not as opulent as this. In such places you could rent a room or a bed, choose a drug and be under the influence for as long as you wanted, or for as long as it was safe. Trained staff would check on you to make sure your dose feed was right, your vitals in order.

With the advent of new drugs, the Government claimed there was no addiction, and all legal drugs were safe to use. Many were developed in an attempt to cure the suicide pandemic, but none of them were successful. Since a lot of money was invested in the research, they had to do something with all that junk — and besides, how else would they manage millions of hurting orphans? Diagnosing us was a major pain; we had too many things wrong with us to get it right. Non-addictive, smart recreational nano-drugs were a great idea, I thought — better than us all overdosing on some illegal rubbish. I'd heard there was a small dosage of antidepressants with long-lasting effects in most of these new substances — of course, that might have been just one of the thousands of rumours circulating; but maybe it wasn't. Those who wanted to stay off drugs for a while could do so with the help of a pill — a vac, a cleaning lady — available at any pharmacy and anywhere where they sold drugs. This cleaning pill would make you crave clarity of mind, level out your emotions and help you get through day without resorting to perception alteration, which recreational drugs provided. It never worked for me; and the result didn't last unless you took it systematically like birth control. Who had the brain for that? One slip and the pain became too uncomfortable again, and you'd go back to the sweet salvation of modern chemistry. It was a natural thing to do. When people could choose 'safe' perception alteration, there was no way they were going back to real life. Not this life, anyway.

A woman in a lab coat came out of one of the glass cubicles, closed the door and entered a code. After a buzz, a clicking sound followed. She walked by me without so much as a look in my direction, as though I wasn't even there. I walked over to the room she had just left, and peered through the door. On the other side was the thing I had seen in my mind's eye in the ad: a man lay unconscious on a bed in the middle of the room, and overhead a wreath of purple and turquoise light danced. His body twitched from time to time, his eyeballs moving under his eyelids as the wreath of energy changed shapes and colour.

Suddenly, the energy erupted and hit the glass in front of me. I recoiled, losing my balance, but someone's strong hands grabbed my shoulders, preventing me from falling. I pivoted on my heels.

A man in a dark suit towered over me. 'Captivating, isn't it?' he said.

He walked over to the next cell, leisurely, a subtle smile on his clean-shaven face, enriched with shallow wrinkles expressing profound satisfaction.

'It amazes me to see what we are made of. The multiformity of our layers. So many interconnected relationships operate in one body – a body so primitive it can never truly experience the gifts it bears.' The disappointment in his voice was superficial.

He stared into the glass cubicle, at the swaying mass of energy, hands clasped behind his back, a golden watch flickering from under the cuff of his white shirt. A dark-grey tie matched the colour of his three-piece suit, and was elevated from his chest with a golden collar bar. He stood erect, his chin up, eyes steady on the subject of his interest. He didn't waste a single motion – I imagined he even inhaled and exhaled at precisely the same intervals.

I looked around the lab again. It teemed with tech I'd never seen before. The clients around the place were wearing clothes that cost more than a car, and the man in the cubicle before me had more money invested in implants and jewellery than my apartment was worth. These people didn't come here to satisfy their sickest pleasures or indulge in some sophisticated drug-induced delirium. I'd expected to discover something along these lines – it wasn't the first time I found myself in an exclusive club – but this was a whole different level. I felt like a little kid in a wonderland, and nothing scared me more than being a kid again.

'A soul – what an intricate module,' the man continued. 'I'll use my human ignorance license and allow myself to call it, perhaps, one of the most beautiful structures in the universe.'

While my skin prickled, repelling the man's energy, my brain swallowed what he'd said and was asking for more, and my ears were open to anything that would come out of his mouth. He stirred my impatience by remaining silent for a time, allowing me to accumulate desire slowly, to work a little for what he would make me want.

'Human soul?' I asked.

'In its luminous glory,' he said, and grinned.

'Where is it?'

'They travel anywhere they want,' he said, and pointed to another cell, at a bright conglomeration of light particles. 'Look at her. First true steps towards absolute freedom.'

'It can't escape the cell?' I asked.

'No. You don't want your soul to leave you for ever, do you?'

*How would it feel to see my own soul? Could I talk to it? Could I control it?* I wondered.

'Outside our physical bodies our abilities are limitless,' the man said. 'We can go through fathomless distances, travel in time, access dimensions we could never think of.'

'Do these people remember anything after they wake up?' I asked.

'They have some feelings, but nothing compared to what they experience when they access a much larger world. Inside us, consciousness is suppressed, so we don't have the capacity to handle information of this kind. We would lose our minds.' Looking me straight in the eye, he went on, 'That moment when your soul becomes free... It changes you for ever. That one moment is worth living for. Or dying for.' He smiled and motioned to the door.

The need for this experience spilled into my every atom.

We left the lab and I followed him down the corridor to the front part of the club.

'We are the only institution that provides services of this kind in a safe, controlled environment. We don't accept every client. We checked your medical history before we let you in, of course. We take precautions to protect our clients. Your profile indicated seventy-nine per cent probability for successful completion of the soul-flight.'

'What's the price?' I asked.

He took a small piece of paper from one of the leather boxes on a table, wrote something and slid it over to me.

'For this price,' I said, indignantly, 'I assume this is not some bullshit simulation?'

'Miss Jennet, for this price you will get a chance to feel what a soul is without a body and mind. It's a fair, if not humble, price – wouldn't you agree?'

The price was exorbitant. I didn't have this amount, and my expression revealed it. It would take me at least a year to save up such a sum, and that's if I didn't spend money on drugs, booze and entertainment, which obviously wasn't an option, as I had to live somehow.

'Think about it. We are at your disposal should you have any questions,' he said, and, without any effort, merely by looking me in the eyes and holding himself the way he did, he delivered a final message: he didn't need my business; I needed him.

This sensation made me sick – it was a need on the verge of dependence, and it made me so, so sick. Everything that was in my stomach was now rising to my throat. I detested men like him: men with power and influence. I was afraid of them. And yet, the strangest feeling overpowered me – I didn't want to leave. If someone had told me I'd been hypnotised, I would have been relieved, because I had no explanation for what I felt. I wanted to lunge forward, grab the man's wrist and make him promise that he would let me back in and discuss with me how I could go on a soul-flight without paying this ridiculous amount of money. But of course I didn't – I couldn't just grab him and start begging; that would be ridiculous. I had to leave. A bouncer was already waiting for me in the doorway.

* * *

I was walking nowhere, feeling dizzy and nauseous, the streetlights blurring everything into a stew. My thoughts were in the glass cubicle. I imagined lying there, looking my soul in the eyes, asking it the question that had been on my mind since the moment I should have died but hadn't.

When my parents tied a rope around their necks and got themselves a ticket out, I was confused and scared and sad, but most of all I was very, very angry. And when the anger passed, I began suspecting that maybe I had had something to do with it – maybe I wasn't a good child. What could be so terribly wrong with me that my own parents – my own mother, who gave birth to me – would leave me? More – leave me completely alone? I was twelve – old enough to find many reasons, some more ingenious than others, to blame myself for their death. Therapists at the orphanage helped me taper my guilt and some of my anger, but not the loneliness. The feeling of loneliness was heavy; it was exhausting to carry it inside all the time. And then there was the fear. A lot of fear. Being with other kids in the same situation made it easier, but not by much; we were all mature enough to understand that the world had changed and none of us would have the lives we'd imagined. There was no one to take care of us any more. It was a collective sensation of doom. We reminded each other that our circumstances were not unique, and at the same time, we fortified each other's integration into this new frightening normalcy.

Here is how my generation was raised: whenever a new kid arrived at the orphanage, the first thing you'd ask was, 'How did your parents kill themselves?' A round of stories would follow, and everyone would share again and again, so we heard all sorts of means by which adults took their own lives. By the time you left the orphanage at the age of eighteen, you'd feel comfortable talking about death, and you'd form your own special relationship with it. Fantasising out loud about how you'd kill yourself was a common practice.

A lot can happen before your eighteenth birthday. A few things happened before mine. I didn't think my story was unique, but I never heard other kids talking about similar experiences, which made me feel all the more isolated. During my first year at the orphanage, I met a priest. He was supposed to help me cope with pain and restore my faith in life. What cruel irony. With a prayer for my parents on his lips and animal lust in his bulging eyes, he invaded my body. That was the moment when my body and soul became alien to each other. I was disgusted and ashamed. I avoided mirrors, wore layers of clothing to distance the world's eyes from my skin. I didn't want to exist.

I failed in my suicide attempts, but some of my efforts were more successful than others. I overdosed on something I purchased from a dealer at our orphanage – she was a youth care worker, about thirty years old. I bought drugs from her frequently. One day I told her I wanted to die. She sold me something and advised me to mix it with my antidepressants.

The thing was, she said, I had one shot at killing myself. If I failed, they'd put me on a watchlist. They'd fit me with a bracelet that would monitor my vitals and biomarkers, and they'd be able to prevent another overdose. But before that, if I fell into a coma and survived, I'd spend months in the Neuroscience Institute. People didn't wake up from comas these days – at least, very rarely, and every case was carefully studied. People died much more frequently under general anaesthesia, too.

I almost succeeded. Almost. I was in a coma for two months, and somehow survived and spent another three months in a lab with a bunch of whitecoats studying me like a rat.

I don't remember what my soul did while I was in the coma, but for some reason that bitch decided to come back. So I'd give everything to look it in the eyes and ask – *Why?*

My soul came back, but it was me who had to live. It was me who had to wake up every morning, hurting, hating, crying, feeling sorry for myself. Time, meds, alcohol and drugs morphed my pain and anger into numbness. That was even worse. I still hated the world, but without pain, I couldn't find the motivation to kill myself any more. I didn't know who I was – all fond memories of my childhood had been erased by the time I turned fourteen and earned a new label: coma survivor. I had no identity, I reasoned, so whom would I be killing? I'd already murdered myself. Now I was simply trying to bring myself back from the dead; I needed a validation for my existence, because I was tired of drinking or getting high every night, of defeating numbness with oblivion.

My heart raced, I was sweating, and no matter how fast I breathed, the air failed to satiate my lungs. I wanted the soul-flight, the possibility of recognising myself as something other than a worthless sludge that floated aimlessly in this world like a turd in the ocean. I saw it as a door that led from a place I referred to as the present – a place where nothing happened, where I didn't think I even existed – and into the future, where my life would finally begin. I needed to walk through this door right now, immediately, away from this interim quagmire of vague misery.

Money was a problem. After my eighteenth birthday an advisor from the orphanage recommended that I sell my parents' apartment and buy a smaller one to live in, putting the rest of the money in a bank. Unfortunately I made the mistake of allowing the stupid woman to talk me into locking up my own cash, and as a result the bank would only release monthly instalments until my thirtieth birthday, when they would pay out the remaining balance, if there was any left. Supposedly such arrangements provided orphans with better opportunities, making them more likely to gain higher education, and facilitated better integration into working life. Nobody wanted kids to blow their cash in one week and start increasing the crime rate and homeless population. For the same reason I couldn't use my apartment as a collateral for a loan, either – the only way for me to get a loan was to get a job and start building credit history. Screw that.

I should never have signed the damn papers. I should have kept the money and died before spending it all.

# 2

---

I returned the next day around ten o'clock in the evening. An hour passed and they still hadn't opened the door. *Dirty Castle.* I traced the letters with my finger. I knew they would let me in eventually – they would have never allowed me to enter this place to begin with if they couldn't use me for something. I looked into the eye of the camera that was staring back at me; whoever was watching me must have been amused by how desperate I was to get in. I waited patiently, soaking up the tension – not because I had patience, but because I had no idea what would happen next; I didn't know what kind of bargain I would have to make, I only knew I would regret it later. But what happened later didn't matter, because later I would be a different person.

The door finally opened and a guard escorted me to the office where the man I'd met before relaxed in a leather chair behind an antique wooden desk. The massive old table would have been completely out of place in this high-tech environment if it had not been for a built-in wooden bookcase filled with books whose gold-stamped spines bore signs of heavy use. As pretentious as it looked, at the centre of the office the desk fulfilled its function of establishing authority.

'Welcome back, Miss Jennet,' he said. 'I apologise for the wait. Please,' he said, gesturing at the chair in front of the table. 'You know what makes us special?' he said, getting right down to business, not bothering to be particularly creative with his pitch. 'We let our clients discover yearnings they never knew they had.'

'Don't we all want the same thing?' I asked.

He moved his eyes in the way people do when they're reading information from their implants. Besides smart lenses, I couldn't see any other modifications on him, although I noticed a thin seam running from the top of his thumb down to his wrist, where it disappeared under the cuff of his white shirt. He was one of the few people who wanted to remain a man – he probably still believed in human superiority, but couldn't resist the lure of technology.

'Oh yes, we do,' he said. 'There are a few things that we all aspire to have or experience.' His lips tensed involuntary as he finished reading whatever he was reading and focused on me. 'That is, until you travel. This is the magic of it – our clients don't just get what they want here, they discover their *true* desires. And trust me, what you think you want in your flesh is far from the cravings of your soul. But I assume that since you are here, I don't need to tout.'

'What's the catch?' I asked.

'The catch? I'm a businessman, Miss Jennet. You came to me. If you don't want what I'm selling, the door is behind you.'

'I don't have enough money,' I said.

'I understand – the price is steep. After all, you are paying for technology no one else has. And for a team of top scientists – and such talented people don't come cheap.'

I swallowed. 'Can I pay you some other way?'

'Miss Jennet, you are an attractive young woman, but I don't require sexual favours.'

'Do you do payment plans or something like that?'

He clasped his hands and leaned forward, resting his elbows on the table, smiling. At least he didn't laugh in my face.

'Give me a loan,' I improvised. 'I can work at your club to repay it,' I said. I had no intention of keeping the job after I got what I wanted. 'I can dance. I can sell whatever it is you are selling to these junkies.'

He looked at me appraisingly – or rather, with curiosity.

'Take off your clothes,' he instructed.

I got up and took off my coat and my dress.

'Are you going to hide your breasts out there, too?' he asked.

I took my bra and panties off.

His eyes remained on my face. No lust – no interest in my nudity. He pointed to the table with his chin. 'Dance.'

I have never felt shame from being unclothed, and I wasn't ashamed to stand naked in front of him. It was something else – I was suffocating, in a very particular way, as though the man was in control of every mote of air and didn't let any of it reach my lungs. I had to earn it – I had to earn the privilege to breathe. So I danced. As far as I was concerned, the sexual pretext could not be separated from a scene like this, and yet there was nothing sexual about it, and I really didn't like the feeling of it. I'd rather be objectified than forced into submission by an unexplainable yet very perceptible mental manipulation. It felt unnatural.

'I don't just give out loans,' he said. 'But I try to work with my clients.' He pushed himself up from the chair. 'Work for me for some time. Prove you are trustworthy. Then we'll see if an arrangement can be made.'

'And how long will that take?' I asked.

'It will depend on you, Laura. A week… a month.'

'Then I'd better get started,' I said, fastening my bra.

'Come back in the morning.'

'I can start now,' I insisted.

'You will start in the morning,' he repeated.

I didn't dare to argue.

'Do you have a name?' I asked before leaving.

His lips started stretching in a smile, very slowly, as though he was still debating whether he should reveal a secret. 'Craig. Craig Nolan.'

\* \* \*

I knew I wouldn't fall asleep tonight, so I didn't even try.

A big guy opened a door and the room I entered seemed like a place where people drink, fuck and forget. Exactly what I needed. A long rectangular bar in the centre was busy and too large for one person to service. The bald, muscular bartender didn't waste time, but didn't rush either. The burn on his face reminded me of a map. It was large, with scads of branches strangling his thick neck, decaying somewhere under his black T-shirt, which was too small for his bulky arms.

Nobody complained. The sight of a human pouring shots and mixing cocktails was satisfying, and so customers waited gladly, enjoying a smoke and the worn but real leather under their asses.

'Laura?' said a voice behind me. It belonged to a tall black guy in a sheepskin jacket.

'Who the fuck are you?' I asked. I'd never seen him in my life.

I wasn't on social platforms, so you'd have to do a bit of digging to ID me. It didn't happen often, but I really didn't like it when random people called me by my name. I didn't know what it was – maybe the quality of a certain voice awakened unconscious associations, like a smell can evoke memories – but sometimes when I heard my name, my whole insides shuddered. This man had this effect on me.

'John,' he said, almost unsure. His stare slid down my face like a bewildered leech.

'Am I supposed to know you?' I asked, glancing sideways at him. He looked tired. One lapel of his sheepskin jacket was covered in mud stains, and he emanated the faint but unmistakable scent of the city river.

His eyes twitched, then grew wider. His hand froze in the air, a cigarette between his index and third fingers, his full brown lips slightly parted.

'What will it be?' the bartender asked.

'Vodka,' I said.

John waved, the bartender nodded and pulled two bottles from the second and third shelf. He placed a shot of clear liquid in front of me and pushed a whiskey over to John. John raised his glass, mumbled an awkward nice-to-meet-you and downed his drink.

I ignored him. He was well-built and could potentially be a good fuck. No wacky body alterations, either. But he wasn't what I wanted tonight. I rarely screwed men for pleasure, and today I wanted pleasure.

The vodka was perfect – after a few gulps of the stuff my gut was burning. It felt good; I was ready to explore more of what the surroundings had to offer.

Two men and a woman chatted on a sofa. One of the men, who had a shaved, tattooed head and glow-in-the-dark eyes, touched the menu screen installed in their table and selected another round of shots. He squeezed the woman's thigh as he pressed 'send'. The other man placed his prosthetic arm around her shoulder. She liked it.

Sitting next to them was a girl, alone in a pastel-pink dress printed with cherry blossoms. Red light washed over her face. She stared into nothingness, smoking, sinking deeper into her chair. She lifted her head, just a bit – just enough for me to notice her invitation. I sat on top of her, stole the cigarette from her mouth and took a drag. She smiled. Tracing the curve of her neck with my nose, I smelled berries. She obviously had a skin screen that added smell and taste to her body. I licked the sweetness of blueberries and honey off her lips; the alcohol kicked in stronger, and my hand felt just right on her lacy bra. It was an absolute freefall – no force, only gliding motion: the type of ecstasy when you are wet and relaxed at the same time.

*I love you today, blueberry girl. I love you.*

I closed my eyes and imagined nothing but deep black. I felt her skin, the silk of her dress, her lips and sweet smoke.

*Please don't make me see anything else. No monsters – just a blueberry girl.*

'I love you,' I whispered into her ear. 'You are so beautiful.'

Her skin suffused with the colour of dark amber, and her face morphed into the freckled face of the woman from the hidden ad from Dirty Castle – the ad for the soul-flight. I got goosebumps, my belly filled with more heat, and I seized this hallucination before it dissipated.

When I detached my mouth from hers, the features of the woman from the ad were gone and the blueberry girl was back. She didn't say a word as I exposed her chest. Her nipple changed colour to bright purple, and faint flowers appeared around it. She was too high to make her skin screen do anything else. If I had an implant, and if she'd let me, I could have connected to her screen and imagined my own world on her body. But I didn't, and my mind was clogged with too much darkness to create anything beautiful.

\* \* \*

The sun was almost up. Autonomous taxis picked up tired bodies. People gathered in front of food trucks; fast food tasted better just before the sunrise. The smell of pork-flavoured instant noodles and deep-fried imitation-beef sausages dominated the air.

I buttoned up my coat and started walking, hoping to exhaust myself so I could fall asleep – I didn't want to stare at the ceiling all day cursing insomnia. Sleeping pills didn't always work. Falling asleep was a gamble.

'Had a good night?'

I glanced back and saw the guy I'd met at the bar, John, catching up with me, sucking the smoke from a stub. The entire bottom part of his sheepskin jacket was wet and covered in mud; so were his suede lace-up boots.

'Been for a swim?' I asked.

He put on something that looked like a smile – only it looked like it was from a face that didn't belong to him.

'Want to get a coffee?' he asked, nodding towards a coffee shop across the road.

He didn't look like a creep – if anything, he seemed strangely normal. And hot coffee sounded good.

We took a booth by the window. There were no menu panels on the tables, and you had to order and pick up your coffee at the cashier desk. John must have liked some things the old-fashioned way.

'So, Laura, is it?' he asked.

I ignored this redundant question. I didn't want to get into why he'd looked me up. I had no intention of hooking up with this man.

He lit up a cigarette, inhaled the grey smoke, leaned back and closed his eyes.

I looked out of the window. Some people were still drunk; some were just ghosts. I hated being sober – I hated the parasitic emotion that used to be pain but had transformed into impenetrable numbness a long time ago. I couldn't bear early mornings that shapeshifted into long days, illuminating the surface of the streets with worthless sunlight. The hypocrisy of light – how it shone and shouted that life went on was cruel. Everything had stopped; there was no life, so why did it still shine?

I glanced back at John. He was resting, the light from the window emphasising the thick stubble on his dark face.

'Hey!'

'Yes?' he said without opening his eyes.

'Did you try to jump or something? You smell like sewer.'

'No.'

Silence shrouded the room once again. We sat in this silence, half awake, almost unaware of each other. My sobering mind took me back to the hidden ad for the soul-flight. I saw the placid face of the girl, the bright wreath of energy hovering over her. And as I imagined lying there, watching my own soul flying above me, taking me far away from this reality, my body grew lighter and slumber wafted its haze over my head.

Dreams would often disturb my few chances at peace. A pack of dogs. Again. Skinny, battered and hungry, the dogs ran back and forth on deserted streets, trying to scare someone away. But there was never anyone else in my dream, only dogs. The dreams were permeated with emptiness – every particle of matter was abandoned by life itself. The dogs barked, barked and barked into the void, and even when the dream was over and the dogs had gone, the feeling of loneliness remained.

When I woke up, John wasn't there, and my head was splitting in half. I reached for the cup of coffee, expecting it to be cold by now; but it was warm – hot. I looked around. John was still there, talking to the bot at the cash register.

'You OK?' he asked when I approached them.

'Feel like shit.' I grunted.

'Better than feeling nothing,' he said. Not a bad conclusion. 'I'm gonna head out,' he said. 'Take care of yourself.'

He opened the door and looked back at me. There was a well of grief in his eyes, and it made him look so human. He was hurt like everyone else – everyone had lost someone – but his eyes were not empty like mine: there were memories – a presence of something real – in them. I hadn't seen this very often, and it always struck me how some people found strength and chose to remember good things, even though it must have hurt them. This man must have loved someone very much. I envied people like him. I wished I could grieve; I wish I could pretend that I loved someone, that I missed someone. I wished I could say there had been someone who'd loved me once.

# 3

The performers in Dirty Castle were all mesmerising. Some were beautiful, some bizarre, all flaunting the work of top surgeons and bioengineers. There were people with wings and tails, golden skin, purple skin, leopard skin; some wore tiaras and diamond-encrusted underwear. I saw bald heads tattooed with gold and manes of black locks cascading to the floor. A person with large translucent breasts passed by me; inside their breasts fish swam in a shining liquid. Another had blue skin, equally large breasts and male genitalia. Their stomach was transparent, and inside was a red metal ribcage, with a hummingbird fluttering from rib to rib.

'Queens of the universe,' said an older woman, seeing me looking around. Her voice was deep and husky, and she wore a black see-through robe. She smiled, and the light bounced off her golden teeth. Her face was dry and wrinkled, and she was even shorter and thinner than me. 'Let's see what's so special about you,' she said, grabbing my chin. Her bracelets clinked as she pulled my face closer to her milky blind eyes. She palpated my cheeks like a butcher examining a piece of meat, tugged at my black bobbed hair and laced her fingers through my fringe, jerking my head back so hard my mouth opened. 'Turn around,' she ordered, and I did. 'Mmm, not much.' She accompanied the disappointment in her voice with a grimace. 'We see later. Jeff! Jeff!'

A big clumsy man with a distorted face came in.

'Give her the pills.'

He pulled out a few bags. One was filled with pearls – those were drugs – and another with clear gel beans. The gel beans were self-dissolving chips. The way they altered reality was incomparable to anything. Through them AI ran simulations that placed you in environments and situations you couldn't imagine with a human brain. I'd only tried it once – the price was exorbitant. I assumed it was a part of the show here.

'You do tables only,' the woman said. 'I don't want to see your skinny ass on that stage.' She grabbed my elbow and walked me to the dressing room.

Tables under big square mirrors edged with LED panels held all kinds of boxes, jars, tubes of make-up, brushes, fake eyelashes, nails and nail polishes, body paints, glitter and other stuff. A separate section was dedicated to wigs and jewellery. Nearby there were racks of clothes, and next to those stood two displays – one held body parts, including wings, horns, tails and penises; the second contained skin screens, external vocal amplifiers and other tech I wasn't familiar with.

'You put on anything that's black – nothing else, understand?'
'Yes,' I answered.

The woman and Jeff left. I picked some lacy bondage lingerie and a pair of heels, put it on and made my way to the main hall.

On the stage appeared a being with white wings that reached to the floor. Their almost-exposed breasts were generous, and their luminous porcelain body moved through air like a boneless reptile. My job was easy: to blend into the background and spread pills under tongues, which were already hanging out. I couldn't see faces under hoods, and I avoided looking at those who didn't have a hood on. I didn't think about them or these otherworldly performers – the bright wreath of energy occupied my mind; I couldn't see anything else.

During my break, I returned to the dressing room and saw a young woman standing in front of a mirror. When she turned around, a chill ran down my neck. It was the woman from the hidden ad again. She had light-brown skin and her hair was cut short, leaving less than an inch over her perfectly sculpted head; freckles scattered across her face like galaxies trapped in honey, and her chin and part of her neck were covered with a metal plate. The shape of it was fluid, like silver had flowed around her features then suddenly solidified. In the ad her hair had been long, and I didn't think she'd had this metal plate on her face, but I had no doubt it was her.

We stared at each other. An icy sheet of perplexity crackled between us. I felt dizzy. Something about her stirred my emotions in a way I couldn't explain; I couldn't breathe, and my heart raced in my chest.

* * *

While I was getting guests their treats, the woman from the ad appeared on the stage. She wore tight mini-shorts and a crop top, through which a pierced nipple showed. Besides her neck and chin, other areas of her body were covered in silver plates too: her arms, part of her legs, her left breast. She resembled a machine more than she did a human. I stopped what I was doing and stared.

Her performance didn't start with a sparkle in her eyes and a smile; she wasn't trying to seduce – no, she radiated anger. And she moved so fast, speeding up all the time. When she reached an unstoppable speed, she started changing shapes like a hologram without flesh. Every jerk of her body produced a new character – a girl walking along a dark street, shaking, trying to cover her naked body; a girl swallowing pills; a girl in a red dress, hands covered in blood; a girl fighting a… priest?

My heart froze, and time stopped passing, as though someone had killed it. I couldn't hear anything except the swoosh of her movements, and didn't see anything except the distorted faces of the girls she showed. It was hard to distinguish the features of the girl and the priest, with the figures changing too fast, but that coincidence threw me completely off balance.

*Can she read my mind?* I thought.

It felt as if these stories came from me, from my head. And I knew many stories like this. I used to read articles and watch videos about child abuse. It was my self-prescribed psychotherapy. Many of these stories were so much worse than mine – and they made me feel better about myself, if only for a short period of time. Soon my pain would come back to the surface and I would have to watch something even more brutal.

She finished her act floating lifeless in the air. If I were on drugs I would think I was hallucinating. But I wasn't, and she was really levitating.

The air returned into my lungs. I looked around, shaking, scared for her. Would they punish her? Would they kick her out? Would I ever see her again? My thoughts scared me. But there was no time to analyse why I was so concerned about this girl. I'd fix the damage first, then think about why it mattered. There was too much discontent in the air – the show wasn't right for the audience at all; it didn't amuse them. I rushed around the tables and distributed more pearls to smooth over their irritation. On the house.

When I came back to the dressing room, I found her sitting in a chair, with no expression on her face. She raised her head and our eyes met. An electric wave surged from my fingertips to my cheeks and belly.

'Aleece, come with me,' the old witch I'd met earlier called from behind me. Two guards came to stand by her side. Aleece got up, and they left.

My heart sank. *What will they do to her? Why do I care?*

\* \* \*

I closed the Dirty Castle door behind me. A drink was on my mind – as was Aleece, and I wasn't too surprised when I saw her outside. I'd hoped she'd be here. In my mind's eye I had found her leaning against the brick wall out front, and here she was, leaning against the wall, her oversized bomber jacket wrapped around her arms, revealing her slender athletic shoulders.

She nodded to me, turned around and started walking. I followed. We walked in silence, side by side. She made me nervous and comfortable – a pleasant sensation, overall – and by the time we reached the river the nervous tension was gone altogether.

She bent forward, rested her forearms on the railing and looked out at the city dipped in the neon bloom of giant holo-banners. Buildings glimmered, big and small, stately and battered, drones flew in flocks, distant sobs of sirens came in lazy outbursts. In the sky behind the muddy clouds of smog hung a faint reminder of the white moon.

When she finally turned to look at me, I asked, 'Who are you?'

She kept her eyes on mine as she turned my question over in her head. That's when I noticed how strange and deep and beautiful her eyes were: pools of some ancient wisdom camouflaged by strings of green and hazel.

'Are you human?' I asked.

'That depends on how you define human.'

That was a fair point. Some took a firm stance on the issue, while others sought a balance, striving to retain a sense of humanity while exploring ways to transcend the limitations of our nature. Politicians and corporations politicised and commodified our divisiveness and uncertainty, which only deepened the confusion. I wouldn't be able to define what it meant to be human, and the point at which you stopped being one – the definition had never been important to me. What good would drawing a line do?

Now I thought about it. Aleece resembled a machine, but it wasn't the amount of synthetic parts in her body and gadgets expanding her mind that determined whether she was human or not – it was something else. She had that timeless quality about her; a piece of classical sculpture – atavistic truth captured in a body. Humans ended; she went on.

'I saw you in the ad,' I said.

'What ad?'

'The hidden ad for the soul-flight.'

She squinted, and her eyes traced the skyline, as if chasing memories.

'Did you go? On a soul-flight?' I asked.

'Probably' she said. 'I'm not sure.'

'What do you mean? You either did or you didn't.'

'When you don't know what you are most of the time, it's hard to say what you did or didn't do,' she said, keeping her eyes on mine. I felt my spirit was about to leave my body and drown in them and never come back. 'I've been through so many experiments and procedures. I really don't remember.'

I believed her. It didn't even occur to me to question what she was saying; I couldn't imagine that her mouth could paint anything but the truth.

'Do you want to go on a soul-flight?' she asked.

'Yes.'

'Why?'

'The same reason anyone would want to go – to see what's out there. To discover what I am. *Discover my true nature. Free myself,*' I said, citing the ad, smiling. She smiled back, but it was clear she had no clue what ad I was talking about, even though she was in it. 'And there is nothing left for me here, so I just have to figure out how to make some money quickly and pay for it, so I can be done with this job.'

'That's why you work at Dirty Castle?' she asked.

'Yeah.' I pulled out a pack of cigarettes and offered her one. She took it. 'And I could use a job.' No idea why I said that – to seem 'normal', whatever that meant? I didn't want a job; I didn't enjoy showing up at a certain time at a certain place. It was my first day and it already felt like torture.

I watched her lips and long eyelashes as she leaned forward to dip the tip of her cigarette in the flame of my lighter.

'Soul-flight is not an experiment, right? I mean, they're selling it, so it's safe – to some extent, at least?' I asked.

'Nobody will give you a guarantee for this kind of experience,' she said. 'It's been tested, but not legally approved. But then, I don't think you'd expect it to be, in a place like that?'

'I guess not.'

'You have family?' she asked – an opening salvo in nearly every conversation between fresh not-quite-strangers.

'No, no one. Some distant relatives, but they have their own problems; I'm not in contact with them,' I said. The truth was I'd been so ashamed of being raped that just the thought of meeting someone I knew, especially a relative, made me anxious, and I cut all ties with my extended family. Most of those who I had trusted with my secret were religious and didn't believe me when I told them about the priest. They thought I was traumatised by my parents' passing and had misinterpreted what had happened. That stung, but fuck them. My aunt tried to visit when I was in a hospital after one of my suicide attempts, but I told doctors I didn't want to see anyone, and I proved my point by screaming and knocking down some machines and monitors that stood by my bed. They got the message.

'I'm sorry,' she said.

'That's fine.' I shrugged. 'What about you?'

The question confounded her. I watched how she tried to salvage an answer from the current of her thoughts.

'I don't think I have anyone left. I don't remember much about my origins,' she said, and stared straight out in front of her.

I snatched the opportunity to study her profile, the prominent shape of her nearly shaved head, the silver plate that hugged her neck and chin like a silver turtleneck.

'How did you do it? Change your body like that?' I asked. 'Like a hologram?'

She held out her hand and looked at her palm, the cigarette between her index and middle finger. Her brown skin started glowing, then became translucent, strings of light replaced her muscles and tendons. I'd never seen anything like it.

'I can modify my body. I don't know exactly how it works, but all it takes is thought.'

I had to hold back the urge to touch her transparent hand.

'I used to be a scientist. Although I don't have memories of that either; I just know it. It is as if someone put that knowledge in my head, but I don't actually remember the experience of being a scientist.'

'You don't have any memories at all?' I asked.

'Some images emerge occasionally, but they are just incoherent fragments,' she said. 'For example, I remember I used to have long hair. Really long.' She gestured at her waist. 'And a fringe like yours.'

It wasn't hard to imagine her with long hair, since in the ad her hair was long. But I didn't want to bring up the ad again.

'There are some memories I can't piece together,' she went on. 'They are more like illusions, and don't stay in my head for long – for some reason my brain rejects them. Sometimes I have visions that I know don't even belong to me. I have to revive my memories, whatever's left of them, every other week or so.' She lowered her head and shoved the toe of her boot into the gravel, took the last drag from her cigarette and threw away the stub.

We stared at the river for a while. Thin veins of acid yellowness in the water made me aware of the stench that had been here all along but started bothering me only now that I was more relaxed and could spare my attention.

'You don't look like you have any alterations – not even an implant?' Aleece asked.

'No, nothing.'

'That's quite rare.'

'Yeah, well, I wouldn't know what to change. Except everything. And I doubt that would make me feel any better. And an implant – I'm not giving some assholes a way to monitor me. I was in a coma for a few months, and in a lab for another few months after I woke up. For as long as I have a choice, I'm not letting anyone study me or my brain again – no one looking into how I feel and why I feel the way I feel ever again. Nobody cares about how you actually feel, they just like to collect data. And I'm sure as hell not going to serve my mind up to them and pay for the privilege,' I said. The stink of the river was becoming too intense. 'Do you want to get a drink?' I asked Aleece.

'Sure.'

We hit a few bars. In each of them she ordered cocktails that were either pink or orange. When the first one arrived – bright pink, served in a martini glass – I realised it suited her more than I'd thought it would.

Aleece talked, and her sentences jumped at me like puzzle pieces. I placed them together, trying to construct a coherent story of one person. She knew she used to love science; she knew it because someone had told her, not because she actually remembered. Quantum physics and nanotechnology had been her interests. She did remember being often alone in a big fancy apartment when she was a kid. She also talked about two little girls. Twins. In her memory they were very young – maybe five or six years old. They were not her sisters; she was somewhat certain about that. When she spoke about them her voice was soft and her whole expression was one of pure tenderness – they must have had a special place in her heart. They could have been her childhood friends, I thought, since she didn't have – or didn't think she had – siblings.

As I searched for something to tell her about myself, I realised I had large memory holes, too. Years blurred into each other without any distinguishable events – perhaps down to all the drugs and booze.

In a way we were alike; she didn't remember much about her life or who she was because of an accident with some technology she had been working on, which must have wiped her memory. And I couldn't paint an adequate picture of my life because I'd spent the last fourteen years drinking and getting high, trying to forget my past. So our conversation came in spring showers, induced by sudden images one of us managed to salvage from our broken minds.

During moments of silence, I acknowledged how my skin prickled when I looked at her, how my belly filled with sweetness, and I could tell by the shine in her eyes that she was experiencing something similar.

# 4

It'd been ten days since I started working at Dirty Castle, and I'd never been so aware of time. Days dragged out, slow as snails, as if on purpose. I was becoming paranoid that maybe I would never go on a soul-flight, that maybe the place would get raided and shut down, or perhaps it might burn to the ground, or Craig would simply not let me go for some reason – or of course the world might come to an end. The latter would have been OK by me ten days ago, but now I didn't want the world to end – not before I got what I wanted from it. It didn't help that whenever I tried to talk to Craig the guards outside his office had only one answer for me – he was too busy to see me.

So I waited. Until finally I was escorted to see him.

'When can I travel?' I asked abruptly.

'Mmm, Miss Jennet, your manners. Didn't your parents teach you to say hello?'

'No – and they didn't teach me how to say goodbye either.'

'Oh, you see, that's exactly what I'm worried about – if you get what you want before paying me back you might leave without saying goodbye,' he said.

'I've been working here for more than two weeks!'

'Ten days, to be precise, isn't it? I told you it could take months.' He shifted his eyes slightly to read something that popped up on his smart contact lens. 'You haven't earned it yet.'

'I need a guarantee,' I said.

'Have they treated you badly here?' he asked, returning his gaze to me.

'No.'

'I didn't think so. You see, we are a big happy family here – we don't lie to each other.' He was feeding me a bunch of bullshit, and didn't even make an effort to hide it. He was humiliating me on purpose – probably deriving pleasure from it. He knew I had to swallow this phony crap and got off on my submission. 'When you have worked enough to prove your determination I will let you know. Or I could implant a chip into your little head and blow your brain if you don't pay me – but here's the problem: I know you don't give a damn whether you live or die, so it won't do me any good.'

He was right about that, sort of. I didn't want to die, but I didn't want to live either.

'I guess you will have to trust me, since as we both understand I can't trust you,' he said, and motioned towards the door. 'Of course, you are free to leave at any time if you doubt my word. Please – no one is stopping you. You will be compensated for the time you have worked.'

I didn't have an argument against that, and I definitely didn't want to leave.

I went to the dressing room, where I found Aleece. I hadn't seen her since our first encounter, although I'd been waiting for her. Her absence made my time here even less bearable. I caught her eyes on me as I changed from fancy lingerie set back into my slip dress. The traces of her eyes on my skin soothed the irritation Craig had contaminated me with. Her presence swapped the tension in my muscles for a pleasant tingling in my chest and belly. I liked the subtle lure of her gaze.

'Want to grab something to eat?' she asked.

'Sure,' I said.

We got two orders of pot stickers and yakitori from a food stand, found a free bench in the park and ate in silence.

'Had a rough day?' she asked after we finished our dinner, picking up on my annoyance.

I shrugged and let her question hang. 'How long have you been working at the Castle?' I asked.

'For as long as I remember.'

'Which in your case—'

'Can mean anything,' she said. We both smiled. 'I believe I've been there for quite a while,' she said.

'You know Craig well, then?' I asked.

'I don't think anyone really knows him.'

Our eyes met. The energy she radiated rolled through my body, leaving my tongue thick and my groin burning with the anticipation of our first touch. Her lips parted, calling to me.

I removed an unlit cigarette from my mouth, and my eyes jumped from her lips to her eyes, my heart pounding in my chest.

'Would you like to see my place?' I asked.

There was a pause.

'I'd love to see your place,' she said.

We took a taxi to my apartment.

I pressed my thumb against a touchpad, and the door slid open. It was a one-bedroom apartment, an OK size, in a decent area. It was decorated with minimal furniture, which had come with it; I never bothered adding a personal touch, so it stayed dark grey and bleak. The view, however, was good. I had to have a view. The stars were rarely visible because of the smog, but the city lights were my stars.

'Do you want a drink?' I asked.

'No,' she said.

She followed me to the balcony. A holographic billboard hovered in front of us, showing two women, their bodies breaking down into glowing particles and forming a new single body.

Aleece touched the side of my palm. An electric charge shot up my arm. She took my hand and pulled me closer, and our lips sealed. I felt the smooth moves of her body against mine as she slowly pushed the straps of my dress off my shoulders and her hand brushed lightly against my breast. She took off her top, revealing more of her amber skin. The neon light of the banner, advertising a new model of an implant – a fusion of human mind and artificial intelligence – illuminated our bodies. Bright merging silhouettes in the ad reflected in Aleece's metal plates.

Her breasts were small and perfect. One was covered in metal and was cold and another warm – I found the combination attractive. I leaned towards her nipple and circled my tongue around the little silver balls, squeezing her round flesh hard. Aleece slid her thumb into my mouth and around my lips, pulling my head back up to her face. She looked me in the eyes, then her hand moved down my crotch.

The pleasure was immense – it was enough for me to forget about this life for a moment and all the pain it contained.

I didn't have a habit of returning pleasure. I was usually just a greedy bitch looking for someone to give it to me – I never felt the need to give back until that night. That night I wanted, needed, desperately desired to see Aleece lift her chest up, throw her head back and gasp for air.

And so she did.

\* \* \*

We lay in bed under warm sheets. I watched Aleece, this peaceful, otherworldly being.

*Who are you, Aleece? What happened to you?* I wanted to ask, as I ran my fingers over her skin, her surface changing from flesh to steel, from warm to cold.

'Do you feel anything here?' I asked, touching the silver plate on her hip.

'I do. When you touch it.'

'What are these plates for?' I asked.

'To keep what's left of my soul from escaping my body,' she said.

'Is that really what you think, or are you trying to be mysterious?'

'I'm not trying to be mysterious,' she said, and turned to her side. Her face was like a winter lake: serene but teeming with life beneath a frozen surface. I couldn't imagine her laughing hard or crying, but I could feel the highway of emotions concealed between the multiple layers of her complicated soul.

'Can I ask you something? Or have I asked too many questions already?' I asked.

'Ask. I'll tell you if I know the answer,' she said.

'The girls you projected that night – who are they?' I couldn't shake off the feeling that she'd dug those stories from my mind rather than hers.

'Victims of some really horrific crimes,' she said, her voice slicing through air without sorrow, but her eyes swelling with sadness.

'Are they someone you know of – or heard of?' I asked.

'I never met them,' she said. 'Although it's hard to say. I can't always distinguish this reality from visions that come from other times, other places, other people.' She raised herself on her elbow, propping her head against her fist. Purple light coming from the street glided over her chest and face. 'Sometimes I can hardly tell who I am. I hear other people's voices; I have thoughts in my head that are not my thoughts. It's exhausting.'

I took a breath and held it, unsure how to respond. I wanted to know what the hell had happened to her, but she'd already told me she couldn't remember anything.

'They are just girls – abused, taken advantage of. There are many of them; always have been and always will be. Not just girls – young vulnerable kids in general. But for some reason my memories are mostly of girls,' she said. 'The girl on the street with the long hair. Did you see her?'

I nodded.

'Her ghost is still here.' She stared ahead as though watching the scene unfold again. 'Her father raped her – multiple times. He made her walk naked on the street before putting a bullet between her eyes. It was a long time ago.'

I knew that story – I remembered the girl. I remembered because I'd focused on her time and time again when I was younger, thinking that she had had it so much worse than me. When Aleece showed the hologram of her on the stage, the image moved too fast; I thought I had recognised her, but I wasn't sure – her features were indistinct. Now I saw her face clearly, as if I, too, was witnessing it all unfold in Aleece's memory, more slowly and in detail.

'I know this story,' I said. 'I saw her in some old videos. How did you isolate that specific one? …And the priest?' I said, and paused, then asked. 'Can you read my mind?'

She thought for some time.

'If I can see the thoughts and memories of others, there's no reason why I can't see yours, I guess,' she said. 'Does it bother you? I can't read your mind at will. Things just come to me.' She closed her eyes. 'These ghosts, they don't just disappear; they never leave – their energy blends with the air we breathe. All their misery, sufferings, shame and despair: all of it is knitted into us – they are eternal. We pass their spirits on to our very few children; our children pass them on to their children. But it doesn't stop there. Their pain is forever embossed in the subsoils of the universe, and it will always be a part of anything that is ever born.'

I couldn't think about it any more – it was becoming painful; my wound was about to open and remind me of itself. 'So, things just come to you out of nowhere?' I asked quickly, to keep myself talking and not thinking.

'Something like that. I gave up on trying to control my mind – I must numb part of it, otherwise I would go mad. Hearing everything is… exhausting,' she said, penetrating me with her eyes, dissecting every grain of me. 'I'd like to see more of you, though. And one day I'd like you to see what I see when I look at you. It's beautiful.'

We steamed up the room one more time, and in the dark lakes of her eyes I tried to catch a glimpse of what she saw when she looked at me. Did she really see something beautiful there, and not just a wretched mess? Did she see someone other than an orphan, a victim of sexual abuse, a wreck?

\* \* \*

A bright wreath of energy still hovered over me when my mind started shedding the mist of slumber. I wanted to fall back asleep and keep dreaming about a soul-flight, but no matter how hard I tried to keep the neon wreath in my head, it slowly faded away with the rest of the post-dreaming haze.

Aleece was asleep. I got out of bed and put on the slip dress I'd worn the other day. It didn't smell good, but I didn't want to wake her up looking for fresh clothes.

It was still too early for the first signs of dawn. I walked on the streets, killing time, looking for a distraction.

Being with Aleece made my obsession with the soul-flight more acute, because now there was another reason why I wanted to cure myself of my past. I'd been avoiding getting close to anyone – I knew there was no way I could have a chance at a relationship; I was too broken, and I had to fix myself first. Aleece coming into my life made me feel like I needed to fix myself as soon as possible. My heart was still locked – there was no question about it. Even though I imagined I could fall for Aleece – there was a base for it, a connection, an ease I'd never felt before – I still controlled how I felt about her. But the mere possibility of an attachment made me anxious.

My body shook. I wanted someone to come up to me and slap my face. *You idiot*, I thought to myself. *Don't even think about it. Not even as a remote possibility. It's not your life! Love? Are you joking?*

But if I fixed myself, maybe it could be my life? I needed to pacify my mind so it wouldn't torture me like this. And I knew one good way to divert the frustration.

\* \* \*

I went to one of the clubs I'd discovered recently. The dark ambiance allowed for the illumination of just the right amount of flesh so I could find someone to fuck my brains out with – but not to see so much of them as to be utterly disgusted.

I remembered the bartender very clearly, that big burn covering half of his face and neck, and he wore an eyepatch.

*Good for him – that eye was freaking scary.*

I ordered a double shot of vodka. He filled a glass with clear liquid, and I drank it all in one gulp. It was nasty stuff – burned my guts instantly.

I made my way into the darker corners, scouting faces. Some big guy responded to my calling and followed me to a less crowded part of the club. His plaid shirt, tucked into blue jeans, strained so hard at the seams around his shoulders that I was curious if it would rip if he lifted his arms. A metal plate covered the top part of his head. Add a leather vest and he would look like a member of a cheap Cowboys in Space strip show.

'How—?'

'Shut up,' I cut him off, and unbuckled his belt.

He conformed to my mood quickly and unceremoniously. He lifted me up against the wall and caged me with the mountain of his body. The expression on his face changed from a horny dog to a hungry hyena. A light band flared in his eyes. *Shit, I hate that crap.* I assumed he'd just mapped my face and in his mind modified my features to a look he desired, or replaced my face with something entirely different. For all I knew he could be staring at an alien monster right now.

He squeezed my breasts like they were a piece of meat. His pounding inside me was rough. I didn't enjoy it. I hated it – it hurt me. And that's what I came here for: like medicine, a shot of pain and disgust that would put my mind back on track and my heart in its place – in a safe with a lost combination.

Groaning into my ear, going faster, the man clenched my neck. I tried to push him away, but he was massive – I didn't stand a chance to fight him. My vision became blurry, and I couldn't breathe. I was chocking. I thought that was it – I was going to die. *Wasn't that something I wanted?* The thought crossed my mind, but didn't stick. I kept fighting until I lost consciousness.

I opened my eyes again when my body fell to the floor. Coughing, through tears I saw someone fighting the cowboy guy, putting him down with a few punches.

'You OK?' the someone said, squatting over me. I recognised him immediately. John – the mysterious normal-seeming guy who knew my name. 'I hope I didn't ruin your plans to die tonight,' he said, as he helped me to my feet.

He escorted me outside, where the cold of the air hit me. I took a few greedy gasps, which only irritated my throat more, and I croaked like an injured crow.

'Let's get you some water,' he said.

\* \* \*

We went to the same coffee shop we'd gone to the first time we met.

'You've got some skills,' I said, musing on his knocking the life out of that big mass of meat.

John didn't comment.

'Where did you learn to fight?' I pressed.

He ignored my question but didn't take his eyes off mine. He brought a cup of coffee towards his face, inhaled the nutty smell and took a sip.

'What exactly were you trying to do?' he asked.

'What did it look like I was doing?'

'Getting hurt. Diverting your attention from whatever is going on in your life,' he said, bluntly.

I remained silent.

He pushed a button on the table, and the bottom part of a built-in ashtray detached, rotated and slotted back in, presenting a new clean bottom panel.

'Why did you intervene?' I asked. 'You don't even know me.'

'You think we should only help people we know well? Leave the rest to die even if we can save them?'

'Nobody needs to be saved.'

He mumbled something as he lit a cigarette, then said, 'You were fighting him. You didn't want to die.'

'Those were just reflexes,' I said.

'Really? I don't think so.'

Why does everyone assume there are only two states: life and death? What about finding yourself not wanting to die but hating life at the same time? That was surely the most common condition then, anyway. Something might change, you think – you hang on for a while, see what happens, wait for a miracle; you can always kill yourself later.

'You didn't want to die. At least, not tonight.' He exhaled a long column of smoke. 'Sometimes the world may seem pretty empty and scary, but there is always something worth sticking around for.'

'Sometimes? If it was only sometimes, I wouldn't want to die,' I said. 'What do you live for?'

'I don't mind living overall.'

'Well, I do,' I said. 'And how do I know if my reason to stay alive is good enough?'

'If you have any reason at all it's already a victory – it's already a good-enough basis for hanging on to life. I'm still breathing, I'm still conscious, so I can hopefully still do some good – that's my reason.'

He made me feel strange. One part of me resented his concern; another part was drawn to it.

'Whatever you're going through, don't hold it inside,' he said. 'It's important to talk to someone about your feelings.'

'What are you, a shrink? I hate shrinks,' I exploded.

'I'm a neuroscientist,' he said, finishing his coffee.

'I hate scientists too.'

'Yeah, we're not a popular breed these days. That's why if you want to be a scientist you'd better learn how to fight. I gotta go.'

That made sense. I had personal reasons for disliking scientists. They gutted my mind after I'd woken up from a coma, and not a single one of them asked what had led to my overdose in the first place – they were interested only in data. They had my story on file – I imagined there were many authors who co-wrote, altered and contributed to it – so why bother asking me? A shrink would fix me up later, right? I wasn't talkative or friendly; I was sealed off from the outside world, which I assume isn't that unusual for a teenager who has been raped by a priest after her parents killed themselves. And although I never volunteered anything, it turned me inside out that none of these scientists who drew my blood and took pictures of my brain every day made more effort to find out how I'd reached that point. That made the experience of surviving worse. After I was discharged from the hospital I felt even more worthless and alone. So I didn't see why I had to like or trust them.

Some people hated scientists and tech people particularly vehemently, however, and it often got physical – scientists and engineers were blamed for pretty much everything, from failing to solve the mystery behind the suicide pandemic to inventing gadgets that actually stole our souls. And the Church knew how to pour oil on to this fire.

Without thinking, I followed John to wherever he was heading.

'I can recommend a few competent therapists I work with,' John said.

'Is diagnosing strangers your fetish or something?' I asked.

'I can give you a few numbers to call,' he went on, ignoring my remark. 'Maybe one day you'll feel like—'

'No thanks. How many people did they save?' I snapped.

'Aha, OK, let's address that. You're right, not many. That's because there was nothing they could do. And you are not lost to life, you've just been through a lot. You need a little guidance and some willingness to work on yourself. But I understand the scepticism. If you show warning signs, which you do, there are ways to manage them. Not all people who die by suicide exhibit warning signs. And the abnormal suicide is a completely different phenomenon – very little of what we know about suicide applies to these victims. Their impulse to end their lives is a sudden one – sometimes it comes only minutes before they act on it. They don't plan their death. They don't want to die.'

'Oh, bullshit. If they didn't want to die, they would still be here.'

'I'm not going to tell you what to believe. There are certainly plenty of theories to choose from. But in my professional opinion, and I've been studying suicide for a while, I don't think they acted with deliberate intent,' he said. He stopped walking, and indicated that it was his destination.

We were in front of a round marble skyscraper. Above the heavy wooden doors golden letters read 'Saint Angel's Cemetery'. A never-ending tower visible almost from every part of the city, it was likely the most visited building.

I had been here once or twice when I was twelve – my parents' ashes rested here. I remember thousands of small cells spiralling up along the perimeter of the cylindrical hall. Looking up from the middle, it seems as though the round hall leads straight up to the sky, showing lost angels the way home.

'Maybe… OK, maybe they didn't necessarily want to die. But they could have fought the impulse!' I countered. 'If they thought they had something to live for, if they loved something enough, they would have fought it.'

'If it is determined that a person died by abnormal suicide, then nothing led to it, Laura – there was no impulse apart from that final one, which was a very sudden sensation. It was difficult – I believe it was impossible – to control this impulse. And before that there was nothing to fight.'

I felt my throat narrowing, and tears approached my eyes. I blinked and lowered my head.

'Whoever you lost,' he went on, 'try not to… I know it's not my place to tell you how to feel about it, but based on the extensive research – and there were millions of cases studied – when it comes to abnormal suicide, there really was nothing people who took their lives could do to stop it.'

I wiped my eyes with the back of my hand. My head was still bowed, and my knees were getting weak. The reproachful stare of the heavy doors of the cemetery weighed heavily on me.

John squeezed my shoulder. 'Let me give you my number.' He reached into the inner pocket of his sheepskin jacket.

And all of a sudden I collapsed. Whatever usually gave my muscles strength left me, and I fell to my knees.

John kneeled before me and asked what was wrong and if something hurt. I screamed at him to leave me alone. He tried to calm me down, but I pushed him away. He backed off.

The realisation of how different my last fourteen years could have been had I not spent them hating my parents all this time, had I not lost faith, had I not stayed away from every possible human connection was overwhelming. Of course I hated them – they had betrayed me, left me on my own. To confound things the priest was supposed to guide me, but he raped me instead – and that had happened because of *them*. It was their fault that I was raped. How could the memory of my parents be the same after that? They left me alone. They didn't explain anything. They didn't protect me. They led me into the devil's snare.

*But if they didn't want to die…*

It was hard to digest the implications of such a fact.

*They didn't want to die.*

But of course they did. If they didn't, they wouldn't have done it. But they did. Nobody made them put a rope around their necks. They were not sick. They did it to themselves. It's not like they didn't know what they were doing. How could something cloud your judgement so much you don't notice you're putting a rope around your neck? Bullshit. How dare John show up and start coming out with this bullshit? I wanted to kill him. He was just another fraud. What did he know about my parents? How could he known they didn't want to die? That all these people didn't want to die? His theory was crap, invented to help poor suckers come to terms with their loss. Blame it on something else – yes, go ahead, blame it on anything but those who actually did it. Our loved ones who left us. Nobody forced them. They did it.

*And if I'm wrong? What then?*

A brief moment of relief teased my heart – but then a new pain ripped it into pieces again as I realised how fragile my superficial shield was. For years I'd been erecting a wall between me and my past, between me and the outside world, between me and myself. Brick by brick I'd been protecting myself, only to find out that my wall could be shattered with a brief allusion of hope that my parents didn't leave me willingly – which means that maybe they loved me, maybe I should have grieved, maybe I shouldn't have hated them.

Merciless feelings washed over me. I felt as though I had been thrown into the storming ocean with nothing but a broken raft, and I was drowning.

Regret crawled out of the fissures of my heart like a swarm of cockroaches. It bit me till everything inside me bled. I tried to resist, but it turned into a whip and struck ruthlessly until I finally allowed myself to believe that maybe John was right.

All I could do was say, 'I'm sorry, I'm so sorry,' again and again.

It had started to rain – I hadn't noticed it start, but I was already wet. I felt someone's hands on my upper back. It was John.

'I'm so...' I began, but a blast of tears stopped me from finishing.

'Let's get you somewhere warm and dry,' he said kindly.

'I can't...' I said, looking up at him and shaking my head.

'Yes you can – come on,' he said, holding out his hand.

'I can't stand up,' I said. 'I can't feel my legs.' I really couldn't – my whole body was numb. 'I can't feel anything.' If I were not so emotionally crushed, I would have started panicking, because for a moment I didn't feel my body at all.

He wrapped his big arm around my back and helped me to stand up. My body seemed to be functioning after all, so when he asked me if I could walk I told him I could. Then he asked if I'd like him to take me home. I told him I didn't want to go home.

'Would you like to go to my place and talk?' he asked.

I agreed to that. We took a taxi – it was a short ride – and I calmed down a little on the way. It felt good to have someone to talk to, I admitted to myself – I didn't want to be alone.

John's apartment was on the sixteenth floor. It was spacious but homey. The open-plan living room was furnished in light colours – mostly white and grey. The floor-to-ceiling windows presented a wide view of the city. It was almost surreal how warm and *normal* his place was. It made me feel out of place.

John took my coat, told me to make myself comfortable and brought two cups of coffee over, and fetched a blanket.

'Here,' he said, wrapping the blanket around my shoulders. He sat down in a chair next to the sofa I was sitting on, and waited for me to start talking whenever I was ready.

It didn't work – it was hard for me to start. It was hard for me to open my mouth and start talking on my own.

'What happened?' he said, trying to help get things going.

'What you said, is it true?' I asked. 'Is it proven?'

'About suicide?'

'Yes. People who killed themselves... you said they didn't want to die.'

'They didn't,' he said. 'In the case of the abnormal suicide, I believe they didn't.'

'There is evidence?'

'Of course. There are numerous multi-disciplinary studies that all point to the same conclusion. Experts from various fields all over the world have worked together and gathered an extensive amount of data: interviews with friends and family, analyses of risk factors, psychological assessments, medical histories, crime-scene investigations. By now millions of simulations have been created. I myself worked with many professionals, from psychotherapists and epidemiologists to forensic scientists and VR engineers to recreate the final moments of the suicide victims and attempters, and to investigate their mental states at the time. Our findings were consistent with those of other studies, and showed that in the majority of cases there was no previous intention to self-harm. On top of that, many people who survived their attempts said they didn't want to do it – they were confused about what had happened, and indeed many had no memory of it, but many said they remembered a sudden impulse that came out of nowhere, and they were afraid that it would happen again and they wouldn't be able to do anything to stop it. Most of them tried again and succeeded.'

It was hard to accept what he was saying after thinking something very different for fourteen years. The strange part was that I knew all that – I had seen the interviews, heard these frightened people talk about it. They were terrified because they wanted to live, but something had taken control of their bodies and guided them to the edge, into the river, towards pills or the knives. And there were notes discovered with horrifying messages like, 'If I'm found dead, please believe I didn't do it myself.' It was true – all this information was available, and I'd seen it – but I was still shocked by what John was saying, and my mind was trying to reject it. It always had done. With the rational part of my mind I could explain that it was possible that my parents didn't die willingly, but that possibility made me more angry – it always did – and made me reject it all the more vehemently. As a result, I had never accepted it, and now my whole body was telling me I was being deceived. What if John was in denial himself? He'd lost his entire family – how could he assess the situation objectively? He too needed something to believe in, and he believed in what helped him cope with his loss.

Eventually I asked, 'Then what made them do it?'

'There is no official explanation,' he said. 'There are many theories. I can't confirm or deny anything. I don't know what made them do it.'

'So you're keeping quiet about what you've discovered?' I asked, furious – the desperation of my brain trying to find someone to blame was palpable.

'Not at all,' he said. 'All our findings are out there. The research is comprehensive, but it doesn't offer a reason. And people are more prone to believe something conclusive – they want resolution. And we don't have answers.'

I stared ahead into nothingness, trying to replay bits of my life in my mind that I'd long locked away. It was like watching a damaged old video file: my hatred and shame distorted some information, and my later years glitched and froze and turned black in some places.

'My parents killed themselves when I was twelve,' I said after a while. 'All my life I hated them. All this time I believed they ended it because I wasn't good enough. And I tried to kill myself too. There hasn't been a day, an hour, even a minute in my life I could say I enjoyed living.'

'I'm really sorry, Laura.'

'Why haven't you shared your findings?' I asked, on the attack again, my mind initiating its defence mechanism and rejecting what it didn't want to accept. If I accepted it, I would have to construct a very different version of my past, and that would involve a whole new kind of pain.

'We did share it,' he insisted. 'As I said, it's all out there. But there is a lot of other information out there, too.'

'You have to keep telling people,' I said.

'People don't want to hear that their loved ones didn't want to die,' he said, patiently, 'unless they are given a reason why they did it. And I don't have an answer. There are many theories that offer an explanation – although often a connection is unconvincing, to put it mildly: you'll lose your soul if you meditate too much; eat too much of this or that and you'll die; Wi-Fi makes people jump from windows, and if you have any kind of implant you're finished. Then there are aliens, extra-dimensional telepathy, mini wormholes through which people's souls escape into other universes. There are so many social and personal factors that influence what people choose to believe, and it's not easy to change that. For example, do you believe me?'

I took some time to think. My mind was impenetrable. I tried asking myself, but there was no answer.

'I don't know,' I said, and wiped my eyes as tears started falling again. 'It's hard to believe something when you've lived fourteen years with a different conviction. Especially when that conviction made you who you are.'

'Exactly. You will believe your own experience over anything else. Even if I show you hundreds of interviews and supporting documents proving our volunteers had no symptoms and couldn't fight what was coming, maybe you'll think that it doesn't necessarily apply to your parents. In this climate, without having solid evidence to back up our words, it's impossible to be heard and taken seriously. There's too much politics in it. And even when presented with evidence, people still doubt its authenticity. It only takes one person to say that our data is fake, and the rumour will spread like wildfire, and causes huge damage. It's only been a year since cases started to go down – we're not back at pre-pandemic levels yet, but close – and people are just beginning to regain trust in life. I think everyone needs a little time to reconnect with themselves before we start throwing more theories into the mix.'

'So the Church will keep spreading bullshit stories about souls abandoning humanity for its sins?' I asked no one in particular. 'And the priests will be heroes, because they are the only ones who can help our souls find peace? I don't need fucking priests praying for my parents' souls. I need hope that they didn't just abandon me, that they loved me, so I can pray for them myself, so I can remember them. I remember nothing.'

I wept. John was silent. After a few minutes he got up and placed a box of tissues in front of me on the coffee table. I took a few and blew my nose.

'I'm sorry,' he said. There was genuine compassion in his eyes.

I stared out of the window. My mind was quieting down. It had fought and resisted and objected, but that was now recessing. A new battle lay ahead, but before that, time would have to do its job and allow for all these new emotions and discoveries to process and integrate in my head. Maybe today I wouldn't take a sleeping pill and would use the time to think instead.

But I suddenly realised I couldn't go home and think now. 'Shit. What time is it?' I asked. My phone was in my coat.

'Almost ten.'

I was two hours late for my shift. I asked John if I could use the bathroom. He showed me where it was, and I washed my face, cursing inwardly. I looked bad – my face was red and swollen from tears, and mascara was smudged all over.

'Here's my number,' said John when I came out, handing me a piece of paper. My coat hung over his forearm. 'If you ever need anything, or just want to talk.'

I thanked him. On my way out I noticed two photographs on a shelf in the hallway. One picture showed twin girls – not identical, but looking almost the same, about five or six years old, both of them were laughing. There was a sandy beach behind them. The other photo was of John and a woman, probably his wife or girlfriend. He was hugging her from behind, arms crossed at her chest. She had her head thrown back and her mouth was frozen wide open in the most exuberant smile. I'd never seen so much happiness in one smile.

I realised now the warm homey atmosphere in the apartment was kept for them. And it was clear he'd lost them all.

'My daughters took their lives when they were six,' John said, noticing me looking. 'Jess was lucky she didn't witness it. She died in childbirth.'

'I'm sorry,' I said.

The number of women dying in childbirth was declining, but maternal mortality rates had been disastrously high at the peaks of the suicide pandemic. People were only just beginning to have babies again.

'Thank you. You take care of yourself,' he said.

I wish I could say I would.

# 5

---

The streets were grey, dry and empty. Those who hadn't managed to reach home before the effect of drugs wore off sat on the pavement or doorsteps, hiding their faces, crying. Coming back to a sober brain is never a sweet experience. That's why I don't like daytime – the light exposes our lives and makes fun of us; it shines on us but never touches us. The wind picked up and changed directions rapidly, pushing garbage around like a football. Cleaning robots rolled about, occasionally bumping into each other, swallowing wrappers, ketchup-stained paper plates, condoms and broken glass, washing urine and vomit off the pavement. The city was full of us, abandoned people, who did a good job wrecking it every night, reminding it that we indeed existed; yet every morning, when we crawled back to our apartments, it looked empty. And every morning the early emptiness asked to be filled, but there was nothing to fill it with, nothing we could offer to a new day and nothing it could offer to us.

I had to wait for an hour before someone opened the door to Dirty Castle. I'd anticipated that being two hours late wouldn't be in my favour, but it hadn't occurred to me that I could be in serious trouble for not showing up on time. Now I was worried.

Finally the door opened. Jeff let me in and escorted me to the dressing room. 'Craig will see you after your shift,' he said.

Would Craig kick me out? Would I have to work here another month to prove my trustworthiness before I could go on a soul-flight? I was fed up with the place – that is, not with the place itself, with having to show up here every day.

The old witch came in. She observed me with her white eyes while I was changing.

'I don't like you,' she said. 'No use for you here. Better if you don't come back next time.' Her scratchy voice dragged through my ears, leaving a nasty sludge.

She was such a witch.

I turned into a spectre and moved from table to table, offering guests self-dissolving gel beans for a more intense experience of the show.

I thought about my parents. Memories came in fragments: my mother's laughter, my father's eyes, me playing hide-and-seek, a book in my mother's hands. I didn't trust these images yet – I'd spent too long erasing them from my memory. I was cautious not to allow my heart to make conclusions too quickly, as I sensed the prospect of disappointment hiding nearby, waiting to attack. But behind the shadow of fear there was hope – hope that maybe, gradually, I might find the courage to face these memories and assemble them into a different past: a past where my parents didn't kill themselves because I wasn't enough, a past that would help me redefine who I was.

A customer grabbed my hand as I passed by their table, disturbing my reverie. I turned around and looked down, and my heart stopped. My mouth opened, an involuntarily groan escaping, and I squinted, my vision having become fuzzy with tears. It was dark and he wore a hood, but even in the shadow I could never mistake those wet, hungry eyes.

'Hi, Laura,' he said. The wheezing, poisonous voice stung me.

My knees became weak, and I felt as though I might collapse.

'How are you, child? You haven't changed much. Oh, you grew, you grew. A woman now. Still a little girl to me. You will always be my little girl, won't you?' he said, his grinning face already greased with a nasty fantasy. The hood could not hide the abomination of his essence. His aura was black and sodden in children's tears. Even when he died, it would be impossible to wash his filth from the air that circulated Earth.

I tried to free my hand, but he held it tight.

'I pray for your parents every day. You didn't think I forgot about them, did you? Their souls are at peace. They are in heaven,' he said, pulling me closer. 'I will pray for you. Do you still trust God?' He touched my inner thigh. 'Would you like that?'

I wrestled my hand from his grip and ran to the dressing room. Images from the past flooded my head. I saw everything again so clearly – the morning of my birthday, how excited I was; I wanted to go camel riding – my parents promised me we would. And a cake. I ran to the kitchen, where the cake was on the table, decorated with red and purple flowers and two fairy figures in the middle. It was my favourite cake.

I called for my mum and dad, listened, called again. After making sure nobody was watching, I sneaked a taste of the icing with my finger. It was delicious. Then I ran into their room, excited to wake them up and see what other presents they got me.

But there was no present for me that day, only their death.

I made a call to the emergency services. They arrived fast. Later some woman came and explained to me what would happen next. I was assigned to an orphanage, where we had support groups and church visits to help us deal with our loss and regain trust in life. And for some time talking to nuns and priests did make me feel better, and I even started to think I would be OK. I enjoyed praying, too. It made me feel like there was a higher power that loved me and would protect me.

One day a priest told me he wanted to show me something. We went into a room. We were there alone. He told me that I was special, that my parents were still here, always watching over me and taking care of me, and if I wanted them to stay, I had to pray harder. He was going to show me how to pray – a very special prayer, he said.

I was on my knees. He came closer and squeezed my cheeks, slid his thumb over my lips and into my mouth. His black robe that had many buttons was already unbuttoned up to his waist. He moved his thumb in and out my mouth while opening his trousers with his other hand. When he attempted to stick his disgusting hardness in my mouth, I screamed and tried to escape, but he caught me. He held me tight. I tried to break free, kicking and yelling. He bent me over his desk and hurt me. I cried, hoping someone would hear me. He covered my mouth with one hand and told me to be silent and pray while he rubbed himself against my flesh.

Then the door opened, someone came in, he lost focus and I managed to run away.

I remembered the pain and shame. I wanted to rip my skin off my bones, get rid of the filth he'd kneaded into my every atom.

From that moment the memory of my parents was distorted.

I didn't tell anyone until a few weeks later, when I refused to go to the church. No one believed me.

\* \* \*

'Laura,' Aleece called, bringing me back to the present. 'What happened? You're shaking all over.'

'I need to get out of here,' I said. 'Can you leave now?'

'Sure,' she said.

On our way out one of the security guards stopped us. 'Craig wants to see you,' he told me.

'Tomorrow,' was all I managed to say.

'Now,' he insisted, and blocked the door with his tall square mass.

I looked at Aleece. She placed her hand on my shoulder, as if to reassure me that it would be all right.

'I'll wait outside,' she said.

I followed the security guy to Craig's office. He was the last person I wanted to see now – him and his obnoxious antique desk that separated normal people from his power, wealth and genius.

'Well, Laura,' Craig said, pointing to the chair across from his desk. I sat down. 'Looks like today is your lucky day.'

I couldn't reply to this surreal statement. There were no words in my mouth, no expression on my face – I couldn't feel my face at all.

'You don't come here whenever it pleases you, unless you pay. Either you work here when I say or you don't work here at all.'

'Some stuff came up,' I said.

'I'm sure it did.'

'It won't happen again.'

'And I believe it will, darling. I don't think your commitment is serious enough, and I don't have a habit of wasting my time.'

'My commitment *is* serious enough. I'm working for you for free.'

'Well, in that case, I have a proposition for you,' he said.

There was that sensation again: like being chocked by an invisible hand. My throat closed; hair rose on my arms. I don't know how, but I knew exactly what he was about to say.

His lips moved, but my eardrums rejected the airwaves, and I heard nothing.

'I thought your time here was done after you didn't show up this morning. But His Excellency, apparently, has some interest in you.'

I just stared at Craig, unable to speak.

'Laura? Do you hear what I'm saying?'

'Tell His Excellency to go fuck himself,' I finally managed to squeeze out.

Craig laughed. 'This temper will get you in trouble one day.'

'Is there anything else you wanted to talk about?' I asked, standing up.

He came around his desk and opened the door for me. 'No need for you to come back tomorrow, then,' he said. 'Or any other day.'

'We had a deal! I'm not a prostitute.'

'Nobody is – we all do business here.'

'I worked for you for weeks without getting paid,' I said. 'We had a deal.'

'You will get paid for your time, but I'm afraid I can't give you a loan, so you will have to save up if you still want a soul-flight. Of course, I can't promise we will have the same deals and products available. You know how this business is – things change every minute.' The pause that followed was more cynical than his words. 'Or you could fuck the priest and fly whenever you want.'

'How much is he paying you for this?'

'That's none of your business,' he said. 'The question is, how much are you willing to give to get what you want?'

'You are a sick motherfucker! This is not about money for you,' I said.

'No, nothing is about money for me,' he shrugged. 'Never was. I want to know how far you will go to get what you want. Because if you really want a soul-flight – if you really, really want it – the bond of your soul and my technology will be so profound that the result... Mmm, you can't even imagine where it will take you. A miracle will happen. And that's what I live for – to witness miracles.'

'What miracle?'

'You'll just have to work for it and see,' he said.

I was silent for a time.

'I'll take that as a yes,' he said. 'Tomorrow at four he will expect you.' He turned around and went back to his desk.

* * *

Aleece and I found a bar and ordered a few shots, trading her fancy cocktails for vodka, neat.

I told her everything.

'That man was the priest?' she asked, her eyes watery.

'Don't call him a man!' I spat. 'He's a monster.' I gulped my drink. 'This can't be just a coincidence, can it? That Craig found him? Although I wouldn't be surprised if that animal was a regular at Dirty Castle.'

'Why don't you just walk away?' she asked.

'Walk away where? To do what?'

'You can do whatever you want,' she said.

'But I don't want anything! I'm stuck. I need something to shift – in my head... or, I don't know... Something has to change. I can't keep living the life I lived. I'm already not there.' I gestured behind my shoulder, as though my entire past was spread out behind me. 'I'm cut off from what I used to be – I have to become someone new. There is no way I'm stepping back into what I was.'

My thoughts became black, like oil. There was so much darkness in my head. It felt like some dark entity possessed me and filled me with its essence. I was hyperventilating. I covered my face with my palms, scared that if I removed them all this darkness would come gushing out of me like black vomit. I had to kill this beast.

'Laura!' Aleece called.

I lowered my hands a little. When I saw her, when I saw all the other people sitting behind her and in the room around us, I knew I no longer belonged to this world. I had to go on a soul-flight. If I were a machine, I would say I was programmed this way, that it was a part of my code, and that nothing could overwrite it.

'I have to do it,' I said. 'I must. I need to hurt myself enough to erase everything inside me, so I can fill it with something else.'

'I don't think you understand what you are saying,' Aleece said. Her eyes were wide and glistening with tears. 'You are in shock.'

'I've never wanted anything so badly. Something is going to change after I fly,' I said, tapping my chest with my fist. 'I know it. But I have to go through this pain – I need to let it devour me, completely, so there is nothing left for it to feed on any more. I must be gone, and my soul should remain. Clean, pure, without me. Yes, that's it! This humiliation, this pain will destroy both me and this monstrous thing inside me, and all that will be left is my soul. That's what he wants!'

'Who wants that?' Aleece asked.

'Craig – and I feel the same way. I must disappear so that I can be something new. You understand, don't you?'

She started at me, then lowered her eyes, and for a long time she seemed to be thinking about something.

I was overtaken by my revelation. Everything seemed so clear and in the right place. Things were happening exactly as they should.

'You can't trust Craig,' Aleece said.

'I don't. What do you know about him?'

Another reservoir of silence.

'He is my father,' she said.

'What?'

'Craig is my father,' she repeated.

'Your biological father?' I wasn't sure if she meant her real father or a fatherly figure of some sort.

'Yes, my biological father.'

'You are joking? You said you didn't have anyone left. Why did you lie?' She didn't owe me an explanation – but to hide this fact...

'I...' she hesitated.

'Let me guess – you didn't remember? That's very convenient, don't you think?'

'I do remember sometimes. Like now. I've just remembered that he is my father.'

I rubbed my face and massaged my temples to relieve the pressure. She wasn't lying, either – that I knew without a doubt: she couldn't.

'Did *he* do this to you? These experiments?' I asked.

'I don't know. I told you, I don't know what screwed me up. I left this place a long time ago. He holds a fraction of my ghost in metal shackles, but I'm too far gone to come back.' She looked down, blinking her long lashes. What she was saying didn't make much sense.

'He makes you work in the club?' I asked.

'I don't work there. And the club is only a cover for the best lab in the city. It's pretty much where I have to live, if I want to live. I sabotage the stage from time to time. Helps me release the energy. He doesn't like it when I do.'

When she raised her head again, it seemed as if a wave washed out her features. Every cell of her face was naked and blank. There was nothing that separated me from her – she was about to dissolve into thin air.

'I'm afraid,' Aleece said.

'Of Craig?'

'No – I'm not afraid of him. I'm afraid that everything I did, I did for the wrong reason.'

'What did you do?' I asked.

'I can't remember. This thing inside me won't let me remember.' She got up from the table, not looking at me any more.

'What thing? Where are you going?' I asked, but she just ran outside.

I followed.

She turned around, grabbed my shoulders and pressed me against the wall.

'What the fuck, Aleece?' I cried out. 'You're hurting me!'

She let go and rushed away again. Her slim figure grew smaller and smaller, and the fog consumed her, leaving me perplexed and alone, face to face with my choice.

*I will find you again, Aleece, and I will help you find answers, find yourself – whatever you need, I will help you. I just need to help myself first. There is strength in me, I just need to wake it up.*

I went home, fell on the bed and slept.

* * *

'Laura, honey, come here,' the sweet voice of my mother poured out from another room.

'You have to find me first!' I called.

*Oh, no! I exposed myself. Just sit tight and wait. But maybe she didn't realise where my voice came from. Yes, she probably didn't,* I thought, and an ardour returned to me.

'Where is the little monkey?' my mum asked. 'I can't see her anywhere. Did she run back to the jungle?'

*No, no, she didn't run back,* I thought, giggling. I heard my mum's steps and held my breath, lips pursed and ears pricked.

'Hmm, she is not under the table. She is not behind the door. Where could she be?'

Mum was coming closer and closer. I pulled my neck in as much as I could, as if it would help me stay invisible, and waited for her to move the curtain. As soon as she moved it, I would scream and scare her.

As I waited, anxiety slinked into my chest.

'Where is the monkey? I can't find her,' my mum kept saying.

I heard her voice, and her steps seemed so close, but nobody pulled the curtain. I let out a giggle; she still couldn't find me. I tugged at the curtain – *she should notice that,* I thought.

I was a bit worried. *Should I come out?* I was hiding so well, though. I didn't know what to do. That was the longest my mummy looked for me. I had hidden so well, my efforts would be wasted if I exposed myself, but I was getting too scared of being alone now.

Finally I pulled the curtain. Nothing happened – the curtain still hung before me. I tried again, pulling and pulling, tugging and tugging, and more and more of the thick brown satin material fell into my hands and on top of my head. It was a never-ending curtain.

'Mum! Mummy!' I started screaming. 'I'm here! I'm here, Mummy!'

I wrestled with the fabric that now covered me all. It was so heavy I couldn't even stand up, and my legs were deep in fabric. As soon as I tried to get to my feet, I tumbled down and rolled in the fabric. Brown fabric was everywhere – so heavy, so tight around me, I couldn't move at all.

'Mummy, please! Mum!' I screamed, tears blasting from my eyes.

'Laura, honey, wake up.'

I opened my eyes and Mum was right there in front of me.

'You had a bad dream, honey.' She caressed my face, her hands warm and soft. She was smiling.

'I was h-hiding... and you d-didn't... you didn't f-find me,' I said.

'Oh, monkey.' She pulled me towards her from under a puffy duvet and hugged me. 'I will always find you – no matter where you are, I will always, always find you.'

She pressed me harder against her warm body. I felt her familiar creamy smell.

'I d-don't want t-to be alone,' I murmured.

'You will never be alone, honey. Daddy and I love you so much. We will always be with you. We will always find you, even on the edge of the world,' she said. She looked at me, her eyes brown and kind.

'On the e-edge o-of the world?' I asked.

'Yes,' she said, smiling. 'Even on the edge of the world.'

She kissed my watery eyes and wiped the tears off my cheeks. 'You promise?'

'Pinkie promise,' she said, and we shook our pinkies.

I instantly felt better – nothing could break a pinkie promise.

* * *

I opened my eyes. *No. No, no, no.*

'Don't leave me,' I whispered, holding my mum's face in my memory, pressing my hands against my eyes to prevent them from opening.

'Don't leave me. Please!' Tears rolled down my cheeks.

The image of her hurt; all the same, I didn't want to let go of it. I hadn't dreamed about my parents for a very long time. Not like this.

I could still sense my mum's creamy smell. I kept inhaling until the day and the place and the world I lived in bleached it out completely and replaced it with reality. This ugly new day. And my future deed that would burn this day into my memory for ever.

# 6

---

Craig rolled a tiny silver object the size and shape of a kidney bean between his long fingers with lazy fascination. He seemed to be holding an inner dialogue with the object – or perhaps with the universe, or whoever he usually addressed in his dogmatic speeches.

When I sat down across his desk, he brought the dialogue outward.

'People have so many weaknesses, so many buttons to push,' he said, keeping his eyes on the little shiny thing. 'All these buttons we created. And for what? To control one another, to maintain order? Order...' He grinned and looked at me. 'Let's take *dignity* as an example – a trap that I never could understand. It has no physical substance, yet it seems to have so much weight, doesn't it? But *dignity* is nothing but a by-product of a blinded ego.' He paused. 'It sickens me to see how primitive we are.'

He placed the object on the table, slid it forward and gestured for me to inspect it. I picked it up with my thumb and pointy fingers. It was heavier than I expected.

'When you take a soul-flight, you will realise that you belong to a superior generation, free from the crippling qualities that make humans slaves to their crude minds. You deserve to experience real freedom – freedom from a body and its impulses, freedom from persistent genes, from social banalities.'

He got up, walked around me and placed his hands on the back of my chair. His presence made the skin on my neck tingle.

'Using resources that we have to get what we want is our most basic instinct. I could never understand why people try to justify means. Evolution doesn't care about means, it cares about results; it takes mutation after mutation to introduce and adapt a species to an environment. And we've lost interest in our physical environment a long time ago. Our environment is no longer this.' He tapped on his desk. 'It is here.' He motioned his hand through the air. 'And here.' He touched his temple. 'But we can't make a full use of it unless we uncover the hidden resources of our bodies and work with them.'

A long pause followed. Something in his voice made me feel like I wouldn't leave this room. Not in one piece, anyway.

Craig bent over and whispered in my ear, 'You think you are paying a high price?'

I tried not to give away my fear, but my pulsating energy shook the walls of the room. He reached out to my hand, took the silver bean and brought it up to my face at eye level.

'What you will experience is priceless. Look at it. Don't be afraid. Oh, stop shaking! Look. You want it, don't you? To transcend your limitations, to see what's next for the human race?'

He waited for a response, and when it didn't come he returned to his chair. I exhaled.

'I'm proud of you. You are a very strong woman. A woman who understands what's important. Don't let yourself be fooled by barbaric dogmas that were implanted in your brain before you were born. Don't cling to our nature – we've always been only a stage; we are a transformation, one of countless out there.'

I hated to admit it, but I found comfort in his words, was grateful for his mad delirium, which I presently decided to believe in. He was right: who cared about means when I was about to experience a miracle and become a completely different person? I even went as far as accepting his words as my own truth – at least for the night. One crazy thought more in my head, what difference did it make? Anything to help me justify what I was about to do.

\* \* \*

Among the many doors along a dimly lit corridor I found the one with the number I'd been given. The room was dark inside; thick brown curtains blocked all the daylight. I lay on a bed. At first time passed slowly, then everything started happening too fast.

The door opened. My heart dropped. I closed my eyes – I couldn't look. I wouldn't open them until it was over, I told myself.

'Hello, Laura,' the priest said.

The sound of the shutting door thundered in my chest. The smell of sweat, candle wax and old age wasted on sin rather than wisdom intruded.

'Such a beautiful girl you became,' he said, sliding his hand along my thigh and lifting my dress. 'Don't be afraid – God is with you,' he said.

*God is with me.*

He took off his cassock and unbuckled his belt.

'I was worried about you, Laura. You were so young the last time I saw you. I wanted to protect you, to prepare you for life. Real life is hard, child. I hope with my help you were ready to face it. All of you are like my own children to me. It's difficult for me, I'm not going to lie – it is very, very difficult at times for a man like me. My heart is too soft. But we all have duties, and mine are harder than most. It is a burden I promised to carry when I became a servant of our Heavenly Father. You see, child, I must pass on life lessons and share God's love and His punishment. There is no life without suffering. You must learn that.'

I heard his trousers drop to the floor.

'Look at you now,' he said, grabbing my legs and pulling me to the edge of the bed. 'All grown-up, and still seeking my guidance.'

I gasped, but the air was not reaching my lungs.

*Don't think. Don't think. You are not here. It's not you. You will be new. This is someone else — you are not her any more.*

I imagined Aleece, attempting to divert my attention and find a refuge in her beautiful freckled face, but the reality was overwhelming. The disgust and shame I felt now were far more scathing than the memories from fourteen years ago, because now I didn't even struggle, I chose not to.

The priest didn't talk any more, just bellowed and grunted like an animal. He was inside me. I had to hide somewhere from all this: past and present. Hide. Back to the scary dream I'd had this morning.

*Hide behind the brown curtain and wait for this to be over. Shh, quiet. Be still and nobody will find you.*

I sat still, clutching a knife. I wasn't a bit surprised to have a knife in my hand. A sudden and persistent impulse possessed me, a foretaste of liberation flickered on the edge of the blade. My brain tried to resist the temptation, but the memory of my body commanded me to act. I got up from the floor and opened the curtain; the hunched figure of the priest was on top of me, of that other me that lay on the bed. I looked at myself — her eyes were full of horror. She was under the priest, defeated, drowning in shame and humiliation. I stood in front of him with the knife in my hand, and I wanted nothing more but to see his rotten soul leave his body, get sucked straight into hell and burn, skin melting off his screaming face.

In the eyes of my other self I also saw others who had lain under this demon: victims of his nasty carnality, scarred with never-ending pain, shame and guilt that shaped who they had become.

One more step and I drove the blade under his ribs. He yelped. His lips twisted; his eyes were even more ugly now, filled with fright. I pulled out the knife and thrust it in again and again, until the blood spilled from his mouth and he crushed over me.

'It's OK,' I said to my other petrified self. 'He deserved it.'

*What will I do when I open my eyes and see his face grinning at me?*
*What will I do when he finishes and leaves? How will I move through life*
*with these memories? Was it worth it? Was it? What if I meet my parents*
*in that glass cell when my soul flies free? How will I look them in the eyes*
*knowing how much pain is in their hearts? The pain that I caused them*
*because of them.*

Thinking about it made me realise I wanted them to hurt.
Hurting myself all these years, destroying myself beyond repair
seemed like the only way to show my parents how badly they
had hurt me. Even now, knowing that they may not have wanted
to kill themselves, I still couldn't forgive them for what I had
gone through because of them. Maybe it was evil of me, but it
was beyond my control; I pitied myself, and I wanted them to
feel my pain.

My body called me back into my flesh, and I felt the weight
of the priest again. He was heavy and motionless; no pounding
inside me, no groaning.

I opened my eyes. By the side of the bed stood another me.
Or… was it Aleece? I blinked a few times – it was Aleece, but
the face… it was my face. She wiped the tears that sat on my
cheeks. She kissed my lips. Yes, it was Aleece, and my face was
melting into her features.

I felt wetness. I was covered in red… blood.

The mass on top of me was lifeless.

I crawled out from under the priest and recoiled from Aleece
and the bed, where the red stain percolated through the white
yarn of sheets.

'Is he…? Did you…?' I tried to ask Aleece. I was afraid to
hear the answer; the image of me killing him was vivid – maybe
she had changed her shape like she did on the stage and become
me. But I'd felt the knife in my hand – it was my hand that had
driven the blade under his ribs.

'You want to know if I killed him?' she asked, her voice calm.

'Who else could have killed him?' I said. I knew I couldn't
have – I'd been under him all this time. But it had felt so real:

the knife – the same knife that was now on the floor covered in blood – the resistance of his meat when I'd sunk the blade into his flesh.

'Did you want to kill him?' she asked.

'Answer me!' I demanded.

'He was hurting you. For fourteen years.' She made a step closer. I moved away, afraid of her. She was stoic as always, above everything and everybody.

'Just fucking answer me! Why did you have my face on?'

*She set me up. She works with Craig. Of course! She is his daughter – or so he tells her.*

'Do you understand what you've done?' I asked. 'I'm never getting out of here.'

'I just wanted you to be free,' she said. 'I wanted you to feel it.' She came close and placed her palm on my cheek. 'Do you feel free now?' she asked.

I looked at the dead body. The blood dripped on the floor, forming a little red lake. It felt good. Killing him felt good. But not as good as I'd imagined.

She pulled the straps of my bloodstained dress off my shoulders. The dress slid down my body and fell on the floor. I stood completely naked, looking at the dark-brown curtain, at the red lake that was getting bigger, at the mouth-cave of the priest. Aleece brought a dressing gown from the bathroom and wrapped it around me.

I heard steps. Two guards opened the door. They acted like they didn't see anything.

'Craig is waiting for you,' said one.

I glanced at Aleece; she didn't seem the least bit alarmed, and her expression was as calm as ever. I tried to ask her with my eyes, scrutinising every muscle of her face, searching for a sign.

The man started towards me. My impulse was to run, but there was no way I could get past them. Where would I run? How could I run from this? I had just murdered a priest.

Aleece raised her hand and the guard backed off. 'I will never leave you,' she whispered into my ear. 'Don't be afraid. As long as I can, I'll be near until you are safe.'

She dismantled me with her eyes; my body opened up layer by layer. Aleece sucked the distance between our lips and caught my mouth with hers and pulled me closer. I didn't feel the floor – it didn't exist under our feet any more. The distorted face of the corpse, the cold triumph on my face, the horror in the eyes of my other self blurred into one warped vision. The room was spinning. When it stopped, we stood on the edge of a cliff in the tall green grass. Aleece held my hand, and the air was cold and reassuring. Before us, the riotous ocean abutted the horizon. The horizon captured the ocean, eating up every chance of escape. The ocean roared, lashing itself, furrowing its surface with white foaming scars. But it wasn't the scream of the waves I heard. It wasn't the ocean that asked to be released.

Was it the sound of a caged soul?

I glanced at Aleece one more time before leaving the room with the two men. She didn't flinch.

# 7

During the few minutes it took to reach Craig's office, I thought about the situation I was in. As far as I could see, there were two scenarios: I could either go to jail or do what Craig told me to do – I would be his slave, and he would make me do terrible things. What kind of things? That was another question. And how long would I remain in his servitude? My whole life? Until I was ready to go to jail? Was there a particular task he wanted me to perform, after which I'd be released? Was I naïve to think that he would ever let me go?

I lowered myself into the chair in front of his intimidating desk.

'Are you ready for your soul-flight?' Craig asked.

I couldn't understand what he was saying – it was as though he spoke an alien language. *Is he testing me? Toying with me like an overfed tiger with its food?*

'What's with all the drama?' he asked. 'It's all over your face! You look like you saw a ghost – a holy ghost, maybe?' His laughter hurt my brain.

I looked down. There were stains of blood on my hands. I hid them in the pockets of my gown.

'Your room is prepared for you. We can start whenever you are ready,' he said. 'Why wait?'

I glanced over my shoulder to see if the guard was still standing behind me. There was no one there.

'What about... What about the priest?' I asked.

'What about him?'

'What are you going to do with his... with me?'

He leaned back in his chair and for a long time just stared at me. I started trembling – I couldn't help it; my shock was finding its way out of my body. I needed to know the answers to all my questions, or I would go mad. *What will you do with his corpse? What will you do with me? Will I go to jail?* But I couldn't bring myself to ask – my mouth was too dry.

Then something strange happened. Craig closed his eyes and frowned, as though he was in pain. An internal fight seemed to distort his face. His lips twitched; the knots of his jaw muscles bulged; he was clenching his teeth.

'What brought you here, Laura?' he asked. It was his voice, but he sounded like a very different person.

'Craig, I-I-I didn't do it,' I stammered, and started crying. 'It wasn't me. I couldn't – I was under him—'

'Shh.' He raised his hand and asked, again, in the same strange voice, 'What brought you *here*?'

'I don't know. I don't know!' I was so disoriented. *What's going on?*

'Yes you do. And you will see it through.'

'Craig, please—'

He stood up. I heard steps behind me.

'Make it happen,' Craig snapped.

The guards asked me to come with them. I obeyed. They escorted me back to the dressing room. One of them remained outside and another walked inside with me. He told me to clean myself up and get dressed; after that, he said, they would take me to my soul-flight.

\* \* \*

I reached the shower, doing my best not to faint, lowered myself on to all fours and propped my back against the glass partition. Water fell on me, but I was elsewhere. My mind was stunned, and I couldn't use it to think or operate my body. When I finally felt I could stand up, I scrubbed my skin with soap, using a lot of suds to wash off the priest's blood and sweat.

Wrapped in a towel, I sat on the toilet and thought. I was so tired; I wanted to leave – I wanted to go home. I wanted to get drunk and forget. I wanted to get out of here and never come back. But he wouldn't just let me walk out the door. I was trapped and the only way out seemed to be on the other side of life.

It was the first time I could remember feeling afraid to die. I felt hopeless. I wished I had told someone, left a memento of me somewhere. I feared disappearing without a trace.

*I'm Laura Jennet, the daughter of Marie and Daniel Jennet. I didn't kill anyone. I'm twenty-six years old. I am Laura Jennet.*

An instinct told me I needed to focus on who I was – etch it into my memory. Where this instinct came from I have no idea – I have never felt anything like it before; it was so rational and sober. Nevertheless, I followed it, because there was nothing else real enough to believe in. I went over to a mirror and tried to memorise what I looked like: every curve of my body, my small breasts and flat stomach, pale skin, black hair cut in a short bob. Then I imagined my parents' faces. To survive I needed a deeper integration into myself. *Now you must find some dear memories.*

An image of my father emerged. I remembered him teaching me how to play chess when I was four or five years old. I loved the knight and the queen the most, but he explained to me that every chess piece was important – it wasn't a figure that held power, he said, but the player who breathed life into it. At first I gave up each time he took my queen; I would lose motivation and stop playing. But with time and perseverance I learned to keep fighting till the end. My dad would never let me win – I had to earn it. It took me four years of practice and persistence, and it finally paid off: one day I queened my pawn and defeated his king.

\* \* \*

In the glass cubicle next to mine a man lay on a bed, a bright ball of energy flouncing from wall to wall above him. He was unconscious, his fingers twitching as though he was playing a piano in his dream, his eyeballs moving underneath closed eyelids. His clothing was excessive, fashionable, expensive, his wrists cuffed in shiny jewellery, a thin golden band crowning his head − an implant with an astronomical price tag. There was a lot of money on his body, and entwined within it.

And me? How did I get here? An ad had lured me, the voice and the image unfolding in my head like a dream, and I'd followed that dream. The image of the girl who'd stolen my breath away, and the promise to meet my soul.

But me? Here? An experience that could only be afforded by those who own cars that fly higher than drones and pay more for an hour of privacy than I pay for a month's worth of food? But no, I was asking the wrong questions − it wasn't how did I end up here, but why?

Craig walked into the room, followed by a man and a woman wearing white coats − I assumed they would be running the procedure. He introduced them by their surnames.

'Congratulations on your first soul-flight. It is a very special experience,' the woman said, and smiled. 'Before we can continue, I need you to sign this.' She handed me a tablet. On it was a form that exempted the company from any responsibility in case something happened to me during the soul-flight.

'What can go wrong?' I asked.

'Anything,' Craig answered, before either of the scientists could say a word.

I looked through the forms. '… *The procedure will take twenty-four hours. Your body will receive all necessary fluids to maintain a healthy state… Once the experience is over your soul will be returned to your body and you will wake up. It is common to feel dizzy or nauseous. Symptoms will pass after approximately thirty minutes to one hour after you wake up...*' There was a big chapter on side effects: heart failure, memory loss, brain damage, muscle dysfunction...

'Do you have any questions?' Craig asked impatiently, holding out a stylus pen. 'It's a pleasant formality, although we both know it doesn't really matter if you sign it or not.'

I pushed the tablet away.

'As you wish,' he said. 'Sweet dreams.'

He pivoted on his heels and strolled over to the door. He stopped in the doorway and stood still for a minute, hands in his pockets. It looked as though he might turn around and say something, but he didn't, and was soon gone.

'Lie down, please,' the male scientist said, pointing to the bed.

I did as I was told. I didn't feel I had a choice.

The woman ran some basic tests on me and drew my blood. 'We can begin,' she said. She attached a few sticky patches to my body.

'You will fall asleep now,' she said, preparing an injection. She tapped the syringe with a finger.

'What is it?' I asked.

'This will help you relax and allow us to safely detach your soul from your physical body,' she said, and squirted some of the liquid out of the syringe. She set to disinfecting my inner forearm where the needle would go. 'Don't worry,' she reassured me, 'it won't hurt.'

She injected the solution into my vein, and my vision started blurring. I started to drift off as a machine appeared in the room, with many wires and a long silver hose with a needle at the end. The man placed a little silver bean inside the machine, and everything turned black.

# 8

---

The pressure inside my chest pushed a stream of air out of my mouth, but no air was coming back in. Around me were clouds of red liquid. I breathed in water, choking. It was painful. When the pain stopped, I didn't need to breathe, and I was still alive. I tried to turn around, but it was difficult – the liquid was thicker than water. I couldn't see anything besides misty red. I couldn't hear a sound, either. My eyelids slowly drooped over my eyes, but my vision stayed – I could see. I opened my eyes and closed them again. My vision remained. I closed my eyes and put my hands over them; still I saw everything.

I was calm. I couldn't feel much of my body; I knew it was me, but my perception was different. I was rediscovering myself – how I felt, how I saw, how I heard. I didn't think; I couldn't think – I didn't know how to. There was nothing to think about.

I was something new.

The water level was decreasing, first slowly, then more rapidly. My body collapsed on a hard surface with a loud splash. Lying on my stomach, I looked around. The room I was in was white, but the light coming from somewhere, nowhere, made it look red. There were no windows, and the door was locked – I didn't need to try the handle to know that. When I touched the wall it moved towards me, forcing me to recoil. I took another step back and the wall shifted closer again. I turned around – now the opposite wall was advancing as well. All four walls pushed forward, constricting the space around me, until they were so close that I couldn't move.

I was getting bigger – my mass started warping, bending, clashing with itself. The walls crushed my body – or maybe I crushed the walls – and everything went black again.

* * *

Stars flickered around me. Some were far away and tiny, others were bigger and brighter, some were of colours that stretched beyond any description existing in human perception. The space teemed with presence of all kinds. Waves of iridescent energy and blazing particles rolled their fat masses through the black matter, leaving long tails of radiance behind.

My own movement was imperceptible. I was invisible, I wasn't anything of my own, and yet I was all that could be seen. I wasn't present anywhere in particular. I dissolved and merged with everything else and stretched light years apart. The long tentacles of my existence writhed through space like arms of a giant octopus splashing in the vortex of infinite experiences, in many worlds and dimensions. The universe perceived, multiplied, deepened itself, and I shared its knowledge. I heard everything that had ever happened, every thought that had been born. The sound of space became loud, causing me to expand so I could take in all the noise. All the information that the universe contained, all the lives that had existed, every moment that had happened and was yet to take place – I was in all of it. I, on the other hand, didn't hear my own thoughts. I didn't exist in a form that could acknowledge itself. I stopped being *I* and merged with the flow of life.

It was a state where the most destructive storms collided with nothingness, forming distances that last billions of years. I heard a thought that impregnated these distances with life, and I was a part of it too. This impulse created the natural order in every void it permeated. It was in every particle that vibrated in the vacuum of darkness. There was an equilibrium, and it was so complete that if you looked at it you wouldn't see a thing; if you tried to listen to it you wouldn't hear a sound; and if you tried to perceive it your senses would be lost and you would become nothing but a gap between thoughts of a mind.

There was nothing familiar here, nothing I could relate to, yet it felt like home, and simultaneously the insemination of the core of every metamorphosis.

*How do I explain how it feels to be both nothing and everything? How do I explain how it feels to know everything that happened, to be everywhere at the same time, to experience every death and every birth in the universe but at the same time not have any thoughts of your own? How do I explain the sensation of absolute completion, when the frequency of your feelings matches the frequency of life?*

When the bliss turned into oblivion I 'fell asleep'. I slept for centuries, maybe, or for millions of years – I didn't know whether it was million years into the past or million years into the future, and it didn't matter, not to me, not to you, not to the entire universe, because time itself disappeared, and whether I was dead or alive mattered only to those who remembered enough. Their thoughts would form tiny strings of light, thinner than hair but stronger than eternity. They exist for ever, these memories. Even after their owners die, strings of memories, tiny scraps of light, roam the cosmos.

These glowing strings drifted closer. They came from all over. Some were from places I couldn't remember, but some I recognised; I had seen them in lives of others. But some of these strings were new, fresh, bright. They circled around me patiently, pulsating, talking in their own language, waiting to connect to my essence. They must have still been alive, still remembering, still thinking, and their perseverance woke me up at last.

\* \* \*

My hibernation was deep, my awakening long. The giant translucent masses of my tentacles glided back, colliding with debris from comets, picking up the shimmer of young stars, riding waves from supernovas. I pulled my viscous arms from the enormous space of the past and future and shed the histories of countless planets to prepare myself for a different state. Some of my particles came back from lives that were never born but that exist in a space the human brain cannot grasp, therefore cannot see or acknowledge.

With the last few suctions of my essence the ability to feel presented itself. It wasn't possible to distinguish between emotions yet; they all existed in a perfect balance, undisturbed.

Not for long. The blazing strings wrapped around me and called my name. I felt their unrest. I knew by then that I was free: I could exist, or not; I could feel, but I didn't have to; I could go anywhere and experience anything; and I could be born again.

The memories weren't giving up – they circled around, waiting, lice cruising around a whale.

At last, one of the feelings fluttered on to the horizon of my soul, creating ripples on its previously smooth surface. First it was a pinch, then a scratch, and finally a burning torment. It was pain that stretched beyond borders of a heart. It wasn't mine.

My response to the calling was fluid and slow. I plunged back inwards, and the vortex of rapid transformation spat me out into a different ledge of existence.

\* \* \*

'*Laura*,' a soft voice purred somewhere.

I had slept for too long and still needed time to get acquainted with my new form.

'*Laura*.' The voice was getting closer.

A haze defined the shape of my body. I was cold. My mind had visions, and I knew they were mine, but I couldn't connect to them yet.

A woman appeared before me. Her wavy brown hair reached her chest. In the corners of her green eyes tears sat, about to roll down her cheeks. Despite the tears, her lips reposed in a smile.

Something in my chest grabbed my heart and squeezed it hard.

'Mother,' I whispered.

'Laura,' she said, and touched my face. I couldn't feel her flesh, just her energy passing through me. 'My little monkey.'

I looked around. 'Am I dreaming?' I asked. All I could see was blurred lights and my mother. I was probably about to wake up, and then the dream would end. 'You came to me again,' I said.

'I've always been here,' she replied. She struggled to keep her smile, and when she allowed herself to cry, her tears were never-ending.

'Mum, don't cry,' I said, and hugged her. I was happy to see her. I felt so strongly that we were one – that her blood flowed through both of us. We could have seen each other just days before; there was no awkwardness, no sensation that time had dulled our connection. I pulled away and looked into her eyes.

'Why?' I asked her.

'Laura, I'm sorry,' she said.

My form started dissipating.

'No, I don't want to leave! I don't want to go!' I clung to her. 'I don't blame you. I don't, I promise – please don't let me disappear.'

There was a fight taking place between me and another life form – possibly it was my soul, or perhaps it was a greater unifying force, which demanded I return to another world. I fought it. My mother was here; how could I not fight for a chance to stay longer with her, even for another moment? *Why did you leave me?* The question rushed through my mind, but I no longer cared for answers. I knew everything I needed to know – she was here, she had always been here – nothing else mattered. She had waited for me. I wasn't going to waste a single breath blaming her, because every breath I took I wanted to be for her, with her. Looking at her again, feeling her love was enough for me to die in peace.

She pressed me against her chest. Her heartbeat was a familiar sound; I remembered it from the time when I'd been evolving in her womb. I felt her hair on my cheek, her creamy smell. She infused me with calm. I stopped shaking. A force was sucking me somewhere else, into another dimension. I didn't resist any more. I clung to my mum and spent every passing moment feeling her hands. Nothing could ever give me more than her hands had, and the love with which she had welcomed me into this world. Nothing. Ever.

'I love you more than anything,' she said. 'We will always be with you; we will always find you.' She looked at me one last time. 'Even on the edge of the world.'

# 9

---

'Extracting the subject.'

The ocean roared. A field of tall green grass met the edge of a cliff. The wind carried the smell of pine. The ground split under my feet, and everything – the field, the stones, the grass – was crumbling down. The ocean sucked it all in, then spat it back up into the sky, allowing these tatters to enjoy the light one last time.

'Transfer complete.'

In a few moments the blinding light went off and I could see. I was strapped to a bed with thin belts tied around my hands, legs and head.

'Can you hear me?' a man in a white robe asked, examining my eyes.

'Yes,' I said, but no sound came out.

He performed something on the tablet he was holding in his hands and asked again, 'Can you hear me?'

'Yes,' I said, but still no sound came.

'N3 chest shell,' he said to a woman in the same white robe.

She passed him a piece of something translucent and rubbery; he attached it to my upper body.

'Can you feel your body?' he asked me.

I moved my fingers, my toes, my legs. I could feel it.

'Can you feel your body?' he asked again.

'Yes,' I said, and my voice was so loud – so, so loud – it hurt. I clenched my teeth and shut my eyes until the reverberation in my head subsided. I thought my head would split in half. My heart pumped, streams of energy passed through my muscles, fluids trickled in and out of my organs – my whole body was a volcano, moaning and gurgling.

The scientists locked the door, went over to the other side of the room and passed behind a glass wall. I wasn't in the same glass cubicle where I'd started – this was a different place.

'Laura, your experience is complete. You will be released now. It will take some time for your body to adjust. We advise you to remain calm and move with caution.'

The belts that strapped me to the bed unfastened.

'We hope you enjoyed your journey.'

I sat on the edge of the bed and rubbed my palms, waking up my numb fingers. Memories of what I'd seen emerged in my mind gradually, without invasion, although I found it hard to describe these images with words. There were pure emotional sensations, too, and those I wouldn't even attempt to define. I'd been outside my physical body – that was irrefutable – and not in a form of internal energy, but as a separate intelligent organism altogether. Had I found what I was looking for? Had something changed in me? I was calm, balanced and somewhat satisfied. And I felt stronger, both emotionally and physically.

My sixth sense told me this calm wouldn't last; the quiet in the room was too deceptive. I looked at the door. It wasn't going to open for me – that much I knew. I faced the scientists who observed me from behind the glass wall. 'I'd like to leave,' I said.

They remained silent.

My foreboding was strong; one of those feelings when you know that something is going to happen, only you can't comprehend the reality of it yet. And the reality was still ambiguous; it was detached from me, and I was detached from it. But the racing heart didn't lie – something was about to happen.

A dark silhouette approached the glass wall. It was Craig. His hands were crossed behind his back, his posture tall and proud, his expression greased with satisfaction.

'A masterpiece. Created by the universe, perfected by man,' he said.

As the distance between us closed, I saw my reflection appear in the shadow of his figure.

'Harnessed perfection.'

My heart stopped, dropped and almost jumped out of my throat. Parts of my neck and chin were missing. I grabbed my neck – there was no flesh; my hand went right through pulsating streams of energy. I tore off my hospital gown. What I saw I couldn't understand; it wasn't true. I looked down to confirm the reflection in the glass was really me: ultraviolet flows formed my thighs and ran up to my breasts, where something similar to skin covered parts of my chest and stomach.

I stared at the reflection, then at Craig, my hands hanging in the air, afraid of my own being.

*This isn't real, this isn't me.*

But it was real. It was me. Whatever it was, it was me.

'How do you feel, Laura?' Craig asked.

'What have you done to me?' My teeth clattered. I had teeth! I touched them – they were real teeth. A tongue lay behind them. I also had lips – I touched them, too – and a nose. But some of my face was missing, along with my chin. My lips ended and the chin never began; there was air between my mouth and my collarbones.

'I wish I could take the credit,' Craig said. 'Most of it is your work.'

'What is this?' I didn't know the right questions to ask, what to think – I'd lost a body, or a good part of it, anyway. *Have I ever had a body?* That must have been the most terrifying thought that had ever crossed my mind. Why would I doubt that? Of course I'd had a body. I'd been born human. I was human.

'It's you, Laura, perfected to your highest potential. Recreated just as the universe envisioned you. Or should I say, as you envisioned yourself – because I didn't do anything, really – just gave you a little guidance, that's all.'

# CHAPTER 9

'You are sick!' I shouted. 'You are sick!'

'I'm a creator,' he said. 'I dedicate myself to science so that others can experience life.'

'What did you do to me?' I banged on the glass wall. 'What did you do to me?'

I spilled into phosphoric dust and drove my mass into the walls and the floor, and only patches of fake skin held me together while the swirls of my outbursts fired around the room. I couldn't break free – the room wouldn't let me out, and the skin-like material didn't allow my essence to go back into nothingness.

After exhausting my energy I collapsed.

\* \* \*

My awakening came in small doses. A timid breath, a cough, drunken eyelids opening and closing, a moan, a tear – and finally my mind insisted that I face the reality. I got up and came to the glass, where I could see the vague reflection. Steel plates now covered parts of my legs and arms, some of my neck and chin. My left breast was also shackled with steel; whether there was an actual breast underneath it I couldn't feel. The rest of me looked like me – skin so impeccable I wouldn't be able to tell the difference. My hair was shorter, but my facial features were all a perfect copy.

I touched my face, squeezed my free breast, placed both hands on the sides of my neck; my arteries were throbbing.

A clicking sound indicated that the door was now open. And what could this open door do for me? *You are free*, it seemed to say. *Go, do as you please.* But go where exactly? Home? Where was my home? The grey apartment with its sofa and chairs, table and bed? The streets? Or maybe a flight down from the tenth floor? *Where are you sending me through this open door?* I walked out, knowing very well I wasn't free; I was a lab rat let out in a field.

*Go, little mouse, go.*

# 10

---

Drizzle was falling. The city lights, the smoke, my lips on a cigarette – all of it was an illusion, wasn't it? I stretched my hand out and felt tiny drops of rain. Could I believe what I saw and felt? Would it be reasonable to assume that my experiences were mine? Just the other day my hand had gone through my neck because there had been no flesh there; what guarantee did I have that I was still me, not an illusion? I tested these ideas in my mind, and came to the conclusion that I was real and wasn't dreaming. Whatever I was, I existed in real world, just like Aleece. She had gone through something very similar – she must have – her body had been modified in a similar way, and she was real. She was very real, I knew that – I had proof of that: I'd kissed her here, on this balcony; her body had been next to mine right here.

*Are we the same now, Aleece?* I thought. *You must know, and you must come and tell me what he did to me. Please come. Please don't leave me alone.*

He took everything from me. He – God, the priest, Craig – stole my life and I handed it to all of them on a bloody plate.

*What's next? What else will you take? What else can I give you? I don't even know if I have a body of my own any more. What can I give? I've got nothing left. You took it all.*

I looked at my hands. I probably stared at them for a good fifteen minutes, then went to the kitchen and grabbed a knife.

That was one way to see what was inside me. Ultraviolet streams, I wondered, or blood.

I plunged the blade into the side of my palm. Blood – red, and certainly real – seeped to the surface of my skin. Blood, then. It made no sense at all. Why was there blood and not those strings of light I'd seen in the lab?

I couldn't think about it; my mind refused to operate. *Enough*, it said. *I can't deal with this. It's too much, and I don't know how to process and identify what has happened to you. Let me rest*, it begged. I left it alone.

* * *

Alcohol and sleepless nights made me sick. During the next few days I slept anywhere – between the toilet, my bed and the balcony. When I tried to open my eyes I couldn't; they were too swollen. My body was definitely made of flesh: I had the worst hangover.

Shaking, a cigarette between my fingers, I went on to the balcony. The light was soft and grey, but it was enough to hurt my eyeballs. I needed to get out, I concluded, to see people, see suffering in their faces, remind myself I wasn't suffering alone. It was morning, and there were plenty of afterparties to choose from. A lot of spots specialised in the morning-time depression, the worst kind, and offered the right cure for it.

I put on my favourite strappy silk dress, some red lipstick and mascara. I looked so different. I couldn't decide whether I liked how the soft silk of the dress draped against the metal plates on my breast and thighs and parts of my arms. It exposed too much of this body. I couldn't think of it as mine. The view was shocking – it would take time for me to get used to seeing this in the mirror. *Will I have to get used to it?* I thought.

I changed into jeans and a shirt, grabbed my long black woollen coat and went outside.

People didn't rush. Some were wrapped in their coats, ready to go to bed. Others were still high and searching for more fun.

A group ahead caught my attention. Their gender was fluid; their sex appeal screamed. The two boys looked like nymphs, fragile and elegant. The girl inherited her looks from the Far East, her slender shape emphasised with an unbuttoned oversized tuxedo that didn't differ much from the boys'.

She glanced at me, her eyes black against her pale face. 'Hey,' she said. She was beautiful, cold, almost like a machine covered in white skin. 'Are you alone?' she asked.

I was, more than she could imagine, more than I'd ever known, for now I had lost the one last thing I had – my body.

'Would you like to come along?' She radiated confidence. 'It's a cool place – you'll like it.' Her bright red lips opened slightly, showing the gap between her white teeth.

*Why not?* I thought. She was hot. I threw away the stub of my cigarette and followed her without saying anything.

We approached a set of stairs that led down to a door, which a big security guy opened for us. A wave of some warm, sweet smell poured out into the street; it swarmed between our bodies and into my nostrils. Enticing and spicy, it tied a lasso around my chest and pulled me in. I looked around. Everything, from the walls to the chairs and sofas, was covered in oriental rugs. Some tables and beds were separated by large pieces of fabric flowing from the ceiling. Inside these tents, people convolved into sculptures of orgies, digging out unforeseen desires from the wrinkles of each other's minds.

A robot processed our payments. It was an all-inclusive place – the drugs were in the air.

'Breathe,' the girl whispered into my ear.

I followed her into the depths of the club, but soon lost her in the crowd of people. Every mouth here was open for more air, and the air made you feel good, quickly. As I walked through a labyrinth of rooms and corridors, my body moved slower and slower and my mind relaxed. I was overtaken by a pleasant euphoria.

In the end of a corridor I saw a woman with long, dark hair and a freckled face. *Aleece? Is it you?* I ate the distance between us, but she kept drifting away, teasing me. A few more turns. A few more rooms.

She leaned against the wall, took my hand and pulled me closer.

I rested my head on her shoulder and melted into the comfort of her familiar warmth. Tracing the line of her neck with my mouth, I inhaled deeply. Her thick hair brushed against my cheeks as my lips reached her ear.

'What did he do to me?' I whispered.

'It doesn't matter,' she said.

I pulled away, and the face of the girl who'd invited me here looked back at me. It wasn't Aleece. She took my hand and we found a bed inside one of the tents. She dropped her tuxedo, revealing her boyish chest, and released me from my shirt. She moved quickly. Her mouth was on my breasts, her tongue pushing against my nipple, her hands squeezing my ass.

I felt horny but too stoned to show initiative. She didn't mind taking control.

Her skin was illuminated, and red and purple flowers were scattered across her stomach, chest and neck. Her skin was an expensive screen. A dragon-like lizard enfolded her waist, swam up to her shoulders and down her back. I followed it with my tongue as it reached her breasts.

She moved down to my hips and in between my thighs.

'Do you like cock too?' she asked.

'Yes,' I answered.

She took a prosthetic penis from her handbag and attached it to her crotch. At first it was soft, but instantly responded to the state of her aroused body, and it even picked up some of the flowers. Her mouth brushed over my lips and chest once again before she entered me and filled me with pleasure. She moved slowly, savouring every moment of the action. Breathing faster and deeper, getting more of the sweet drug into my lungs, I lost the sense of place and time.

'Do you like it?' she asked.

'Yes,' I whispered.

I pushed her on her back and sat on top of her. I moved faster and faster, seizing all the pleasure I could get. She clenched my free breast; her other hand was on my steel plate, and I couldn't feel her touch. I placed my hands over hers and squeezed them, and the jerks of my body became rough. Her eyes changed colours while she moaned under me.

I couldn't see the room any more; everything was spinning. I extended beyond the body I was trapped in.

When I looked down at the girl again, it was Aleece that looked back at me. *Aleece.* I leaned forward and kissed her lips. *Aleece.* I wanted to inhale her, suck her into my body and never let her leave me again.

Strong hands grabbed my ass. I wasn't riding Aleece, but John now. He moved my hips back and forth. I was reaching the peak of pleasure. He sensed it and climbed on top of me. Taking my nipple between his lips, he circled his tongue around it, and passionate licks mixed with delicate bites.

His face was blending into Aleece's face, and little red and purple flowers appeared on his shoulders. She was going faster and faster, and after my final exhalation Aleece and John disappeared.

The girl's skin became white again. She pulled out from me and rolled on to her side. We lay in silence for some time. She caressed my body, her gaze filling with curiosity. When she touched the metal parts, I didn't feel anything.

'What are you?' she asked. Her voice echoed in my head, disappearing somewhere in a different place and a different time. Eventually her '*What are you?*' reached me in some other dimension and pulled me back.

'I don't know,' I answered.

# 11

I waited on the street for someone to walk into John's building. First, a lady told me no one by the name John lived here, and tried to hit me when I attempted to sneak in behind her. I had a better luck with an older gentleman.

'Yes, John – a good fellow. Come in, come in. He will like the surprise, I'm sure. He might not be home yet. You can wait at my place if you want.'

I declined the offer and took the lift to the sixteenth floor. I located John's door and knocked. Nobody was there. It was late afternoon – he was probably at work, but he'd come home eventually.

'Laura?' A voice woke me up.

I opened my eyes and saw John. I was sitting on the floor leaning against a door. For a moment I was confused about where I was and why I was there.

John held out his hand and helped me to my feet.

'I didn't mean to show up like this,' I said. 'I wanted to call, but I don't know what I did with your number.'

'You OK?' he asked, his gaze sliding over my chin and neck.

As soon as my sober mind caught up with reality and remembered everything that had happened to me, a wave of emotions brought tears to my eyes. I shook my head.

'Come in,' he said, looking around before closing the door behind him.

I threw myself on his chest as if his shoulders were the last branch saving me from falling off a cliff. 'I don't have anyone else,' I said.

'You did the right thing,' he said, leaning away from me a little so that he could see my face. 'Want to tell me what happened?'

I nodded.

We sat at a dining table across from each other. I told him everything: about Craig, about Dirty Castle, about my soul-flight experience and my altered body – everything except the priest.

He listened without interrupting. His smart contact lens flickered a few times. When I finished, for a moment he continued to read something on his lens, his eye twitching a little. He wasn't surprised; I got the impression he knew what I was talking about.

'Are you sure the man is Dr Craig Nolan and not someone pretending to be him?' he asked.

'I'm sure,' I said. 'I checked.'

John reached for a tablet and typed something in.

'This man?' he asked, turning the screen to face me. 'He's a well-known scientist.'

'Yes,' I said.

John pulled up a map of the city. 'There are at least seven places with the name Dirty Castle. Which one are you talking about?'

I took the tablet. There were all sorts of places listed, from shops to sex clubs. I scrolled through the list. None of them matched Craig's club.

'Where is it on the map?' John insisted.

I fiddled with the screen and found the location. John switched to the live view and zoomed in. There was a club exactly where I pointed, but it had a different name and a very different look. The entire street looked different. It was full of neon and glamour, not the dark narrow alley I knew.

'This doesn't make sense,' I said. 'Dirty Castle is right here.'

I was getting emotional, my heart rate increasing. I scratched behind my ear nervously.

'Keep calm, OK?' he said. 'Clearly something happened to you. It could have affected your memories. Does the name Chilasa mean anything to you?'

'Like the butterfly?' I said.

'Yes, like the butterfly.'

I thought for a moment. 'No, why?'

'It was here before this club opened,' he said, tapping the point on the map where I'd pointed. 'It was famous for about ten years, maybe longer, but closed down two years ago.'

I thought, but I couldn't remember anything to do with the name Chilasa.

'Wait,' I said, and took the tablet. I moved the map slightly, another location popping into my mind. 'Could it be here?'

'You think you were here?' John asked.

I couldn't tell with certainty where I thought Dirty Castle was, and that made me nervous. But both of these two locations burned in my mind very clearly.

'That's where Craig's second lab is,' John said. 'His main research facility is here.' He zoomed in on one of the skyscrapers downtown and glanced at me, checking to see whether I had a response to this image. I didn't have any memory related to this location. 'So you think all this could have happened at his second lab?' he asked.

I closed my eyes and covered my face with my palms. I was certain I'd been there. However, thinking back, most nights I'd walked home from work, and this lab was on the outskirts of the city. I'd occasionally taken a taxi, but it had still been a short ride. From this location it would have taken at least thirty minutes to get to my place by car. The only explanation I could think of was that I'd been transferred from Dirty Castle to Craig's second lab. I suppose it was possible that I was so disoriented after the procedure that I didn't remember taking a taxi home. I'd been in a state of shock, so it wasn't impossible. But then, where was Dirty Castle?

'John, I know Dirty Castle is a real place. I worked there; I met real people there.'

'And that's where you met Craig Nolan the very first time?' John asked.

'Yes,' I insisted.

'And he asked you to work for him and serve drugs there?' he asked.

'You don't believe me, do you? Because I'm just some junkie talking garbage about a famous scientist, right?' I got up and went to the window.

*No one will believe me. No one believed me about the priest; no one will believe me now,* I thought. I should have thought twice before coming to John. He was a damn scientist – of course he would take the side of another scientist.

'Laura, it's not that I don't believe you,' he said. 'I believe something happened to you, obviously. But I worked with Craig, and I know him quite well.'

'You know Craig?' I said, and turned to face him.

'Yes, I worked with him for many years. We used to be good friends. But we reached a point where we didn't agree professionally any more, and we parted ways. I haven't seen him for... I don't know. I don't even remember when we last spoke. He is a complicated man, and he has suffered his share of pain. Trauma can change you, but...' He bit his lip. 'Pff. To perform an illegal experiment on you, without your consent, basically kidnapping you... It's hard for me to digest.'

I pulled down my jeans and took off my shirt. I wasn't wearing a bra – I very rarely did – and I stood before him in my underwear. 'And this?' I asked, gesturing at my body and it gleaming metal plates. 'Can you digest this?'

His eyes widened. 'May I?' he asked, coming towards me.

I nodded.

He examined the metal plates on my neck, thigh and shin, and went around me touching the edges, where the silver surface met the skin on my back. His fingers were warm and rough. After a time he handed me my shirt.

I got dressed. Out of the corner of my eye I saw him shaking his head, as though he was having an internal dialogue and was in a disagreement with someone.

'Laura, when you... after...' he struggled. 'How did you end up in Dirty Castle?'

'I told you, I saw a hidden ad for it,' I said.

'And where were you when you saw that ad?'

'In my apartment.'

'That's all you remember?' he asked.

'That's all that happened — there is nothing to remember,' I said.

'OK, OK, I'm just trying to understand,' he said, and scratched his cheek. 'So you saw the ad, you went to the place called Dirty Castle, and that was your very first encounter with Craig Nolan?' he asked.

'What are you getting at, John?' I snapped. 'Are you somehow involved in this?'

'No. No I'm not—'

'Because now that I'm thinking about it, you approached me out of nowhere in that bar. You knew my name. Are you part of this shit?'

'No, of course not,' he said. 'It's not that hard to dig up someone's name. And as I said, I haven't spoken to Craig for years — I don't approve of his approach. But I don't believe... it is hard for me to imagine he would go this far.'

'Why did you look up my name?' I asked.

'Um...' His eyes darted about and his lips twitched. At first I thought he was coming up with a plausible deception, but it looked as though he was dealing with a painful memory rather than constructing a lie. 'You reminded me of someone I used to know, so I looked you up.'

I replayed everything from the beginning, from the night I'd met Craig till now. I didn't think John was lying — he'd never said anything that would entice me to go on a flight. On the other hand, maybe his task was to gain my trust, and now he had a role to play? But watching him pace nervously, it was hard to believe he was a part of some evil scheme. And I really wanted to trust someone – I couldn't stand the thought of being completely alone.

'So you and Craig aren't friends?' I asked.

'We are not enemies. Our relationship faded. I don't support him professionally, and I don't want to have anything to do with his research. But this – what you are saying he did to you and how he did it – it's a crime. His vision of the future entails a radical transformation, not only of the human body but of the very nature of humanity itself, and I don't agree with him, but he is not—'

'A criminal?' I interrupted. 'Of course not! How can such an accomplished, respectable man be a criminal? I, on the other hand, can easily turn out to be a liar.'

'I don't think you are lying,' he said. 'You've been through something, and I'd like to help you. Have you ever done memory therapy – had your memories blocked?'

'Never. Obviously – because I still remember the worst parts of my life. So now are you trying to say I'm crazy? That I just misinterpreted it all? That I'm so fucked up that I can't tell hallucinations from reality?'

'That's not what I'm saying,' he scrambled.

'Then what's all this bullshit you're saying? I remember everything – my memories are fine.'

'I'm just trying to understand, Laura,' he insisted. 'I believe you. But I've known this man for over fifteen years.'

For a moment we were both quiet, thinking, John's eyes skimming something from his lens.

'Here is what I propose,' he said. 'Let me scan you to see what's underneath all this. We take it a step at a time, slowly, cautiously. And then see from there. Does that sound reasonable?'

I lowered myself on to the sofa in the living room, resting my elbows on my steel thighs.

'So you will help me?' I asked.

'If you let me,' he said, and sat down in a chair next to me.

'If you discover some illegal shit in me, I can't go to the authorities,' I said.

'Why?'

'I might have done something. And Craig can use it against me.'

'You might have done something?' he asked. 'Meaning you're not sure?'

'I'm not sure. It's not straightforward. But it can be portrayed as if I did it,' I said.

'Well, first let's see what's inside you,' he said.

'I need you to promise,' I said. 'A promise doesn't mean much, but I don't know what else to do – I'm not exactly in a position to ask anything, I guess. I don't know if you care – you obviously have your reasons for helping me – but Craig can get me in a real trouble.'

'And this is not real trouble?' John said, gesturing at me.

I looked down and remained silent.

'I don't have a secret motive,' he went on. 'I'm helping you because I want to, because you need help.'

'No,' I snapped. 'You are helping me because you need to save someone, to compensate for what you couldn't do. For people you couldn't save. But I don't care. As you said, I need help.'

'If it suits you to think that,' he said. 'I'd much rather see you alive and doing well than miserable or dead. There is not much philosophy to it. People are not all bad – for the most part we are OK. Have a little faith.'

'Faith? What's that but an anachronism?'

John's lips stretched into a smile. He licked them and chuckled. 'I won't report my findings unless you ask me to,' he said. 'Or unless it's a matter of life and death. That work for you?'

I glanced at him sideways and nodded.

'I met a woman in Dirty Castle, Aleece,' I said. 'She said she was Craig's daughter. Is that true? Does he have a daughter?'

For a moment John lost control over his facial muscles: his eyes widened, his eyebrows jumped up. 'What did this woman tell you exactly?' he asked.

'That she was Craig's daughter. That she used to be a scientist. She looks like me. I mean, I look like her now, I suppose, with these metal plates,' I said, pulling the collar of my shirt down to expose the silver of my neck. 'She has these all over her body too.'

I waited for John to say something, but he just gaped at me.

'What? Why are you looking at me like that? Who is she?'

'Um, no, I just... Would you like a glass of water?' he asked, and went to the kitchen without waiting for an answer and poured a glass for himself. I could see him from behind, putting the glass down, hunched over the counter, staring down into the sink for some time.

'You met a woman at the club, Dirty Castle, and she had similar metal plates attached to her body?' he asked, coming back to the living room. 'And she said she was Craig's daughter and that her name was Aleece?'

'Yes. And she could transform her body just by using her thoughts. She did it in front of me; her hand was completely translucent – strings of blue light, nothing else, no skin, no bone. She doesn't remember her past – almost no memories at all. There was some accident, from what I understood, some tech experiment gone wrong,' I said.

'What did she look like?'

'Light-brown skin, freckles, brown eyes. About my height. Does that sound familiar?'

'Well... the description matches that of his daughter, yes,' he said, and pinched the bridge of his nose. 'You know what, let's go to the lab. It's not that busy now, and I don't want to draw attention to you until we figure out what we are dealing with.'

* * *

On the way to the Neuroscience Institute I asked John about his time working with Craig. He had followed Craig's work since university, he told me. Craig's ambitious and innovative approach to brain development had inspired him, and after graduation he'd applied to be a part of the research team. From what John said, I understood they had been close, but due to fundamental differences, and possibly something else he didn't feel like sharing, when they went their separate ways about five years ago they had not parted on good terms.

The walls of the impressive glass and concrete building were scarred with faded graffiti, already covered with fresh marks: 'MURDERERS', 'DON'T STEAL OUR SOULS', 'STOP INVADING OUR MINDS', 'HELL AWAITS'.

John noticed me looking at these messages, but didn't comment.

The automatic doors slid open and we walked through thin frames of security gates.

'Hi, Dan,' John said, waving to a receptionist robot who was designed to look like a middle-aged man. He wore a blue shirt and a light jacket.

'Evening, Dr Lowe. You have a visitor?'

'My new trainee,' John said.

'Please sign in here,' the bot said to me, pointing to a finger-print scanner.

I placed my palm on the touchpad. The receptionist looked at a monitor in front of him, wearing the fake smile engineers had gifted him. His eyes started running from left to right, reading the information the machine squeezed out of my fingers.

'Thank you, Ms Jennet. Have a good evening.'

'Thanks, Dan,' John said.

'Have a good evening, Dr Lowe.'

John pressed his palm against a touchpad at a checkpoint gate and we took a lift to the sixth floor.

As the floors flashed past, it occurred to me that John was testing me already, and the fingerprint scanner in reception told him something. 'My fingerprints could have been anything – or could have been unidentifiable,' I said, opening my palm and holding it out.

'So you're a privacy-rights advocate now?' he said, dismissively. 'We'd say you messed up your fingerprints, or if they came back as someone else's, we'd say someone hacked your data. Dan would have asked you for two photo IDs, which I assume you don't have on you, and we would have gone home. Anyway,' he shrugged, 'at least now we know your ID is intact. It is likely there is some illegal tech inside you, which could be traced back to whoever is responsible, and there is no reason for them to draw attention to it. If you are here, whoever did this to you wants you in the field, otherwise they would have kept you in the lab. This happens more often that you think. Illegal testing on people is a big problem.'

It annoyed me that he refrained from saying Craig's name, but I realised I had to be smart about it. No one was on my side here. I had to think for myself. John was a good resource: I needed a scan – I had to find out what was inside me. But I had to be vigilant and make my own decisions.

The lift doors slid open and John motioned for me to get out.

'I'd appreciate warning next time,' I said.

'It's not a big deal,' he said.

I stopped. 'It's my life,' I said. 'Don't make decisions for me.'

He stopped in his tracks, looking surprised. What was so surprising? That I was tired of someone or something taking my life and throwing it into a meat grinder? I'd like some control over what was going to happen to me – was that so strange?

'Note taken,' he said.

We walked over a bridge, then through a corridor with a few doors. Some had holographic signs showing things that were prohibited in the room. Stopping in front of a door, John scanned his palm. The door opened, the lights blinking on automatically. He changed into a white medical coat. A long panel on the wall played a promo ad of a medical-supplies company. Behind a glass partition a few clear monitors lit up, but I couldn't see any more than that through glass, which worked as a one-way screen.

'Could you get in trouble for this?' I asked John.

He shrugged and only pointed to the table in the middle of the room, which sat in front of a scanner. 'Please take your jeans and shirt off and lie down,' he said.

I did what he said.

'I'm not in trouble until I know what's in you,' he said. 'And then, who knows, maybe I misinterpreted it, or didn't notice, or... I don't know. We will see. When I know what kind of trouble I'm in, I'll decided what to do about it.'

The table started rising.

'When you are inside the scanner the light will go off, except for these panels on the bottom. A laser beam will circle around you. Keep your eyes closed – or I can give you covers if you want?'

'It's fine,' I said.

'You will hear a sound like a heavy wind – it's completely normal; the sound seems much louder than it is. You don't have to be absolutely still, apart from when I ask you to be, but don't try to get up or make any sudden moves. You can communicate with me. If something feels uncomfortable let me know, and we will see if we need to pause. If you become anxious and want the procedure to stop, squeeze this,' he said, and placed a squishy ball in my hand. 'This will pause the scanner immediately.'

I blinked and gave a slight nod.

'I'll be right there, watching you,' he said, gesturing at the glass partition.

The table finished rising and began to move inside the tube. The scanner clicked and started its first slow, heavy spins. The white flicker accelerated to an almost continuous white noise and my puzzled mind was spinning with it, drifting away.

* * *

I saw what looked like a blurry hologram: light shaped in a human form.

'Laura,' said Craig, standing before me smiling, his hands behind his back. 'How does it feel?' he asked.

*What is it?* I thought.

'Yes, questions. Of course you have many questions; the intensity of your change must be overwhelming. Unfortunately I can't answer them for you. What do I know – I'm only human. But you, you really surprised me. I could have never predicted this. What I can't understand is, why did you come back? The entire universe is at your feet. Why did you need this life? Regardless, I'm intrigued to see what you are creating – what form, if any, you'll chose for yourself. You can't possibly want your body back. I refuse to believe it. I'm sure this is only a little deviation from your goal. And I will help you navigate through all this, steer you in the right direction, so to speak.'

He contemplated me for some time before releasing another chapter of his madness.

'We built another god, intelligence incomprehensibly greater than and different to our own; we showed it where our souls are. We shut our eyes, plugged our ears, we took its hand and led it inside the most superior part of ourselves, an incredibly complex mechanism we are all born with but are too ignorant and too busy to discover. Instead we discover stars; we strive to domesticate planets.' He let out a chuckle. 'Ants expanding their nest, still using the excuse of survival to gain more, to reach outwards instead of inwards. But there is nothing out there that can save us, and if there is, we will never reach it on time. We must look inside. Three billion human lives – this is how much it took for someone to notice that we do, indeed, have a soul, that we are not isolated biological units but part of a more complex structure. One third of the world's population gone. It made me angry at first – helpless, to tell you the truth. But that sacrifice was necessary for us to have the impetus to make the first big leap forwards in our evolution. I wish I didn't have to admit that, but we needed something to wake us up. And we can't ignore it; we can't let these people's deaths be in vain.'

I felt the energy of his stare brushing over every string of my mass.

'I see you are scared,' he went on. 'This will pass – all of these crippling feelings will pass. You are so close, Laura. Don't let us down. Don't fall into the trap of trying to be human again.'

My reflection contracted in the big, dark pupils of his eyes.

'Because you are not,' he said. 'You are not human. You are a new greater being that gives us all hope. You are the most advanced intelligence we've ever achieved that we can actually control, and now you are captured in a structure that can do you justice. Unlike your brain in its present state, it won't reduce and categorise your consciousness, it will expand it, expand you, and it will still allow you to remain aware of yourself.'

*Don't fight it. Let it take you beyond the horizon of what you think you are.*

I no longer heard Craig's voice; his thoughts resounded inside me. He watched me choke on my own substance until the last drop of me vanished.

\* \* \*

The tubular machine was moving me out of its cave. I tried to raise myself up on my elbows, but John bent over me and pushed my shoulders down, saying something.

'Laura, do you hear me?' I could finally hear his voice. 'Calm down. Calm down. Do you hear me?'

'Yes… yes… I… I… I know… I was…'

'You need to relax. Breathe.' He covered me with a white robe.

It took a few moments for my mind and body to settle down. John's eyes looked as perplexed as I felt.

'John, I was… I went… I was out…' I kept trying to sit up, but he kept pushing my shoulders down and telling me to relax. I slapped his hands away. 'I am… Listen to me! I am not… he said it. He said it! He said I am not human.'

'Who?' he asked.

'Craig. I was somewhere else. Outside this body. It's not my body, is it?'

John was silent.

'Tell me!' I said.

'You... this... OK... um...' he tried.

'John, tell me!' I demanded.

He was obviously struggling – perhaps he didn't understand what was going on either, or maybe because he thought I couldn't handle what he had to tell me.

'This is... this might be your body. The DNA matches the one on your file,' he said. He paused and stared at me.

'Go on! What's inside me?' I asked.

He raised his hands as though to calm me. 'There is a foreign structure in your body.'

'What sort of structure?' I asked.

'I don't know exactly what the nature of it is yet,' he said.

'In my head?'

'No, not just in your head. It's not centralised – it's inside your whole body.'

I got up and staggered, and the robe fell. John tried to steady me, but I pushed him away. 'Is it a brain implant?' I persevered.

'More than that,' he said. 'Why don't you get dressed and come with me.'

I put on my clothes and followed him into the other room.

'See these fine glowing particles – looks like dust?' he said, gesturing to the monitor. I saw my brain on it, and the whole thing was covered in this dust. He shifted the image: now we were looking at my abdomen. He zoomed in. 'These particles are inside your skin, in your organs. Bones. Hair.' He zoomed in closer. 'They are independent, but connected.'

'Why don't I feel anything?'

'You don't feel any different at all?' he asked.

'No, not at all,' I said.

John brought the image of my brain back on the screen.

'What's that?' I asked, spotting a cylinder attached at the top of my spinal cord.

John zoomed in on the cylinder, breaking it into layers of different materials. Inside the cylinder was a tiny bright ball – like a star, but the size of a pea. 'Looks like a part of the interface,' he said.

'Can you track it? Where the signal is coming from, I mean?' I asked.

'I'm not sure. I'd need some help with that,' he said, zooming out. My whole body was now on the screen, and it flickered with a colourful light.

I gasped. 'What's happening to me?' Shining particles moved inside me like swarms of fireflies, making me dizzy. Between clusters of these particles sprawled thin threads like fine mycelium.

'I can't give you an answer now. I see it's evolving – it's changing its own architecture. But I can't say what's it doing to you yet. We need to monitor it. And I'd like another opinion.' He copied the scan to an external drive and erased the original file from the computer. 'I need more time to look at this. I can't do it here. Our integrated security and infringement system may pick up an anomaly,' he said. 'This should definitely be reported, and there is only so much I can *miss*.'

\* \* \*

We sat across from each other at a small table in the corner of a dark room at the back of a restaurant. It was a simple spot offering a modern version of Vietnamese cuisine with vegan options and prices higher than average. I looked through the menu and ordered; John followed suit, reading something on his smart lens, occasionally squinting and tensing his lips. My own composure was melting. Initially I took the news of the strange structure implanted in my body with relative coolness. Filaments of light in place of flesh... what I'd seen of the soul-flight had prepared me for this, but glimmering dust spread throughout my brain and organs wasn't something I could easily accept – but I realised I had been expecting something along these lines.

Still, slowly but firmly anxiety was taking hold of me. I wasn't the type to remain calm under stress. I only exercised self-control when I needed to avoid emotional connection, and never considered it worth the effort otherwise.

'What do you think?' I asked John.

'It does look like tech Craig and his daughter worked on. It's been five years since they finished it, but they were never cleared to move on to human trials. I've just checked the list of tech banned for testing, and there are a few listed that have similar descriptions. Of course, I'd need to look into these—'

'Why don't you believe me? I know who did it to me! I was there, in Craig's lab. Everything happened in his lab. He did it to me.'

'I do believe you. I do. Shit. I just can't wrap my head around it,' John said, and leaned back, rubbing his face, then crossed his arms across his chest.

'Well, you'd better hurry up and accept it,' I said. 'Because from what I saw on those recordings you made, this stuff is doing something to me.' I shuddered and stretched out my arms. 'I feel it all over me now.'

'OK, let's not panic,' he said to both of us. 'I'll look at it more in detail as soon as we get home.'

The waiter bot – a steampunk type made of square and round shapes rather than a humanoid design – brought our drinks over.

'I saw Craig,' I said. 'I was somewhere else – I think back in his lab. There was a hologram, light shaped like a body. I assumed it was me. Craig was there. He said I wasn't human. Am I human, John?'

'Of course you are! What else would you be?'

'But all this,' I held out my arms, 'it's not even... what's inside is... something else is in there.'

He leaned forward and took my forearms in his hands. 'Yes, there is. But you are still you, and let's keep it that way. Someone— Craig might tell you many things. But it's not just him. If this is indeed what I think it is, it was designed to take us outside our bodies. It's the instinct it has – to stay outside human flesh, not inside. This thing is run by an incredibly sophisticated AI, and it will try to manipulate you in any way it can, and in every state – both while you are wide awake and in the deepest sleep – to achieve its goal.' He squeezed my hands. 'This is you. Feel it?'

'Yes.'

'Good. We will run a few more tests and see the progression to determine what this thing actually does to you. In any case, I have to start collecting evidence, so that, if the worst comes, I have something to give to the authorities so they can raid Craig's lab.'

I hid my trembling hands under the table. My skin prickled all over, and I was hyperventilating. 'Please don't report me,' I said, the image of the priest's corpse on the bed crystalising before me.

'What if your life is in danger? Hypothetically...' he said. 'Well, no – let's be clear about it: your life *is* in danger. This thing can mess you up. You'd rather lose your mind or die?'

'I don't want to die. I want to survive this,' I said without hesitation.

'That's good to hear.'

'But I don't want to go to jail,' I said.

'No one is going to jail. Do you want to tell me what you think you did?'

'No.'

After a moment he said, 'Did it happen before or after you were acquainted with Craig?'

'After.'

'Could it be a set-up, do you think?'

'I don't know,' I said, and thought about it. On that day it had certainly felt like something strange had gone on, and it could be… But I saw the figure, saw my face, as the knife was thrust into the priest's gut. It must have been me. How else could I explain that? The most disturbing thing about it was that I'd felt that knife in my hand. 'There is chance, yes, I suppose,' I said.

'We'll take it a step at a time,' John reassured me. 'I won't report anything. I won't do anything behind your back, OK? I don't want to make the situation worse for you. But you have to understand: even though you feel fine now, this can change quickly. This is very, very powerful tech inside you. I can't just extract it or switch it off. First of all, I don't have the equipment. Secondly, it is merged with your organs, and I have no idea what disconnecting it will do to your brain and the rest of your body. And I'm afraid of what could happen to you if Craig were to kill this thing remotely in order to cover his tracks. That's why we need to have enough evidence and be prepared to act fast. I can hire you a lawyer – you can discuss your options. Let's give it a day, then we'll do a second scan and see what has changed and take it from there. You agree?'

'I guess,' I said slowly.

The waiter bot brought our order.

We sat in silence for a while, digesting the food and the news, stubborn mouthfuls fighting their way down our throats. I ran scenarios in my mind, and came to realise I only had one option: I had to trust John. He already knew what was inside me, he had a recording of it, so even if I tried to run away, they'd find me. I was fucked one way or another.

When we finished, our waiter processed John's wallet and we left.

'Do you want to get a drink?' John asked.

'No. I want to sleep,' I said. I didn't feel like drinking, and I was tired from the emotional turmoil.

'How about you stay at my place for the time being?' John suggested.

'Afraid I'll run away?'

'Yeah?' he asked, incredulous. 'How would you run?' he asked.

Right. The visceral fear of prison coursing through me was likely my mind's attempt to bury a truth it was struggling to accept – that I was fused with an artificial structure; I certainly couldn't run from it, since it was now a part of me.

John's gaze was sympathetic. There were no sinister motives in his eyes – at least, I couldn't sense any. Maybe my situation was so hopeless that I'd find hope in the most obvious trap. I didn't believe it was the case with John, though. He meant well – somehow I knew that. There was a lump swelling in my throat, and I couldn't say a word.

John touched my back and guided me towards the road, already stretching out his hand to hail a taxi.

In the cab I looked out of the window and saw exactly what I'd expected to see: puffy tear-stained faces were transformed into night masks – just a few hours ago they had been wishing to die or cursing those who had left them behind, but now they wore beautifully painted smiles and paraded about, carefully thought-out costumes clinging to their skinny, curvaceous, augmented bodies. Digital skin screens projected flowers and snakes over the traces of their tears so no one could see their grief and pain, but everyone knew it was there underneath. Of course, some hadn't spent the day weeping – perhaps they were stronger than others, or there was the rare occurrence of those who hadn't lost anyone. Maybe they never had friends and family and had been lonely all along, or maybe they weren't victims, but predators preying on those vulnerable souls, and when they found a soul that was in a darker place, a drop more hurt, a bit more desperate, they would make their move and, in one way or another, devour them. Closer to the walls of the building homeless people and genuine lunatics were settled. Their belongings – a tiny tent or sleeping bag, a shopping cart or card box, a pile of clothes – sat next to them. It looked like many didn't have a clue about what had become of the world. And between all those immediately visible layers of society, at least to my eyes, there were also those that might be called 'normal', who maintained some kind of normal life, whatever that meant – but I never noticed them. They filled gaps on the streets, but they were so different to me I barley registered their presence.

So the streets were as busy as they'd always been – everyone was there. Except me. I was missing. I had a very strong sense of my absence. But if I wasn't there, where was I?

I glanced at John, his big hands resting on his thighs. Was my life somewhere between these two palms? I didn't know if I liked that thought. Maybe he was right – maybe there were good people, and he was one of them, but my dependence on him scared me. I both hated it and needed it, and I had no choice but to accept it.

'Do you know Aleece?' I asked John.

'Um… yes,' he said, avoiding my eye. I waited for him to elaborate – tell me a story or something about her – but he didn't. He looked ahead, between the front seats, and was silent.

'Was she working with Craig on this thing that's now inside me, then?' I asked.

'Yes.' I felt that the conversation about her was making him nervous – I'd noticed that when we spoke about her in his apartment too.

'Did it mess her up?' I pushed. 'Did she try it out on herself?'

'That I don't know.'

I turned towards him, making it clear I wouldn't be deterred. 'Why is it such a touchy subject for you?' I demanded.

He licked his lips and turned to face me. 'It brings back memories, that's all. She knew my family, my wife, my kids. She was very close to my girls.'

'Was she?'

'Yeah. They had real bond. She was like an older sister to them.'

'Must have been your daughters Aleece told me about. She only remembers a few things from her past – that's what she said, at least. And I don't have reason not to believe her. I don't know how to explain it, but I can't imagine her lying – seems impossible. Anyway, she said she remembered two girls, twins, about five or six years old, and there was such tenderness in her voice when she spoke about them.'

John bowed his head and his lips quivered. He turned away from me and looked out of the window. I didn't press him any further, although I had many more questions, but it was clearly difficult for him to talk about it.

\* \* \*

John offered me a drink when we arrived. I refused. He poured himself a glass of whiskey on a few sharp cubes of ice.

'Let me show you your bedroom,' he said.

He gave me towels, a dressing gown and a T-shirt – one of his. After a long shower I lowered myself on to the bed and unwrapped the gown. The sheets were stretched tightly over the mattress and smelled fresh, the subtle scent of a flowery laundry detergent lingering. I dived under the duvet and fell asleep.

# 12

———

Thick curtains kept the light out. I looked at my phone – it was almost midday. I felt rested, and for the first time since I could remember I woke up without a headache.

I put on the T-shirt John had left for me, which ended bellow the middle of my silver thighs, and went through to the living room. John sat in front of a computer screen.

'Good morning,' he said, getting up.

'Good morning.'

'Did you sleep well?' he asked, going through to the kitchen. He poured a cup of black coffee and handed it to me. 'Hungry? I don't have much to offer, but I can order—'

'It's all right,' I cut in, 'I don't eat breakfast.'

He shrugged and refilled his coffee cup.

'Did you find out anything new?' I asked.

He rubbed his eyes. It didn't look like he'd had much sleep. 'I'd like to get a second opinion,' he said. 'Tomorrow we'll do another scan and make some decisions. You feel any different at all?'

'No,' I said, flatly.

'Most likely the tech is making your brain interpret everything as "normal" so you don't feel like anything strange is happening,' he said.

I didn't feel the urge to ask anything else. Quite the opposite, I'd rather not know the details. I felt calm, and I didn't want to disturb the peace of not knowing – at least, not for a time; for a while I'd let myself breath air that wasn't charged with fear and panic. The storm will hit again, I thought – something would happen soon; possibly even this evening some bad news might strip me of hope and I would be back to shaking and crying and hating everything. But for now, I could enjoy what little I had: a quiet day, a mug of hot coffee, the company and support of another human being and his clean apartment, with its trace of a happy family – proof that such concepts as happy families and love existed.

'I need to go to the Institute,' John said. 'Why don't you put my number in your phone?'

I pulled out my phone and saved his number, then called him. Now he had my number too.

He disconnected an external drive from the computer and turned it off.

'Thank you. For everything,' I said.

'I haven't done anything yet,' he said. 'Here.' He handed me a bundle with a key and a chip. 'In case you need to go somewhere. Don't take any drugs. Take it easy today, OK? And if the chance to get in trouble presents itself, please walk the other way. You've got enough going on right now.' And with these words he left.

I took a shower, then set out for my place to get some clothes and other necessities.

Compared to John's apartment, mine was a mess. Scattered around the mirror were the bloodstained bandages I'd used to mop up my blood after I had tried to find out what was underneath my new skin. I picked them up, and went round throwing away empty bottles, cleaning the ashtrays (some of which were not ashtrays but mugs, which I must have turned to once the trays filled). I wasn't sure when I'd last vacuumed or washed the floors, and I set to on the living-room floor. I saved the bedroom for later – one room at a time.

Next I set to packing a bag, starting with toiletries. Toiletries were easy – there was only one of everything – or, in the case of moisturiser, two. Make-up was also easy: mascara, black eyeliner, shade palette, lipstick. With clothes a few decisions had to be made — potential future circumstances like the weather and occasions — and I picked a few T-shirts, a pair of jeans, a dress or two — the green one and the red — underwear and socks. For how long would I be staying at John's, I wondered? I needed something warm. A sweater — the brown one. I spotted my strappy silk dress that I loved, and went to pack it, but when I pulled it off the hanger through which it had been stuffed, it breathed the heavy smell of sweat and cigarettes, and I quickly changed my mind — I had to wash it before wearing it again. I could take it with me and wash it at John's — but would it be weird to take my laundry to his? I decided to leave it, afraid it would transfer its odour to the bag and everything inside it.

Packing was clearly a mental activity. I'd never thought of it as such before — but then again, I'd never thought of it very much at all. The last time I packed a bag was eight years ago, when I'd moved from the orphanage to this apartment — and that had been easy, because I'd just packed everything I had and transferred it all; here I had to make choices — even simple choices. It was a pleasant distraction; it made me feel normal, human — grounded in the simple tasks humans have to do.

A physical body has to be taken care of, to be clothed and fed. I had never stopped to think about this before: I ate same thing every day — either noodles or chicken, occasionally a salad with mango. Now I wanted to do something nice for my body, eat something healthy, something that was good for it, and feel how it broke the food down and extracted nutrients it needed to function properly. I never cooked at home, so my fridge was empty, save for a couple of bottles of soy sauce and chilli oil and a few packets of condiments from street vendors.

I made myself a cup of tea. I didn't drink tea, as far as I could remember, so I wasn't sure where the packet had come from. It was stale, and barely had any residual taste or aroma, so it must have been ages old. I sat down at the kitchen table and enjoyed my tasteless tea. The warmth of it, the feeling of it trickling down my throat and into my stomach, was soothing. My belly became warm and relaxed, then, my thighs craving the heat, I placed the cup between them. It was surprisingly pleasant. The skin of my legs tingled. I pressed the cup tighter to my pubic bone and my whole crotch absorbed the heat, and it started to spread out across the rest of my body.

I sat like this, the cup between my legs, until it was lukewarm. I craved the company of another human, and if there were someone nearby I would have touched their arms, their chest, their face, and let them touch me too – they would have seen that I was also human, with the same basic needs and desires for simple pleasures. But there was no one, so I touched myself. My fingers favoured my skin, which responded with ticklishness along my palms and the insides of my forearms – but even when I touched the metal of my breast and thighs and chin, I wasn't repelled by its cold surface; touching something solid was good enough.

* * *

On my way back to John's I looked around and observed the people I shared the street with. There wasn't as much detachment in their eyes as I was used to – on the contrary, there was a destination in their faces, and their visages were brighter. The day wasn't as grey as usual: the streets had a silver shine to them, and the air had lost the haze of dust and was easier to breathe.

When I reached John's apartment I went out on to the balcony. The sun was rolling its way down to the horizon, backlighting the sharp silhouettes of the cityscape. In the window of a neighbouring building a couple were talking emotionally about something. A few windows to the right, a woman was setting up a table for more than two. One floor below a child sat at a desk watching something on a tablet. Up above, on a terrace, a woman was looking down, arms crossed, a thick sweater wrapped around her shoulders, enjoying the cool evening, watching people below, watching the city live.

\* \* \*

I was asleep on the sofa, wearing John's white T-shirt. The sound of the closing door woke me up.

'Had a good day?' John asked, his eyes running over me, head to toe.

'Yes,' I said, getting up. 'I went home to get some stuff.'

'Good. Got everything you need?' he asked. A sleepless night and long day had licked life off his face, his voice was hoarse and his eyes were red. 'I tried to call you a few times.'

'I must have missed it,' I said.

He placed a metal case down by the table and took a beer from the fridge.

'Any news?' I asked.

'I applied for a badge for you,' he said, 'so we can go in and out of the Institute without attracting too much attention. It should be ready tomorrow – they have to do a background check.' He took a long sip of beer. 'You've never been arrested, have you?'

'No.'

He finished his beer and threw the bottle in the bin.

'Want to grab a bite to eat?' he asked.

'Yes. I'll go and change.'

I looked for my bag in the bedroom, but it wasn't where I'd put it. I returned to the living room and checked by the sofa.

In the mean time John had sat down at his computer. 'Lost something?' he asked.

'Yes – the bag I brought from my place,' I said, perplexed. 'I left it by the bed, but it's not there.' I kept looking.

After a few minutes John joined me, getting up and searching the living room. Having no luck, we checked the bedroom that belonged to his daughters, we looked in his bedroom and the bathroom. Baffled, I went from room to room, looking again.

'Laura?' he called from the kitchen.

'Yes?' I asked. 'Did you find it?'

'How did you get to your place?'

# CHAPTER 12

'I walked,' I said after a pause. 'And I walked back here too.'

'You walked?' he asked. 'Are you sure?'

'Yes!' I said, convinced.

'You walked… what is it, like eight, ten miles? And you walked back, too – are you sure?'

I stopped for a moment and tried to think. Yes, I walked, I could remember walking there and back. 'Yes,' I said, 'I remember being in my apartment, packing and walking back. I carried the bag on my shoulder!' I went through to the bedroom again, adamant, and checked the bathroom again – nothing. I stared in the mirror, trying to persuade myself that I wasn't going crazy. I could still feel the weight of the bag, the friction of the strap, having to adjust it a few times.

'Why don't we drive to your place and check?' John said.

'There's no way I could've just dreamed it!' I said. 'I even washed the floors and had a cup of tea. Green. Jasmine. And then I walked back to your place.'

John looked at me hard. 'Are you sure you remember walking?' he asked.

'Yes! I mean, it is a bit vague… Am I losing my mind?'

He blinked at me, obviously making an effort to choose his words as best as he could, and said, 'Laura, your mind is not entirely your own. You have to be prepared for a few memory slips or hallucinations… or perhaps worse.' It was evidently a kind way of telling me to pull my shit together.

I digested what he had said and agreed to go to my place. I found a pair of my jeans and put them on, stopped briefly to remark on the fact that I was still wearing John's T-shirt from that morning.

* * *

When we got there I opened the door to my apartment and went straight to the bedroom. The empty bag was still in the wardrobe, not even on the bed, where I'd piled things into it.

'It's all here,' I said, confused, chill running down my spine.

John stood by the mirror in the living room, holding one of the bloodstained bandages. 'What's this?' he asked, and, without waiting for an answer, took my hands, turned them around and looked at my wrists. They were clean, but a fresh scar ran down the side of my palm.

'Nothing,' I snapped, yanking my hands back.

'Nothing?' he said.

'It's nothing!' I repeated.

John looked around, taking in the empty bottles and overflowing mugs that served as ashtrays. I'd cleaned them earlier today and I'd thrown the bottles away – I could swear to it – but there they were, regardless. My clothes were still scattered everywhere, dirty dishes and glasses sat on the table and by the sofa, and the knife I'd used to cut my hand lay by the mirror, next to a crumpled pair of socks.

John noticed the knife lying on the floor, and bent over and picked it up. 'What's this?' he asked. 'Have you been thinking about ending your life after Craig did this to you?' he asked.

'No,' I said.

'I need to be able to trust you,' he said. 'I don't want any surprises. Really, Laura, I witness enough death—'

'I haven't! I just wanted to see what was under this skin,' I said.

John rubbed his tired eyes. 'So all your stuff is still here?'

'It is, but how is that possible? John, I tell you I was here today. And I cleaned – all this, I cleaned it. And then I packed. This dress,' I said, pulling out the silk dress and smelling it, 'this dress...' I trailed off. It smelled of sweat and cigarettes – I knew I had smelled this disgusting stench earlier, I just knew it. I kept it tight against my nose and inhaled, inhaled and inhaled, as though it was a respirator and the sweet gas inside would put me to sleep, to wake up and find everything changed back to normal. And I inhaled and inhaled, afraid that if I stopped I would lose the connection with myself and nothing would remain of me.

John took my hands in his and gently pulled them away from my face. I resisted, clenching the dress, and inhaled, inhaled, inhaled.

'Hey, hey,' he said, pulling my hands a little harder.

'No!' I shouted, struggling. It was all I had of me: the smell of me. I would be lost without this smell. I could never find myself again. 'Let go of me!' I pushed his hands away and manoeuvred around the bed so he couldn't get to me so easily.

'You want the dress?' he asked.

'Yes.'

'You can take it with you.'

I was suspicious of everyone – especially men – and although he didn't look cruel, his pleasant face could be a mask. But he was so much bigger than me, I thought, that if we were to fight he would have no trouble getting what he wanted. I had only one option: to take it with me and hope he was telling the truth.

'Is it OK if I don't wash it?' I asked.

'You don't have to wash it if you don't want to,' he said gently.

I hesitated. Maybe if I were fast enough I could squeeze by him and run outside.

'Where is your bag? Let's put it in there right away,' he said.

I pointed at the wardrobe.

'This one?' he asked, pulling out a dark-brown bag. I nodded. He unzipped it, set it on the bed and held out his hand. Reluctantly I gave him the dress, and he folded it and put it in the bag. 'Here. Do you want me to help you pack? What else do you think you need?'

I smiled, relieved; I could trust him, and I felt safe again. I told him with renewed enthusiasm what else I needed. 'The green dress, a pair of jeans, another dress – the red with a black pattern on it – then I need some socks and underwear. I also need my toiletries, my shampoo and both moisturisers, eye cream, face cleanser and a toner. A toothbrush, toothpaste. And I don't know how long I'll be at yours, so I need some tampons – oh, and painkillers for my menstrual cramps. And also my mascara, black eyeliner and a lipstick. Eyeshadows, the palette – the darker one. And a sweater – I need something warm. The brown sweater, please. And can I also take my black sweatshirt?'

'Of course,' John said, laughing, 'you can take anything you like. OK, so... a green dress, you said. Let's see...' He shuffled through the hangers in the wardrobe. 'The red dress...' He turned around and showed me a red dress with a black pattern on it. 'Is this the one?'

I stood rooted to the spot, unexpectedly shocked seeing him searching through my wardrobe. He met my eyes, and I lowered mine.

'Can you wait for me in the other room?' I said in a small voice. He opened his mouth to speak, but I took the hanger from his hand and cut him off. 'Give me a moment, please.'

'Laura, this is to be expected,' he said. 'And I'm good at pa—'

'Please!' I snapped. 'Just give me some privacy.'

He nodded and left the room. I swallowed the lump in my throat and started putting clothes in the bag, stopping to remove the smelly dress and tossing it in the laundry bin. In the bathroom I scooped up my toiletries and cosmetics, tampons and painkillers, pausing before the mirror to confirm that I was indeed a grown-up woman of twenty-six and not a child. This thing inside me was messing up my identity, and my self-perception was wobbly; I had a fear of John – of men in general – which I presently was trying to suppress. My grasp on reality was ebbing away. What if this, the second time of packing, was not really happening either? I folded a sweater and put it in the bag. How could I know for sure that this was real?

I heard the sound of clinking glass. I leaned out of the bedroom doorway and saw John throwing an empty bottle into the rubbish bin. He walked around, taking in the mess, presumably drawing conclusions about me – and, being honest with myself, I felt as shattered as my apartment looked, so he probably wasn't far off.

I retreated back into my room and slid down on to the floor by the bed and rested my head in my hands.

Five or ten minutes passed. John appeared in the doorframe, knocked gently and came in and squatted in front of me.

'What is happening?' I asked. 'I'm not myself. I'm losing control over who I am.'

'Your body is going through an unusual transformation,' he said. 'Your mind is doing the best it can – and actually it's doing pretty well.'

'Am I hallucinating?' I asked. 'Everything here is exactly the same as when I came earlier today – every single detail.'

John shrugged. 'You could have been here – just like when you saw Craig when I scanned your body. Or perhaps you recreated it from your memories.'

'Will it happen again?'

'Probably. I'd expect more out-of-body experiences, blackouts, hallucinations. Be patient with yourself. Your mind will be different to usual – it would be unreasonable to expect it to be otherwise, considering there is something very alien orchestrating processes in your body now.' He took my hands in his and helped me to stand up.

'What am I turning into? I don't want to lose my body – I don't want to lose the sense of touch and smell and taste. It's fine, this body, even with all this metal – I'm OK with that. I just want to have something solid – I don't want to be reduced to nothing. Can I keep this body, do you think? I will take care of it, I promise.'

As I spoke my voice got higher and higher, like that of a younger girl again, and I cringed. John opened his mouth to speak, but I cut him off before he started. 'Don't answer! Don't talk to me like I'm a child.'

He gave a subtle nod and remained silent.

'What are my chances? Be straight with me – I don't want to be in the dark,' I said.

'I will,' he said, 'after I do another scan and see how this thing has developed. Right now I don't know enough to make a prognosis.'

'Don't tell me what you don't know, tell me what you think,' I said.

'Unfortunately there's not much I can say. I have no experience with this tech. I can't make a prediction without more data,' he said, his eyes shifting over my shoulder and back to my face. I followed his glance – there was a half-empty bottle of vodka on my bed.

'Is this ready to go?' John pointed at my bag.

'Say it! Don't just think it – go on, say it!'

'Say what?' he asked.

'That I'm such a mess, a genetic failure without a seed of self-esteem. Why would I even want to live, right? You know what's going on with me – how can you not if you worked with Craig? But you won't tell me because you're afraid that I can't handle it – that I'll overreact, get high, do something to myself, because I don't know how else to deal with problems other than to get drunk and fucked!'

'No! That's not what I think. I believe you want to live – that you're ready to fight for it.'

'You are a fucking liar,' I shouted. 'As soon as you saw a few little specks of blood on those bandages you assumed I had tried to slash my wrists.'

John nodded, as though to say my statement was fair. 'I might have made the wrong assumption there. Based on a few conversations we had before, and… possibly fear – I'm afraid, too. But I'm glad I'm wrong. And I'm not judging you. I'm not great at managing my emotions, either. I know I drink more than I should.'

'You have no faith in me! Judge me all you want, I don't care. But don't lie to me. Don't help me because you need to save someone. Help me to save myself. I have no other choice but to trust you with my life, so don't keep me in the fucking dark, I don't want surprises – I hate surprises. I want to be in control of whatever scraps of me are still here. I've got nothing else.'

'I know,' he said. 'That's exactly why I'm being careful. It has nothing to do with taking control away from you, or thinking you can't handle it. I know you're strong, I just don't know if you are capable if exercising that strength. Your mind is not fully yours now, and I have no idea what sort of poison Craig – and most importantly the AI that's running this structure – is feeding you. Remember, it is trained to break us out of our physical form. My guess is if you get in the way it will try to stifle your identity and erase your grounding in your physical body, and it'll probably leverage your childhood trauma to achieve this. Dealing with loss takes time and work, acknowledging anger and fear, grieving. It takes months and trained therapists to achieve even small results – and I'm not even certain whether that's the right approach here. You have a pool of unresolved emotions, and I don't know if it's safe to plunge in right now. All I can suggest is that you focus on something important – something that matters to you. You said you want to have a physical body – why? Why is it important to you? Anything that fuels your attachment to this body – keep it close. It can be very simple things – in fact, the simpler the better. It will be more difficult for the AI to manipulate simple associations into something they are not. For example, what's your favourite smell?'

'The sea,' I said, without thinking. 'And pine trees.'

'And do you have a memory to go with these smells?'

I shook my head. 'I just like them.'

'That's good enough. You remember that. If you feel lost, think of these smells.'

'Some AI-driven dust is manipulating my brain, and you tell me to think of the sea? Should I also try drinking chamomile tea to calm my nerves? How do I even know these are my thoughts? That it's me who likes the smell of the sea? What if it's already someone else? I feel like I'm losing myself in someone else's dream. Where is the real me? Where does she begin and where does she end? Today she jumped out of my body and went out for a walk without letting me know. I had no clue. Did my physical body just lay on your couch all day, then? Or did it also do something? What will I do tomorrow? Give me some real tools, John, not a sea breeze and pine trees.'

John came up close. 'There are no real tools, not within the timeframe we have to work in,' he said. He took my hand and brought it to my face. It looked tiny and pale in his big brown hands. 'You like how it feels – the touch?' he asked. I nodded. 'Yeah. Feels good, doesn't it? The warmth, the smell.' He inhaled audibly. With his deep brown eyes he looked at me for some time. 'There is no magic pill I can give you. To deal with something like this, an AI of this calibre, you'd normally go through years of special training. You don't have years. You'll have to work with what you have.' He squeezed my hand, released it, then cupped my head in his palms and leaned forward, almost touching my forehead with his. 'All your tools are here. And they are pretty good tools. You want the truth? Maybe you're right: maybe I need you to survive for me, too. I'm still healing myself, you know, and every day is a struggle – every day you put up a fight and find a reason to keep going. But no matter how much I want you to live, you'll have to save yourself. You don't have a choice. There is very little I or anyone else can do. Understand what I'm saying?'

I nodded. A moment of silence anchored his words in me. They carried insurmountable weight. I wasn't sure whether I was more scared now or relieved. I had no idea what to do with this information.

'Is it OK if I use the bathroom?' John asked.

'Sure,' I said.

He closed the door. I heard the toilet seat opening and clinking against the tank – a strange sound for my apartment. He peed. All that beer he'd downed. My razor blade was on the edge of the bath, and I wasn't sure how clean it was. I imagined there might be black tiny hairs stuck between the blades from my legs, underarms, private parts. The thought sent a pleasant rush to my belly, and I had a strange impulse to go to the bathroom, collect all the hairs from my razor and present them to him to prove I was real, and save them somewhere safe – a jar, perhaps, or a matchbox. There must be also loose hairs from my head all over the bathroom, and particles of my skin on my bed – on the pillows, on the sheets, under the blanket. So much of me was scattered around here.

The toiled flushed, and I heard John wash his hands. 'I won't leave you alone for that long any more,' he said when he came back out. 'Someone should always be with you. Tomorrow we will do another scan, and we can decide what our next steps are based on what we discover.' He pointed to the bag. 'Are you ready?'

'Give me a moment to finish this,' I said. I packed my hair-brush – full of my hair – and my razor blade, and zipped up the bag.

\* \* \*

We had dinner at the same Vietnamese restaurant with the steampunk feel we'd been to the other night and went to the club where we'd met the very first time, and where he'd rescued me from the cowboy guy who'd nearly choked me to death. The one-eyed bartender poured us two shots. John ordered a second round right away. Neither of us felt like talking; I was frustrated, he was tired. He sat still like a hill in the rain, breathing slowly, elbows on the counter, big, clasped fists under his chin. If he was even a little worried it didn't show on his face; his eyes were the eyes of a man who'd had a very long day and wasn't thinking about anything. My mind, on the other hand, was restless, and it feared for itself. Could my body know that it was in danger? That someone was trying to eliminate it because it was no longer useful? All these millions of years of evolution for the human body to become what it was, only to one day be declared obsolete by humans themselves.

I gulped down another shot, and when the alcohol relaxed my mind, I took a trip around the club, moving slowly, absorbing the energy of the people around me who had clearly been there for some time. *Am I human or am I not? Are these just memories? Projections? Is this my present or fragments of the past?*

Through a doorway leading to a smaller lounge I saw a couple making out. On the other side, drowned in red light, people swayed to an uneven electronic beat. I joined them. Bodies touched and mixed, exchanging smells, leaving traces of desire in each other's eyes.

I found myself leaning against a wall, separated from the dancing crowd by a man who was licking my neck. His hand moved up from my waist to my breasts. The frustration of my day hung heavy on me, and my body asked to be numbed with the emptiness of random sex. He unbuttoned my jeans, unzipped the fly and felt my crotch. When he attempted to cover my lips with his mouth, I turned my face away from him and saw John staring at us. He walked a few steps in my direction, tearing a cigarette stub between his fingers, looking me straight in the eye while the stranger's hand went up and down inside my underwear. I wouldn't have minded if he'd joined us – I wanted him to. I released a moan and bit my lip. Seeing that I desired his company, John came to a halt, turned around and started walking towards the exit. I felt ashamed, which was ridiculous. I pushed the man off me, and the moment of wondering whether to run after John or not stretched into a minute, two minutes, five minutes. But he was gone, and I stayed.

\* \* \*

The lights were on when I got to John's place. I followed the sound of running water into the bathroom. The door was ajar; I opened it silently. He stood in the shower, like a rocky mountain, icy streams cascading down his broad back across his bottom, frosting the entire room. He was facing the wall, pushing against it with both hands – and if he'd only pushed a little longer and a little harder, it would have probably moved.

He glanced over his shoulder, and, seeing me, switched off the water, reached for a towel and wrapped it around his waist. He seemed the very embodiment of physical strength, the composure in his eyes atop the steep rise of his body. It was a big body. I looked small and fragile next to him.

'Excuse me,' he said.

I stepped out of the doorway to let him pass to his bedroom. He waited a moment – he wasn't waiting for me to leave, surely, since he'd seen me naked, or nearly naked, multiple times – then he threw his towel on the bed and pulled on black tracksuit trousers and a white long-sleeved T-shirt. He reached over to his sheepskin jacket, and, pulling a pack of cigarettes from one of the pockets, went out on to the terrace. I watched him lean against the railing and release a cloud of smoke. I wanted to join him, but it was obvious he wanted space, so I saved my questions until he came back in, but I didn't take my eyes off him for a second. Bending over the railing a little, the outline of his muscles showed through his T-shirt, and his legs were crossed at the ankles. When he was done, he threw the burning stub into the dark void.

'Is it about the guy in the club?' I asked, almost as soon as he walked in.

He sat down behind his computer screen without so much as glancing at me.

'I can see you are upset,' I said. 'What – you don't screw around?'

He fixed me with a long stare. I expected to see contempt in his eyes, but it wasn't there.

'I'm not upset,' he said. 'I just didn't like seeing what I saw.'

'Why?'

'I just didn't.'

'Are you jealous?' I asked.

'No, of course not. It's none of my business.'

'Explain then. I saw the look on your face. You were not indifferent.'

John bowed his head and rubbed the back of his neck. Just as he looked like he was about to talk, he pressed his palms to his eyes and released a loud sigh. 'Oh, Laura, it hurt me to see it, that's all.'

'Hurt you? Why?' I couldn't understand what was going on. Whatever it was, it wasn't jealousy.

He clicked his tongue against his teeth and looked out of the window. 'It just did,' he said, and pressed his palm to his eyes again.

'Are you crying?' I asked.

'No, I'm not crying. It's been a difficult day and I've had too much to drink,' he said. But when he looked at me his eyes glistened. 'You also had a long day,' he went on. 'You'd better get some rest. We'll go to the lab the first thing in the morning.' He directed his gaze at the screen before him.

Goosebumps rose on my skin at the sight of this mountain of a man nearly crying. I stood there, waiting to talk about it, but he didn't return his gaze to me. He hid between the lines of whatever it was he was pretending to read, clearly hoping I understood he'd rather be left alone. I turned and headed off to my bedroom, haunted by the picture of him rubbing his watery eyes.

# 13

---

When I woke up the sky was already blue. My eyes were wet; I must have been crying in my sleep. I sat on the edge of the bed, clinging to my chest. It took me a moment to realise I had pain where my heart was. The pounding inside was too strong, too loud. The pain got sharper. I doubled over and fell on the floor, and I was certain my heart stopped. Had I just died? My body became lifeless, no heart beating inside, but, strangely, I was crying. How could tears fall from the eyes of the dead? I gathered my strength and crawled to the bathroom. Without life coursing through it, my body was heavy and stiff. Rearing up, I gripped the edge of the sink and pulled myself up. I gasped. My face twitched and melted into Aleece's face. She looked back at me from the mirror, sharing my tears, sharing air that I no longer devoured with my lungs but with my whole skin, experiencing my environment in a different way to usual. There was no separation between touch, smell, sight – my body was a conglomeration of particles, and each of them experienced the totality of the surrounding.

Aleece was not as I remembered her; her hair was long, and metal plates didn't cover her body.

'Aleece, where are you?'

*I'm right here*, she said, without making a sound, and touched my lips with her lips, wrapping around me like a snake of warm fog.

I dabbed my face, which was also her face, gliding my fingers over her features, feeling how she was touching me at the same time.

'Aleece, what happened to you?' I asked.

*Shhh...* She took control over my hands and caressed my waist, my breasts and neck. She touched me as if rediscovering my body – her own body, for in that moment we shared a physical form. She wasn't just inside me, she was everywhere: in the air, and in the water that was filling the room, reaching already to my knees. The rising water didn't frighten me, because she was there, and I trusted her with my life.

The current intensified, changing directions, reaching up to my hips. I clung on to the sink.

'Aleece, how do I survive?'

*What for?* she whispered. Her face of timeless presence stared at me from the mirror.

*What for? What for?* my thoughts shouted.

A power shortage in my brain, a moment of blackout, confusion and a flare of some knowledge that I immediately forgot threw me out of balance. I let go of the sink, and the current pulled me beneath the rule of air. A few chokes, and I learned I didn't need to breathe.

*Aleece, don't leave!*

The blackness of her eyes didn't contain life. Instead, there was a tunnel connecting worlds, blending layers of realities, melting boundaries of dimensions, uniting everything into one omnipresent thought.

*Please, don't leave me now. I'm losing myself.*

*The opposite is true, Laura. You are almost here,* she whispered. *I'm sorry. You came back for me, but I can't stay. I'm too far away.*

The water level suddenly dropped, smashing me against the floor. I lay in the doorway between the bathroom and the bedroom.

The darkness outside was unfamiliar: the sky was not painted with pink neon; the skyscrapers did not emit light. The window started vanishing, presenting the view of nothingness. The walls followed, concrete mouldering in the acid of blackness.

Soon I lay on an empty space of black matter, the last cells of my body dissipating.

\* \* \*

A quake woke the flows inside my arteries. Streams of fluids and air inflated me like the shell of a lifeless doll. I opened my eyes. A man was leaning over me. I couldn't understand or feel anything except the serenity that tried to suck me back in.

'Laura?' he called. 'Laura, can you hear me?' His hand was on my neck. 'Laura, look at me.' He waited for a response that didn't come. 'You are drifting away, Laura. Focus. Look at me.' But the blackness was too beautiful. 'Your parents. Tell me about your parents.' I heard him say the words, but they meant nothing. 'When was the last time you saw your parents?'

I closed my eyes and dived inward, where I stopped seeing, hearing, feeling.

Not for long. I felt a sharp pinch that caused me to open my eyes, and my body spasmed.

'How did your parents die?' he demanded.

I started recognising the man, although I couldn't identify who he was just yet.

'Laura, your parents, how did they die? What happened?'

I sucked in a lungful of air. Pain attacked somewhere inside.

'Good. Tell me what happened. Did they kill themselves?'

I shook, my teeth clattered and my muscles danced on my bones.

'How did they die, Laura?'

The pain in my chest, awakened by his words, brought memories that tore the rest of me apart.

'Why did your parents leave you?' he kept on, hurting me.

I wanted to yell, but my mouth didn't open, my body didn't respond to the impulses of my mind.

'Why did they leave you alone?'

A gale of rage forced a scream out of my throat. I threw myself at John, pushing him hard. He caught my hands before I could hit him again and pressed me tight against his chest.

'It's OK, it's OK,' he kept saying.

It took me some time to realise where I was. I stopped struggling as the tremors in my muscles subsided. Tears mitigated my anger. I buried my face against John's chest, and he brushed his hand over my hair. Everything stopped: the fever, the rage, the tears – all gone, replaced by an after-the-storm quiet.

'You know it was necessary, right?' John asked.

'Yes.'

He eased his arms around me. I crawled out of his embrace and looked down at my body. There were silver discs attached to my arms, to my stomach under my T-shirt, to my legs and on one of my cheeks. Next to John lay some device.

'What is this?'

'A muscle stimulator. To remind your mind where your body is. It helped. This time.' He reached over and removed the disc from my cheek and then peeled off the circles from the rest of me. After helping me to my feet, he went to his desk, opened the metal case he'd brought home the other night and put the discs and the device away inside it.

This time I remembered everything, every detail. I remembered Aleece, infinity in her eyes, and my own experience of it, as much as my mind could translate it. And there was so much more. I couldn't share what I felt with John – my brain just couldn't put it into words, because words were not the right medium to express such an experience – but I wanted to share it; the drive to share the experience felt second-nature, like instinct. As I thought of various other means I could use to convey my feelings, I was overcome with the desire to connect with other brains, to access their structure, their molecules: if I could simply inhabit a mind, I could simulate my experience for them. It seemed easy enough – I didn't need to think about the technicalities of creating a simulation because, somehow,

I already knew how to do it. What I didn't know yet was how to get inside another mind.

I approached John. Alarmed by my proximity, he stopped fiddling with the case and gave me his full attention. I could see the shadows of his thoughts and memories in his eyes; I could almost seep into his head and explore what was happening there – but something wouldn't let me in; there was a barrier I couldn't cross. I raised myself up on tiptoe, propped my hands against his chest, leaned closer to his face and took a deep breath. The contents of his brain intrigued me, and what I could do with it had no limits – if I could only get inside I could alter its responses, modify the shape of neurons, choreograph electrical impulses and chemical signals to achieve results I desired.

John started back. I caught his arms and pulled him closer. He winced.

'Wow, easy,' he said, unclenching my fingers from around his forearms and placing my hand into his. 'Press against me.'

As I pressed down, his hand lowered under my pressure, his muscles bulged, his eyes widened.

'You feel any different?' he asked, freeing himself from my grip.

'I do.'

'How exactly?'

'I want to be one with you,' I said. 'I can't explain why. There are no reasons for it – it seems like a natural thing to do.'

He looked concerned. 'Let's get you to the lab.'

Yes, I thought, it was better if he looked inside me himself – for him to understand me he would have to forget that he had a body, expand the amplitude of his consciousness and recognise that he could be anything, take any form, small or big, and be everywhere. But until then he could only look into me through his scanner and let the images on his screen tell him what limited information he was equipped to interpret.

# 14

---

When we arrived at the Neuroscience Institute all I needed to do to get inside this time was slide my new badge through a card reader at the checkpoint gate. The receptionist robot followed me with fake eyes that looked real enough to be mistaken for human.

'Laura, this is Rick,' John said, introducing me to a young man wearing a mustard beanie and a lab coat over a green sweater. Rick bowed his head a little and waved. He was in his mid-thirties, an awkward, bony guy, too smart to be talkative. His neck and hands twitched. One of his shoulders was quite a bit higher than the other and it twitched occasionally. 'Rick will be helping us,' John went on, and gestured at the table in front of the cavernous white scanner. 'You know the drill,' John said.

I nodded, took off my clothes and lay down.

The procedure seemed faster than the last time. I was wide awake the whole time. John was already waiting near the scanner when the table rolled back out. His face was hard to read, and he didn't say anything until we approached the screens with the recordings of my insides, and even then it took him some time to start drafting intelligible sentences.

My body looked like a time-lapse of a bird's-eye-view of a city nightscape. My veins were reminiscent of shining highways, and strands of what were supposed to be arteries flickered with red and yellow lights like bridges cramped with cars. My skin was a night sky full of constellations. I glanced at my hand and wondered how, with this light show firing inside me, did I still maintain a human form on the outside? The answer was immediate. I could take on any shape, but if I deviated too much from a human form I would be caught. No skin screen looked like this yet. I'd spend the rest of my life in some lab. Maintaining a human appearance was a disguise – a decision made in order to survive and gain a more favourable position in my environment. Who or what was making this choice, this thing inside me or me, was another question.

Rick was zooming in on various parts of the image, biting his knuckles, wiggling in his chair. He was making me more nervous than I already was.

'You can see this thing evolves... you evolve very fast,' John said, his words coming out clumsily.

'John, speak – what's happening to me?' I asked. The dichotomy between my states was now a physical sensation. I couldn't yet manoeuvre between these states at will, but the separation was undeniable. There was my physical body, and my experience of it, determined by its biological design; and then there was another complex structure that didn't end where my body and mind ended, and which was not defined by my physical attributes.

'Your body is changing fast,' he repeated. 'You can modify your molecules, create entirely new ones, alter your DNA. This thing changes the way your entire body functions – you are basically reengineering yourself.' He zoomed in on my abdominal muscles, then into my viscera, dissecting me layer by layer. The tissue of my organs was interlaced with radiating strings. My body resembled a hive, and nothing was still: tiny particles merged, broke down, merged again. New particles appeared and connected with the existing ones to form something else. 'It changes so fast,' John repeated under his breath, pointing at a close-up of shimmering dust and webs of light inside my head, which danced around in hypnotising patterns. 'The plasticity of this thing – look how it rewires itself,' he said. 'It has a completely new structure form that in the first scan we did – and it looks like it's processing an enormous amount of new data.' John turned to Rick. 'The question is, where does it derive this new information from? What's its environment?'

There was a moment of silence.

'So, Blank?' Rick asked, although it didn't really sound like a question.

'I don't know what else it could be,' John said.

'And it is being tested,' Rick said, trying to suppress his excitement. 'It's out there in the open.'

'What's Blank?' I asked.

Rick glanced at John, then at me. I could tell he wanted to speak – he was more fascinated than he was concerned. If it were up to him, he'd tell me everything and more, but John was cautious, weighing up what information he should share.

'It is an incredibly complex, self-evolving structure,' John said at last, 'that is currently merged with your body and your soul.'

'With my soul,' I repeated.

'Yes, with your soul,' he went on. 'Craig conceived the idea of Blank even before the pandemic struck. He developed it as evidence that something beyond our will can make us do things, but he'd already been studying all kinds of out-of-body experiences. His advocating for the radical change of humans has been condemned by both Church and science, but he still has a large following and very influential people backing him. He worked with shamans, mediums and psychics to create out-of-body simulations and tested them on hundreds of volunteers. Craig sees the soul as one of many mechanisms within a larger existential framework and considers it our front door into this structure. His goal was to build a unit that could connect with the soul and take us into the very gut of our existence, while preserving our self-awareness. That's what Blank is.'

'So, this thing inside me is some super-intelligent mechanism that is connected to my soul?' I asked.

'In a nutshell,' John said.

'I agree,' said Rick. 'I haven't heard of any other tech that can modify itself and the host it occupies so fast. It is testing possibilities of biological shapes. It brings its experiences and knowledge into your physical form. It seems to be very excited.'

'Why is it called *Blank*?' I asked.

'Because initially it's only a structure – a very smart one, but empty, like a matrix or mould,' John said. 'It becomes activated only after it connects to a brain and a soul, which results in the creation of this new intelligence.'

Rick spun around in his chair to face me. 'Why do you think it chooses to look like this, like you, on the outside? Camouflage?'

'Rick,' John said, through clenched teeth.

'It's a relevant question,' he said. 'Is it Blank's choice or yours? Do you think Blank does it all on its own?'

'I don't know,' I said. 'What do you think I should look like?'

'OK, let's back—' John started.

'No, I want to know,' I said, cutting him off. 'What form would you choose for yourself, Rick?'

Rick's lips started stretching into a smile, and I was looking forward to hearing what he had to say, but he caught John's annoyed gaze and returned his eyes to the screen without answering.

'Does this mean I can change into anything?' I asked. Even though I knew the answer, I was curious what the images of my insides revealed to them.

'Anything,' Rick said. 'Well, not *anything* anything, but—'

'Let's focus,' John insisted.

'Like a caterpillar turns into a butterfly. Only, in an instant,' Rick said. 'And this is how Craig communicates with it.' Rick pointed at the silver cylinder at the top of my spinal cord.

They continued to stare at the screen, the recording of my body playing on a loop.

'He wants the best of both worlds,' Rick said. 'Can you imagine—'

'No, I can't,' John snapped. 'It can't happen. If we learn to control our own minds, someone will be able to control all of us one day. There is a reason why the TEA didn't approve it. And it's only a matter of time before this thing gets out of control, if it hasn't already. We don't know what it has become or where it is, who or what it interacts with, what other species and phenomena. We can't track it, and I doubt that Craig can either.' They leaned closer to the screen and scrolled through parts of my body, stretching the visuals, bringing tiny flickering particles to the forefront.

I was drawn to these images. I was a part of some whole other system – I was no longer an isolated biological unit confined to the surface of Planet Earth. John and Rick's voices became a background noise as I stood, mesmerised, watching filaments of light creating patterns inside me. I felt each individual string pulsating with energy, running through my cells, modifying them, turning them lucid. Ultraviolet waves penetrated my bones and replaced the solid tissue with crystal laminae. My vessels grew and spread like fine silvery mycelium.

*Why am I running from this?*

'Laura!' John's voice interrupted my thoughts. They were both staring at me. Rick sank back in his chair as though trying to melt into it.

I looked down. Parts of my body looked exactly as they did on the screen – no skin, only the metal plates that held my sparkling mass together. My surface looked like a streamlet on a sunny day.

'Laura, this is your body, you have full control over it,' John said.

I raised my hand and observed the processes that bloomed inside.

'She is perfect,' Rick said. 'Better than any human.'

'Shut up, Rick!' John snapped, drops of sweat forming on his forehead, his heartbeat fast and uneven.

I moved closer to John and stretched my hand towards his chest – it went right through his flesh. He was stunned. I started exploring myself through him: I saw myself through his eyes, I felt myself through his brain. His mind teemed with uncertainty and wonder and fascination. I enjoyed what I felt inside him: the desire to know and the necessity to restrain himself, curiosity and fear, the agony of choice. So human. I tried to touch him again, this time focusing on the surface of my fingertips, envisioning the sensation of his corporeality. After a few attempts, my hand landed on his chest, loud and precise. Even under the veil of uncertainty, his inner essence was an impressive landscape.

As I explored myself through him, I knew I had discovered myself through others already; spreading through their memories and perceptions, I had attained another life. I recognised what I was, and that revelation shocked me. My brain couldn't process the truth so fast; its illusive boundaries wouldn't allow me to understand the nature of my new form. I focused on my sensations, tried to decode them, but my physical body was returning, limiting my perception.

'John,' Rick said, and I noticed him standing in front of us. 'John, she's coming back.'

Skin grew on my translucent surface. John let go of my wrist and observed the transformation.

'I recorded everything,' Rick said. His smart contact lens flickered.

'Are you... OK?' John asked me.

I didn't answer. This question had no meaning. Was I OK? My eyelids were closing. John walked me over to the procedure table. I lay down. He covered me with a blanket and walked over to another part of the lab. I opened my eyes from time to time and saw him and Rick discussing something behind the glass partition. I might have fallen asleep.

'Rick will take you home – I have to finish something,' John said, coming over to me.

I was sitting on the table, already wearing my clothes. How did that happen? I had no memory of getting dressed.

'I can get home myself,' I said.

'I'm sure you can, but it's better if someone stays with you. I'll be home in a few hours. Then we can talk.'

I was too tired to argue, and I didn't mind having company.

Rick packed a few devices into a bag and we set off. We didn't exchange a word on the way to John's – like two bemused fish wondering how they ended up together in the fishbowl. Rick fidgeted and squeezed his fingers, digging his nails in between his knuckles, doing everything in his power not to look at me. Out of the corner of my eye I could see his knuckles growing white as he contorted his fingers into painful angles. But he seemed comfortable in his discomfort, a cheeky smile curling his lips a few times. Behind his running eyes was a mind that knew the body it lived in was vulnerable and awkward, knew it didn't need his body to be perfect or normal in order to thrive. I realised I, too, was comfortable in my new strangeness.

When we arrived at John's, Rick set up his computer on the kitchen table and hid his face behind the screen. I made coffee and put a cup in front of him.

'So, what shape would you have chosen if you'd had my abilities?' I asked.

He slid back in his chair, his eyes running every possible direction.

'I'm just messing with you,' I said. 'Unless you want to talk about it?'

He shook his head. 'Please stay as you are until John comes back. Don't change into anything, OK?'

'I'll try,' I said. I went back into the kitchen and rootled in the cupboards until I found a bottle of whiskey; I poured some into his coffee to calm his nerves and loosen his tongue. He sank deeper into the chair. I pushed the cup closer to him. 'I can't – I shouldn't,' he said. 'I don't handle substances well.'

'Nothing will happen to you because of one little splash,' I said, pouring some whiskey into my coffee too. I lay down on the sofa and lit a cigarette. The smoke mixed with the bitter taste of coffee in my mouth. I held it in my lungs before letting it back out and watched how it dissipated. 'Is there a final stage of this experiment?' I asked. 'What am I supposed to turn into in the end?'

'Unless you want to change something yourself, you should remain as you are. Ideally. If everything goes well. Physically, you can change many things. Blank will automatically prevent you from altering yourself beyond the point that would make your existence on Earth uncomfortable. You can have a different colour of skin, more muscles, decorative attributes – whatever a good engineer and surgeon can do, you can do. Mentally you should remain yourself. Of course, your perception of self will change, but gradually, as a response to a new environment Blank is introducing you to.'

'Why am I changing so drastically, then? And why do I feel like I'm losing my mind?'

'Because you are a test. An experiment. It's not a final product yet. You are the first human subject. As far as we know. Ideally you should be able to control Blank and not the other way around. You should not become its playground. You use it to travel outside a body and explore other realms. It's not going smoothly. Sorry. Or maybe you are not the best subject, and you are fighting it. And it fights you back. Hard to tell.'

I raised myself on to my elbows and looked at Rick. He placed his cup on the table and pushed it away. Anxiety took hold of his muscles and sent a wave of spasms down his shoulders.

'What will happen if it all turns into a disaster?' I asked.

'Oh, huh, this is a very broad question,' he said. 'You want to know how it will impact you or the world?'

I chuckled. How easy it was to get information out of him. 'Me,' I said. 'The world can go fuck itself.'

'You may become paralysed, unable to feel anything, unable to think, even. Or perhaps there won't be a you any more. Blank will take off and won't return. Hard to say. I imagine there is a lot to explore out there.' His shoulder jerked up to his ear, he clasped his hands and tapped his fingers against his forehead. 'No more questions, please.'

'Do you know Craig's daughter, Aleece?' I asked.

Rick pushed his chair away from the table and rushed to the bathroom as though it was a real emergency. Perhaps nature called. Maybe the coffee did it to him. Or could it be alcohol? Such a little amount?

I waited. After about ten minutes I called, and when he didn't answer, I knocked on the door. 'Rick? Everything all right?'

'Yes,' came the voice from behind the bathroom door.

I waited another few minutes and knocked again. 'Rick?'

'Yes? There is another bathroom if you need to go. In John's bedroom.'

I leaned my ear against the door and listened. 'What are you doing there?' I asked.

'Nothing.'

Silence.

'Are you hiding from me?' I asked.

'Yep.'

'Are you afraid of me? Or you just don't want to talk?'

'You ask too many questions,' he said.

'What if I can read your mind?'

'No, you can't. If you could, you would have done it already. You wouldn't be asking questions. And you wouldn't be here.'

'Where would I be?' I asked.

'Hard to say. For me – hard to say. If you could get into people's minds, you would have impulses. To multiply, to spread. If you got out of control, I mean. You could make us see things, do things.'

I lowered myself on to the floor, leaned against the door and stretched my legs. 'What if I'm already in your brain and making you see things?'

There was a long pause this time.

'It's possible. I wouldn't notice if you did. Do you think you are inside me?'

'I don't know, Rick. How can I establish this?'

'Not sure,' he said. 'The reality you would create would be the same reality to you as it is to me. Unless you deliberately chose to manipulate me. But since you don't know, it's possible that you live in it the same way I do. Unless you are pretending and not telling me the truth, which is very possible.'

'I'm not manipulating you on purpose. I'm not in your mind, don't worry,' I said.

'Well, you can't know for sure – not really.'

'Well, if that's the case, we are both victims of my manipulation.'

There was the sound of a toilet seat shifting. 'Don't be upset if it's true,' he said. 'One reality is not worse or better than another, because at any given moment there is only one reality. Reality is always only one – the one you are experiencing.'

'But what if you wake up one day and realise that the last, let's say, five years of your life were just a manipulation, an illusion?'

'That would be your reality: you wake up and your understanding of your past has changed. Your reality is still just one. Reality is always now,' he said.

'But a different one.'

'No, not different, the same. For my mind, at least. But I believe it works the same way for all.'

'But if you wake up and realise your life is no longer what you thought it was, doesn't it mean you have a different life now?'

'Life – I don't know. I'm not a philosopher. But reality stays the same because it is always one.'

I felt I agreed with him. 'Don't you want to ask me things? Like, how does it feel not to have a body – that sort of thing?'

'I do,' he said. 'But it is better that you don't think about questions I want to ask. I don't want to stimulate you and inspire you to do anything strange.'

I got up from the floor and tapped on the door with my knuckles. 'Let's go get a drink?' I said.

'Go where?'

'Somewhere fun.'

'No, no, we can't go anywhere,' he said, and I heard him getting up.

'Of course we can!'

'John said—'

'Fuck John! We can't sit here like lab rats waiting for him to come back.' I went into my room and opened the bag with my clothes in and changed into my favourite silk dress. Had I packed it? Casting my mind back, I thought I'd removed it from the bag, but I didn't trust my memory – and anyway, it was right here, already flowing down my breasts and hips. And I must have washed it, too, because it smelled nice.

Rick rapped on the door from inside the bathroom. 'Laura? Laura? You hear me? Laura, it's not safe, it's—'

'I am going out,' I said. 'You can go with me or stay here, it's up to you, but I bet John will be more pissed off if you let me go by myself.'

# 15

---

Steam leaked from under the streets, and a roll call of sirens was called somewhere a few blocks away. With every step I made on the shimmering pavement I felt a growing connection to the city and its inhabitants. This city knew me like no person did. I'd spent so many nights crying here. Somehow pain didn't bother me any more − I wasn't afraid of it. I brought forth all my darkest memories, and the more it hurt the stronger I felt, safe inside a body that could bring itself to an epic self-destruction like some far-flung star bursting out in the universe. The only sensible thing to do now, I was sure, was to connect with others; and so I headed for the room of sweet smoke hidden behind the small red door where the girl with the prosthetic penis had introduced me.

The smoke felt thicker than before, as if the oriental rugs covering every surface in the club exhaled additional doses under the pressure of bodies pushing against their fibres. The drug-sodden air flogged the anxiety from Rick's bones. His eyes finally relaxed, and his pupils turned into ripe black apples. Deep beats, high oriental strings and alien sounds defined the movement of everything inside the club, from teasing lips to arched necks, swaying hips and raised hands searching for something, seeing something, feeling something.

I took Rick's hand and pulled him right into the odour of incense and the contagion of trance. We flew with the crowd, drifted, caught waves, gliding on a smooth surface of the collective euphoria. A girl with long dark hair was dancing next to me. Rick stood, captivated by our quick acquaintance; her thigh rubbed against my pubic bone as my lips traced along her neck. I dragged him closer so he could feel the heat my skin generated, preparing me for greater pleasure.

In a swirl of smoke in the corridor I saw the girl who'd invited me here the first time. Her prosthetic dick pushed out of the silver zip of her nude latex trousers. She smiled when she noticed us, and in a few seconds her tight hardness pressed against me from behind, and her mouth reached my ear.

'I'm glad you like it here,' she whispered, landing a kiss on the lips of the girl I was dancing with.

They smiled at each other and connected in a longer kiss, trapping me between them. Someone's hands were on my breasts, the girl with the prosthetic dick exhaled a muddled whisper in my ear and bit my earlobe. I watched her small ass walk away, blending with the smoke, becoming a mirage of this distorted reality, and I was left with this new girl.

Two androgynous boys I'd met last time approached us – it seemed Rick had sparked their interest. His eyes shone, and he embraced his desire, his body opening up for whatever was coming. One of the guys took Rick's hand and they led him to a big, round bed behind us, hidden behind a soft, white cloth hanging from the ceiling all the way to the floor.

My new friend and I joined them. She lay under me, trembling under the splashes of kisses I drew on her chest and belly. New buds of desire blossomed in my mind, asking to be watered and fed. I worked my way down her groin and submitted to their needs.

The two young men treated Rick's body to a feast, which he consumed without hesitation. Their three silhouettes shared every border, every curve and cavity. Soon inseparable, they formed a statue of eternal classics. Evolving and expanding, never to be decomposed again, the conjunction of their bodies created a new element in the palette of the universe.

I did my best to memorise every texture of the girl I was with, her warm flesh responding to my touch so passionately, without restraint or shame, giving me all of it and still asking for more. There was nothing truer in that moment than her sweat, unreachable in elevated states of being but available in great abundance in this primitive form. The simplicity of our pleasure was genius – bold, raw and exposed, it was a declaration of a moment in time and place, the exact coordinates of which were for ever embedded in the passage of life.

The three male bodies interlaced near us, and I couldn't distinguish between them any more. Rick's eyes were hidden behind his eyelids, his lips open for air.

I wasn't craving an orgasm – all I wanted was to make this moment last longer, to enjoy the body I occupied and the body I was loving.

The vision of John disturbed my pleasure. I closed my eyes and opened them again, blinked a few times, wondering if it was a hallucination. It wasn't. John stood in front of the bed looking at me, looking at Rick, his eyes wide, distressed. He was real. I sat on top of the girl, facing him. She squeezed my breast and placed a hand under my crotch. My eyes ran from her face to John's and I moved back and forth, teasing him, calling him, provoking him. I wanted him to see the pleasure I was getting, pleasure free of guilt or regret.

He came closer, squinting, said something to me. The poor thing, he was trying so hard to stay sober, but the drugs were in the air. I grabbed his neck and printed a kiss on his lips. He couldn't help himself responding before pushing me away. 'What are you doing?' he asked.

'Living,' I said.

'Rick… he can't handle this,' he said.

'He's happy, let him be – he doesn't need you right now.'

John stepped back and stared at the mastery of our bodies on the round bed, rubbing his face, doing everything in his power to resist the penetration of the drugs.

When Rick saw John he froze. A sequence of spasms warped his face. His muscles had relaxed during his lovemaking, and I cursed John for waking them up. To my relief, Rick didn't move, and I was pleased to see his shame-fuelled attempt to escape from the two men failing, and he remained where he was, between the two warm bodies that kept offering him more to love and devour.

I got up from the bed, seized John's arm and took him outside the tent. I slid my hand up his chest and around his neck. Guiding his hand along my waist, I traced the outline of his lips with my thumb.

'Laura, no…' he said, and tried to take a step back, but the wall behind him rooted him to the spot.

There was no space between my naked body and John. His face was covered with beads of sweat. I touched him below his belt − he wanted me all the way. He grabbed both my hands, turned me around to face the wall and clasped my wrists above me. He was heavy on me, and I couldn't move. He buried his face in the back of my head, his heart pounding in a fatal race against itself. I anticipated the sound of his belt unbuckling, waited for his hands to grab my hips. But he did none of that. He breathed deeply and loudly, regaining the composure he never really lost. And I loathed him for that.

Before I could do anything else, he shouldered his way outside.

I returned to the bed. The girl lay on her back, her body relaxed, her expression euphoric. I sat beside her but couldn't bring myself to give her more love. My focus had shifted. Images of John made me bitter; his rejection stung.

After the boys finished their beautiful orgy, I crawled closer to Rick and placed his head on my lap. His face was composed of a harmony and verity only known to those who had experienced the unconditional devotion to the reality-defying non-platonic pleasure – and it was the face of an angel to me. I caressed his cheeks and his chin, thinking about the bond we had. He twitched and opened his eyes from time to time to make sure I was still there. Once he saw me, he would relax again and his eyelids would slowly close.

\* \* \*

Rick and I closed the little red door behind us and stepped out into the cold night. John sat on a staircase nearby, three empty beer bottles sitting next to him. When he saw us he got up, and without a word we started walking towards the main road. The drugs released our minds almost immediately, but clarity was still some hours away. I didn't want to stay at John's place, I realised. I turned around and walked the other way.

'Where are you going?' John asked.

'Home,' I said.

He caught up with me, grabbed my arm and forced me to face him. 'What happened?' he asked, his voice hoarse. It was the first time I had heard an edge in it.

'Nothing,' I said, pulling away from his grip. 'We had a good time.' I turned to Rick. 'Didn't we?'

He was still pretty out of it, but he nodded, hiding his eyes from John.

'There is nothing to be ashamed of,' I said, touching his shoulder. 'It's OK to embrace pleasure. It's OK to have desires. Otherwise what's the purpose of flesh?'

'It's not that,' John said. 'That was a lot of drugs for him.'

'He handled it just fine,' I said. 'What are you saving *him* from, huh?'

'No... Laura,' said Rick, trying to defend John, 'he's right. I...'

Screw them both. Rick was nice, but screw them both. I pivoted on my heels and walked away. After a few blocks I noticed John was following me alone – Rick must have left for home. John kept his distance until I reached my building.

'Why can't you just disappear?' I shouted at him before touching the pad to open the door.

'What happened?' he asked. 'Why are you acting like this?'

'Why am I acting like myself again you mean?'

He followed me to the lifts. 'Laura, we need to have a conversation. It's not just about you any more—'

'You've made that very clear,' I said. 'Look at yourself – so strong and composed, but inside you are as fucked up as any of us.'

'What? What are you getting at? Be straight with me, what's up? What's bothering you?' he asked. I remained silent. 'If you spin out of control, it won't just affect you, it will affect other people – many people,' he said.

'I don't give a damn about other people! They didn't care about me when I needed them. Why should I care about them now?'

'What happened to you fighting for your life?' he asked.

'Mmm, right. I don't know what happened to it. Life is for living, I've heard, so I'm living. What happens next, I don't care.'

'This isn't you talking—' he started.

'Bye, John,' I said.

The door of the lift started sliding closed, but John put his boot in the door and stepped inside. He wasn't going to leave me alone.

From inside the glass cabin I watched the flickering windows of the skyscraper across the road; a nest of primitive bodies with their superior ghosts trapped inside.

*Who is more trapped*, I wondered, *our souls, inside us, or us, in search of our souls?*

Primitive was good, primitive was what I wanted. I couldn't handle the pressure of living up to the infinity of the soul; I couldn't imagine living without imperfection in every thought; I couldn't bear existence without feelings. I'd been trying to numb my feelings for so long, resorting to all the wrong methods. Now I wanted to be satiated with emotions, because if feelings were not the utmost manifestation of a human being, then what was? What was more human than hope and despair, love and pain? I didn't know how I could experience love, but I knew how to hurt. A soon as I was alone, I would lie down on my bed and think about my parents and the fucking priest, and I would hate and hurt. And if after hurting and crying all day I decided there was nothing for me here, I would leave this body and go back to the place where my soul was a magical sucker on the tentacle of a giant cosmic octopus.

I opened the door to my apartment and told John to get lost. I wasn't going to let him in, I told him, repeating it again and again. But he kept his hand on the door and wouldn't let me close it.

'I asked for your help, but you've done your part,' I said. 'I don't need you any more. You said it yourself – you can't help me.'

'Can we talk, please?'

'What, are you regretting not fucking me when you had the chance?' I demanded.

John frowned. I took advantage of his stupor and pushed the door, but he leaned his shoulder forward into the gap. 'Damn it, Laura, just let me in! I need to talk to you!'

'Why did you reject me? Why are you trying to appear so proper and strong and so in control? What's the point?'

'I'm not trying to be anything. I didn't reject you. You don't want me, Laura – not like this. And I don't want to be one of those men you sleep with to numb your feelings.' He paused, then asked. 'Is that the problem?'

My neighbour, an elderly woman who somehow looked young enough to be my sister, cracked her door open to see what was going on outside her apartment.

'Fucking psychos. Junkies. Injecting yourselves with drugs and making this mess here,' she grumbled, before creeping back into her apartment.

'Laura, I care about you,' John insisted.

'Why? You want to be friends? How would that work? We could call each other, go on walks, talk about things. What would we discuss? What do friends talk about?'

He stared at me, his mouth incapable of moving, eyes barely open; he was exhausted.

I was exhausted too, I realised. I let him in.

In the kitchen I found a bottle of vodka, poured myself a double and went out on to the balcony. John found a clean glass, poured himself a finger and joined me.

I leaned against the railing and stared ahead. Drones replaced birds, neon lights replaced the stars, thick clouds sealed the starless sky and repelled acid pink and purple back on us. I looked down – an abrupt edge welcomed me. The abyss would swallow my body, allowing me to enjoy a few brief moments of the freefall before the rain washed the blood of my distorted face off the asphalt. The city would grieve for a moment and move on. That was all this love could spare – one tear over my death – for it had so many others to mourn.

'How does love feel?' I asked John. The question made him think, the shadow from the wall deepening his usual gloomy expression.

'You had a wife and children,' I insisted. 'You must know very well.'

'I was ready to give my life for them,' he said.

'Is that what love is, then? A sacrifice?'

'It's just an attribute that comes with it, I guess,' he said, and looked down, thinking, remembering. 'You can't breathe without that person, you need them like air and it hurts inside your chest so much that you'd rather not exist at all unless you can be with them: that's how love feels to me,' he said.

'Do you think someone could ever need me like that?' I asked. 'Like air?'

John pulled himself up straight. I knew what he was about to say – that I was still young, that if I opened myself to it love would come into my life – but I didn't need to hear it, I needed to experience it, so he didn't speak. Instead, he placed his hand on the side of my neck, and slid his thumb across my chin, where the metal plate adjoined the skin. My skin prickled under his touch. He took the glass from my hand and set it aside on a small side table, together with his glass, and brought his face close to mine. Our eyes exchanged a glance, my eyes telling him I wanted it, and he kissed my lips. It was a slow kiss, a mix of textures, flesh warm and moist. When he pulled away his eyes searched for a confirmation again, and again my eyes told him I wanted it, I wanted him.

The next time our lips met, they didn't part. He dropped his sheepskin jacket on the floor, took me in his arms, my legs wrapped around his waist, and carried me to the bedroom. I kissed his neck, his temples, the creases around his eyes. He lowered me on to the bed, and I pulled his sweater and T-shirt off as his hand ran up my thigh, exposing the metal and the skin under my dress, revealing the alloy of my conflicting nature. His fingers explored me with persistence but without haste, slowly, a corner of me at a time. There were kisses that aimed to tease, licks that aimed to seduce, caresses that made my skin ripple and scratches that summoned moans from my chest. And from time to time he looked into my eyes, still unsure, still wanting to confirm that this wasn't just an empty cure for my anxiety, and I tried to make him see that his hands didn't just touch my body, they touched my soul.

I pushed John on his back and began my own exploration of him. Every kiss I left on his stomach and chest fertilised my own fire. The mountain of his shoulders didn't feel so distant and reserved any longer. He quaked, his moans moving avalanches from my heart, freeing the flame inside. He leaned forward and climbed on top of me. I gorged on every cell of him, and borders between our bodies melted.

'I need you like air,' he said, moving faster.

When I felt his body throbbing, I seized his lips.

He cried and I listened.

He fell on me. I wrapped my hands tighter around his back, inviting him to relax his arms and let me carry his weight, which was likely twice my own. Trusting me, he relaxed and let me hold him. After his breath calmed and his muscles stopped trembling, I caressed him and he started growing again. His lips found mine, and he ran his hand through my hair, finding escalating desire in my eyes. I turned him on his back and sat on top. My voice built up into a chorus glorifying the human's most basic instinct, which could only be felt here and now, in this primal shape, and which was to me a measure of perfection.

John guided my hips with his hands, arching under me. He caressed my breasts and my legs. His touch penetrated through my metal plates; my soul sang.

I screamed, and I kept moving until he bent his head back and released an exhalation of rapture. His muscles shook as he moaned.

I'd known the moment I'd made him touch my neck and place his lips on mine that he didn't want me like this, didn't want to share this sort of intimacy with me. He had struggled, but his mind was no match for mine. He had enjoyed himself nonetheless, and for that he would feel guilty. What the source of this guilt was I didn't know, but I felt it hiding in his past. He had secrets, and although today I still couldn't penetrate through his memories, tomorrow would be another day, and I would try again.

I curled up in the cradle of his arms and lulled his mind so that he wouldn't have to think all night about what we had done. I shifted into a dimension outside this world and fell asleep.

# 16

---

It was cold, ice cold when I opened my eyes. I was in the shower in John's arms.

John cupped my head in his shaking hands and pushed my wet hair away from my face, his teeth chattering. He reached up and turned the switch, and the water started feeling warm.

'Are you here?' he asked.

I nodded. I tried to move, but my body was still waking up, and was limp, lifeless.

He pressed his lips against the top of my head, and we sat like this, warming up.

'I'm calling Rick,' he said, using his implant to place the call. 'Hey, she's back. No, it's OK. Thanks, man. Give me a few minutes. I'll call you right back.' Disconnecting the call, he helped me up, wrapped a towel around my shoulders, patted himself dry with the smaller towel I used to dry my hair with, and put his trousers and T-shirt on.

'I blacked out?' I asked.

'I couldn't wake you up,' John said.

After that we must have discussed me and my condition and what we were going to do, but there was also the subject of the night before – I didn't need to talk about it, but John did.

'Last night...' he started.

'You don't have to feel guilty,' I said. 'There's nothing you could've done to prevent it. There's so much guilt in your eyes.'

'It's fear, Laura. Mostly fear. Guilt too, yes, but that's for me to deal with later.' The line between his mind and my mind was thinning. A tiny effort on my part and his brain would open up before me like a flower. But I didn't want to cross that line again. Not yet.

'I'll get dressed,' I said.

John waited in my living room, which was still in complete disarray. I put on the first pair of trousers and sweater I could find and went through and sat next to him on the sofa, leaving the width of one person between us.

John shifted forward, propped his elbows on his knees and rubbed his face. It would take him a few minutes to tell me about his plans, what he had to do and why, and it would take him another few minutes to reveal what he had been hiding from me. It would only take me one brief glance into his mind to know all of it at once, but I restrained this impulse. Words – I wanted to hear words line up into sentences, carrying sense, summarising a thought; a slow and imprecise process that was still a part of what I was.

'I will have to report this.' he said, and paused, giving me a moment to react. When I remained silent, he continued, 'This tech, Blank, is too dangerous. The recording Rick made in the institute, you losing your flesh, is good enough evidence to search Craig's lab. This is too big. It's a threat to all of us. Whatever you think Craig has on you, I will hire a lawyer and we will deal with it. I don't know what you did, or what you think you did. Let's take the worst possible case – murder, terrorism. I know you are not capable of such things, but if, hypothetically, it's true and you really did do something awful, there will be a way out of it – or at least to make the consequences minimal. The Government will want you to cooperate, give them information, tell them about your experience, how Blank works, etc. Whatever you think you did is nothing compared to what Blank can do. If the wrong people were to get their hands on Blank, it would lead to catastrophic events – they would be able to manipulate other people's minds, make them do things. I'm talking on a massive scale.'

He looked straight into his eyes: here he was, keeping his promise and sharing his plans with me; nothing I could say would influence his decision. He was right about Blank: it was dangerous. I was dangerous. I was unstable, my ability to self-regulate emotions was non-existent, and I was merged with the tech that could manipulate people's minds. But knowing this didn't make me feel in any particular way – I wasn't surprised, angry, or scared. None of it touched me.

'OK,' I said.

'I'm afraid there is no other option. I know it's not how you—'

'You want a clear conscience? Blank is dangerous. What you said is true; what you're planning to do is objectively the right thing to do. Blank can get into people's minds. And I'm a breath away from yours. I know you are hiding something from me, and I'd rather you reveal it to me yourself.' My energy, so impatient and hungry for more information, spouted towards his brain. Again, I restrained it. *Shh, let's hear him say it; let's listen while we still can.* 'Speak, John.'

There was a pause. John clasped his hands and looked down. 'Do you remember how we met?' he asked.

'Yes. At the bar. In the club.'

'We knew each other before that,' he said. 'When you attempted suicide and fell into a coma, you were transferred to us. Our department specialises in studying coma cases related to suicide. I was a part of the team treating you.'

'I don't remember that,' I said.

'No, I know. For some reason you blanked everything out. I've been trying to figure out why you have no memories of me – you couldn't have just forgotten me. I'd like to think we were friends.'

'I've never had friends,' I said. 'Certainly not there, anyway. You and all those scientists, you didn't care about me. None of you asked why I tried to kill myself. You wanted data, images of my brain – that's all I was to you.'

'No, that's not true. Maybe I didn't help you as much as I could have, but I asked you about yourself; we talked.'

'Did I tell you about the priest then?' I asked.

'You did. And Laura, I tried to get that son of a bitch – believe me, I tried. I spoke to every nun and every priest I could track down – but no one saw anything. I had no witnesses, no evidence. The woman who led your support group said you had visions and made the whole thing up. Then my daughters were born and my wife died. I became a father to two little girls and...'

'Why don't I remember any of that?' I asked.

He shook his head as if to say he didn't know.

'And why didn't you say something before?'

He glanced at me, at his clasped hands, tiny drops of perspiration forming on his forehead.

'I can read your mind if I want to, you know,' I said. 'But I'd rather hear you speak. I want it to be an exchange both of us can experience in the same way.'

'When you didn't recognise me at the bar, I realised you must have done a mind wipe to erase those memories after...' He licked his lips, clapped his palm to his mouth and squeezed his cheeks so hard his whole face got distorted. He rotated his body towards me and took my hand. 'Laura, this might be some kind of a trigger. I don't know what's going to happen when you remember. We will do our best to save you, but if we are too late, you'll need to fight this thing. If you feel like you are disappearing – I don't know how it will feel, I have no idea, but you'll know, I hope – you've got to take Blank outside your body, otherwise it may cause severe damage to your brain. Irreversible. If you feel everything is closing down on you, find a way to disconnect from Blank.'

And then I was in him, seeing everything he knew. She was there in his memories, Aleece. She did have long brown hair before. Here was her arm around my waist, her lips on mine. John saw this, witnessed us together, years ago, back in the past. We were together; we were so in love. Was I twenty, twenty-one? What happened to us? Oh, how much I loved her then, and now that love was gushing back into me.

'Laura!' I heard John's voice. 'No, no. Too soon. Too soon.'

I didn't need to open my eyes to see that parts of my hands were translucent.

The room was merging with what looked like a club. It wasn't Dirty Castle, it was another place, full of small butterflies caught in amber walls.

John tried to open my eyes, holding what was left of me in his arms: my disappearing head, half of my chest, the left side of my back and hips.

*I will find you* were the last words I think I heard, as I vanished from here and entered a different dimension, where I was about to fight for my very existence, leaving John alone amid a scattering of metal plates. 'I will find you.'

John had been right – my memories had triggered a reaction. I was back in the very beginning of my life; life itself was flowing backwards, and Blank led me into a form it considered superior, advantageous in many regards, at least for itself. Only something resisted it – my soul, I guess. It was greedy and stubborn and I didn't like it, I would find out, and it had an ally.

# 17

---

When everything turned black, the only thing that still connected me to this world was the water in my mother's womb. I was a tiny embryo. The liquid enveloped me and caressed my cosmic energy with its love – love that filled my endless being, pacifying my expansive temper, ready to welcome me to the world. Suddenly I felt the embryo getting weaker. I rushed back into it, bumping into stars, squeezing between dreams and thoughts, fighting the pull of histories, funnelling my consciousness into a sharper focus. By the time I collected the tentacles of my soul from where they were scattered throughout existence, I saw that not much of me was left: battered strings of my dim energy floated between planets like rotten debris of algae in the ocean. The embryo of me started contracting. I had no illusions – I knew I didn't have enough strength to save it, and it would never see the blue sky of Earth. I was saddened by our unfulfilled union because, even though the world where it would have been born had many flaws, it was a world I was eager to experience. I breathed every grain of my essence into the embryo, let it enjoy for a little longer one of the greatest miracles Earth had given back to the universe – the love of its mothers.

Just when my soul was about to be forgotten, as if I had never existed, a splash of some force infused the last motes of me with life. Something made me expand, filling the emptiness of my shell with its energy. And as I grew, I heard the beating of my heart again. The energy that had just fortified my strength and stabilised my foetus was familiar. Its shine was pure as the beginning, and I recognised it: it was Aleece. She started imprinting the history of my existence into her own matrix. Her immense soul fuelled me with her boiling essence. I rejected her, pushed her away; I couldn't let her die for me. Our souls collided, discharges of ultraviolet blazed in a wrestling match, the friction of our energies generating enough light to drown the galaxies we tumbled through. The mass of my never-ending being raged, trying to resist her sacrifice, but without success; in my weakened state I was no equal to her. She was stronger, larger, more profound. The white light of her supernova accompanied her final breath, and the blinding outburst swallowed the last bits of her before shooting the bullets of her energy through my celestial body, pervading me with her life.

When I didn't hear anything besides my voiceless cry, I knew she was gone. She dissolved herself and impregnated the core of her soul with my memories and experiences so that I could live again.

\* \* \*

In the layers of black matter, I spread out my entity without any intention of claiming it – it wasn't mine and I had no right to it. But the myriad holes left in me after the impact were already sucking on the energy Aleece had spewed into them. My soul, independent from my heart that was beating somewhere on Earth, fed on her self-destructive blast, expanding, getting thicker, nurturing its desire to live.

I hated my soul for its greed, for its unstoppable thirst for experience. I hated myself for letting Aleece disappear. I hated the world for being here.

I tried to break away from myself, lunging across the universe. From quasar to quasar I went, asking them to rip me apart. They crushed my atoms and vomited me back into existence, and still she was there, my soul. No matter how much these black holes broke and distorted me, I would always come out with her attached.

After exhausting my strength, I found myself back on to what looked like Earth, my body floating above the ocean and below the sky, where the horizon stitched the two worlds together. My tears drizzled from grey clouds. The holes in my body, now fully replete, contracted, concealing all of Aleece's energy inside. The wind moved my body on top of a cliff. The smell of pine trees awakened my senses, opened my lungs. I would have cried like a newborn if my voice hadn't been spent.

I stood on the edge, staring into the air. A thick haze mantled the promontory, mixed with the smell of wet stones and white foam, and became a part of the ocean.

Then I realised where I was – it was the edge of the world.

* * *

The grass whispered under me. I lowered myself to my knees and combed the green blades with my fingers, touched a bare patch of earth. The earth was cold and hard, tamped down by the rain that rarely ceased. The pulse of a giant white rock resounded below; here came the heartbeats of my mother and father, muffled steady thuds. Clouds released my parents' tears, and their guilt flushed through me, rills kissing every scar and ulcer in my heart. I kissed the earth and dropped my own tears on it. My parents' love was sealed in these cliffs; they'd immured themselves in the white stones and had been waiting for me here, on the edge of the world, just like they had promised.

My heart was torn now that I knew these rocks really existed, and the abundance of love they carried was immeasurable.

'Why are you doing this now?' I cried out. 'Why?' I hit the earth. 'Why now, when I can't have you? Why?' My lips touched the dirt as I screamed. I clawed handfuls of soil out until I had made a hole, and screamed into it as if they could hear me better this way. 'Why show me love now? To torture me for what I did? Yes, I hated you! I hated you. How could I know? How? How could I know you loved me if you never sent a sign? You never came to me when I prayed. You never came when I needed you. And now what am I supposed to do with your love? Take it away from me! I don't want to remember it. Take it away!' I could handle the pain of being abandoned, but the regret was unbearable. The amount of time I'd wasted on hatred – so much time. How could I accommodate all this regret in one body?

'And you?' I looked up and addressed Aleece. She wasn't there, she was gone, but what else did I have to look at other than an invisible scar she'd left across the sky? 'I didn't need your sacrifice! You had no right to do that, to leave me like this, to give your life for me. Why? I want to give it back! Do you hear me!? Take it back. Take it! You had no right. You spared me – for what?' I edged my way to the precipice, the waves and sharp rocks extended their embrace, and I was about to give in. But invisible arms wrapped around me and pulled me back.

'Let me go! It's enough,' I cried. 'How many times do you want me to survive, only to hurt me again? Just let me go!'

I turned around. In front of me stood a woman in John's sheepskin jacket. She looked like me; she was my soul. 'What do you want?' I asked her. I despised my soul for accepting Aleece. Greedy, greedy soul, all it cared about was life – any life, no matter how painful it was for me. It had eaten Aleece's energy without giving it a second thought, without stopping for a second to think what it would do to me. All it wanted was to survive. And for what?

'Nothing,' she said.

'Why are you wearing that? It doesn't belong to you.' I pointed at her jacket.

'It keeps me warm while I'm waiting for you.'

'You don't need to wait for me,' I said.

'But I want to. Who is Aleece?' she asked.

'You know who Aleece is.'

'Do *you* know?' she asked.

'I hate you. Why can't you just die?'

'Your question makes no sense,' she said.

I turned and ran into the forest to hide from her – I couldn't stand seeing her self-righteous face. I stumbled upon something and fell. The dead body of the priest lay on the grass, his skin grey, his dried mouth wide open. I recoiled, my breath peaked, my heart trying to burst out of my chest.

My soul came over and sat down on the other side of the corpse.

'I didn't…' I said.

What was his death to me?

'How does it feel?' she asked. 'To see him dead?'

'It doesn't change anything,' I said.

'What doesn't it change?' she asked.

'It doesn't change the way I feel about myself; it doesn't erase the stains he left in me. It doesn't bring back the time I could have spent remembering my parents instead of hating them. It doesn't bring back the love I could have had for someone. I've been hiding from love, from people, from myself. His death doesn't change a thing.'

'It doesn't – you are right.' She looked down and brushed her hand over the priest's bulging eyes.

All my wounds were open and bleeding. I was a volcano spitting blood, and my crater was widening. Clouds gathered above us. The rain started abruptly. It was slow and persistent. It fell on my head and on the head of my soul, its rhythmic drumming drowning out my thoughts. I watched water trickle from the corpse's open mouth, down the hollow cheeks and into the ground. One day, I saw, all of this would become one: his eroded flesh, the grass and the earth – all would become one substance.

'We need to bury him,' said my soul.

It took my mind a moment to grasp the meaning of her words. The idea of burying the man who had raped me, twice, landed in the middle of my consciousness like an alien ship, and my mind gaped at it, unsure how to react. But in the end I agreed.

We went into the forest and collected sticks and stones. I watched my soul walking between trunks, picking prickly branches of pine trees, so very focused on her task. I accepted this scene effortlessly; my brain didn't even resist, as though it was the usual business for all souls to wander around a forest gathering branches and stones. Without saying a word, we sat on either side of the corpse and began covering it with the pile of foliage we had assembled. As we worked, my right arm started going numb, and the skin began dissolving; and where the skin had disappeared iridescent streams showed. The same thing was happening to my soul: vessels of light wove through her and replaced parts of her face; the skin of her neck was also gone, as was that of her fingers and parts of her arms.

When the last stone covered the forehead of the priest, I was paralysed, and felt more helpless than ever – there was nothing else I could do, no one left to blame. He was gone. I remained. The world was still here to be lived in, but the knowledge that he would never walk on its surface didn't make it easier for me to move on.

I looked my soul in the eyes. There was so much substance, so much knowledge there, but more than anything there was so much *life*. And I didn't feel an iota of it in me.

I got up and went to the edge of the cliff. The ocean seemed wider, as if it had spread its already imperceptible borders.

'Why did you come back?' I asked my soul. 'You were boundless – why did you need this?' I held out both hands, now lucid and veined with ultraviolet beams.

'I never left you. I've always been here,' she said, gesturing around herself. 'I'm a part of all this, just as you are. Can you remove the rain or wind from Earth? No, it's impossible; it's an integral part – that's how this planet operates. It's the same with the union between you and me. The universe contains a web of innumerable relationships and interactions, and they can't be simply removed or replaced. Once I'm bonded to you, I can't go somewhere and come back at will, just as the rain doesn't start on its own; it's a system: everything is designed for a purpose and everything is linked together. And our bond is beautiful, don't you think? When I become your tear, I see your feelings – hues of human existence shimmering through the lens of your heart. Some perceptions come in tides, demanding your attention, our attention, while other feelings never reach the surface of the mind, yet they still flourish in the weave that holds it all together. I suck it all out of you. Nothing is left behind, even the most hidden impulses fertilise the existence. There are so many fractions of life that rest unnoticed between thoughts, and all these accidents of stillness find their way back into infinity, carrying the invisible fruits of our bond back into the ever-changing whole.'

Almost the entire left side of her face was gone now, iridescent strings running around her eye and cheek. She pulled off her top, and I could see only a few patches of skin were left, on her back and stomach. She took my translucent hand and pulled it right through her body and on to her beating heart. My heart. The first beat thundered through me, blew me into pieces, then glued me back together. Flows of energy jumped off the tips of my fingers and entwined with the fire in her chest. A blast, and another dimension opened up in front of my eyes – the space inside me, part of which her infinite being was. She didn't make me who I am, didn't whisper her desires to my ear; our relationship was far more organic. My soul was part of a network of interconnected entities and mechanisms, like the mycelium in a forest ecosystem, exchanging energy and information, contributing to the knowledge, balance and health of the greater whole.

*It is not easy to look inside and see the infinity in your finiteness. But it is there. All you have to do is feel, bleed.*

My soul snaked around me and squeezed every drop of my tears to the surface. I screamed; I felt everything. Fourteen years of numbness drained from me, and my voice gushed from my throat, echoing through the mantle of the Earth. An earthquake hit my world; and in this apocalypse, I glimpsed the disappearance of all boundaries. The labyrinth of my mind crackled and moaned, its walls crumbling down. Traps revealed their teeth; many had been planted to prevent me from remembering. But I was about to remember everything; the past I never thought I had was about to unfold. I heard coils of life stolen from me sing, and my memories called me. I ran as fast as I could and jumped off the cliff. Lungs full of pine air, I met the waves. They devoured me, destroyed me, demolished my particles and spat me out somewhere in the past, where I forgot everything again.

# 18

---

'Happy Birthday, Ms Jennet,' an automated voice chirped as I walked through the body scanner. Today I turned twenty-one, and next month the bank would increase the monthly allowance it paid to me out of my trust fund, so there was something to celebrate.

An electronic beat thumped against my chest. As soon as I set foot into the club's world I was part of it. Chilasa was my second residence – I spent most of my nights here; I also spent most of my money here – it was an expensive place. Shiny robots paired with humans flaunting exotic body augmentations mixed cocktails behind marble and mirror counters, and there was lots of natural leather, and lighting that gave every skin a golden hue. The interior was an aphrodisiac tango of light and shadow, but nothing here ever ended with just a dance. Giant amber partitions cut the space into sections with different bars and lounges. Inside the amber walls were countless butterflies, their bluish wings peeking out here and there.

I went to the powder bar. The bartender, Ornyth, gave me a kiss. Her reptile eyes blinked and changed from orange to green. Turquoise and red snakes slowly moved around her neck and arms. Under her collarbones was a garden of iridescent orchids. This bi-gender creature had been on my mind a lot. We had pleasured each other on a few occasions, and I'd tasted all of her body, snorting powders and sucking liquids she sold me from her breasts and ass and tight stomach. I loved tasting her. Her skin screen was a new model, and she was changing her taste all the time, so there was always something new to look forward to. She often tasted sweet, but today she had a hint of fig, honey and milk on her lips, a comforting flavour which she hadn't chosen for the purpose of seduction: that one was for her.

'Hi, Laura,' she said. 'What can I do for you today?' Her formality was hot – she played it well.

'Hi,' I said, tapping my finger on the glass counter display, inside which various pills lay in mirrored cells, sparkling like precious gems in a jewellery store. I looked at her, deciding if I wanted her tonight or if I fancied something else. 'Surprise me,' I said. She always knew what I needed.

She pushed a button, and from a side panel of the bar came a crystal tube divided into sections filled with powders, herbs and drops. Ornyth scooped up some glittering black powder with the tip of her stiletto nail and brought it to my nose.

I snorted the substance. It was soft, warming.

'On me,' Ornyth said. 'Happy Birthday.' Her gaze shifted from my face to something behind me. My heart started beating faster. She ran her long, sharp nail under my chin and pointed my face to the side. I pushed myself away from the counter and looked. My girl was there, with a group of friends, as usual, drinking cocktails at the main bar. Her name was Aleece, Ornyth had told me. I wondered if Aleece knew my name. She probably did – Ornyth had probably told her. I had asked Ornyth, begged her, offered to be her little bitch and give her any pleasure she wanted for as long as she wanted if she told me everything she knew about Aleece. But she had said I'd have to grow bigger balls and find out on my own. So I waited for my balls to grow bigger.

Aleece was as often at Chilasa as I was. I had a vivid memory of us making out when I just started coming here after I'd been released from the orphanage, but the first few years were such a drug-fuelled delirium that I could have easily imagined it.

I was high for two years straight. The last year or so, however, I didn't use as much. Because of her: I wanted to remember her, to think of her, but when I took drugs I couldn't focus on anything, and she kept slipping away. So one day I took a cleaner pill, and saw her with sober eyes. That first memory still gave me shivers. Luckily, magic pills, available for free at any club where they sell drugs or at any pharmacy, clean you up and stop psychological and physical cravings. If you made it part of your routine, it was easy to stay sober. Of course, nobody did. I couldn't say I enjoyed the state of detachment or euphoria: I didn't like the concept of giving up control, didn't have friends to get high with; I just hated the alternative so much more. Now the alternative had a ray of light in it, and I followed the light. I started practising intervals of clarity, and these intervals grew longer because I wanted to continue the story of her and me in my mind.

Our telepathic connection, as I thought of it, was getting stronger. During the last few months we had exchanged countless glances and smiles, and there were subtle invitations from her to join her and her friends – a gesture, a nod, a wink – to which I never responded out of fear. I could always tell when she had had a bad day: she would avoid me, wouldn't even look in my direction; and it felt like she was breaking our secret bond a little, distancing herself from me. When that happened, I couldn't relax and have fun. I would go home and masturbate, imagining us having an emotional conversation and then making up. Sometimes I imagined passionate sex; at other times it was tender lovemaking. And overall, this happened so often that, naturally, I already felt close to her.

That one memory, or perhaps fantasy, of us making out for real had become brighter and sprawled into a web of fantasies, from her naked body lying next to mine, to her brushing her teeth and drinking coffee in my apartment. I even allowed myself to dream that one day I would reveal to her I'd been raped. She wouldn't pity me, I thought; she would find a way to support me like no one else could. I had to share this experience, the worse of my life, with her – could we ever be genuinely close if she didn't know? That had always stopped me from pursuing a relationship: why try if it was doomed before it started? I'd have to pretend, and they would pity me, and so on. Or maybe they'd be completely indifferent, because life was just that fucked up. Everyone was hurting – why should I expect to be soothed and understood? But I dared to imagine I could heal with her, because she would care and because she would trust in me. She would know how to make me feel better. I didn't know how, or what words she would use, but I fantasised she would know exactly what to say. Maybe our love would be enough – true love that would align all the necessary words in all the right sentences. Maybe we wouldn't even need words, just a few important ones, and her big listening eyes would do the rest.

I'd had so many imaginary conversations with her that I'd already overcome some of my fears – the fear of being close to someone, the fear of falling in love. I felt like we were dating and just needed to find the courage to declare it and make it a reality.

'Enjoy yourself,' Ornyth said, turning to another customer.

I walked around, waiting for the drug to kick in, observing people, watching Aleece. By then she'd already noticed me and my interest and returned a few alluring smiles. I was more sober than I'd like to be, given that it was my birthday. My desire for Aleece, however, was intensifying, and my body did exactly as it wished. I went into the main bar where she was, and she stepped away from her friends and leaned against the counter next to me. I felt a smile growing on my face, and I was so ashamed of the uncontrollable excitement her proximity aroused in me that for a moment I wanted to run away. I couldn't believe this was happening – I'd been dreaming of this moment for so long. She brought a martini glass to her mouth, took a sip and licked the pink droplets off her lips. She smiled. Oh, how I wished I were more drunk. I wasn't sure what surprise Ornyth had intended for me, but the drug only made me feel more sober than I felt without any drugs in me at all.

'Vodka straight,' I told the bartender. Unable to resist any more, I looked at Aleece. She took another sip of her cocktail and turned to face me. She was naturally beautiful. Her flat-ironed brown hair was long, almost to her waist; her sharp fringe accentuated her brown eyes, a generous splash of freckles sweetened her face and, apart from a few rings in her ears and a little diamond in her nose, she was wholly made by nature. At least on the outside.

'Hi,' she said.

'Hey.' My heart was pounding so hard I was afraid she'd notice my silk dress vibrating against my chest.

The bartender brought my vodka over, and Aleece clinked her glass against mine. I swallowed the clear liquid.

'I like your dress,' she said. 'Looks nice on you.'

'Thanks.'

'I'm Aleece.'

'Laura.'

She smiled, nodding her head to the music. 'Are you here alone?' she asked.

'Yes,' I said. 'I'm always alone.'

'I noticed.'

'Those are your friends?' I nodded to the group of people behind her sharing drinks and conversation.

'Just some people I know,' she said. 'Want to meet them?'

'No. I've got everything I need right here.'

She smiled and bit her lip, encouraging my ardour. I was sober and exposed, and I couldn't help it – I wanted her so badly my groin was moaning like a cat in spring.

'So what's the plan for tonight?' she asked.

'Wanna help me celebrate?' I asked.

'What's the occasion?'

'My birthday.'

'Sure!' She pulled out a lighter and sparked the flint. 'Let's start with a wish.'

I thought for a moment and blew out the flame.

'Don't tell anyone what it is,' she said. 'Otherwise it won't come true!'

'I won't,' I said, and looked at her lips. There was only one wish on my mind, and she had probably guessed it.

Aleece took my hand and pulled me on to the dance floor. The sound was infectious, cocooning our bodies, supplanting the blood from our veins, turning us into night butterflies – the souls of Chilasa.

The presence of Aleece next to me made me drunk. My hand was on her lower back, my stomach rubbing against her stomach, my heart raced anticipating the touch of her full lips that were half open, ready to kiss me. We teased and seduced one another. Aleece moved her finger up my hip and lifted my dress a little, pressing her thigh against my pubic bone.

'Let's see if I got your wish right,' she said, and pulled away to look at me. That look snuck into my head and triggered every chemical responsible for the arousal of a body.

We agreed to get a pod. Behind an amber panel stood Chilasa's wall of sex, composed of six rows of cabins, most of which were already taken. Self-cleaning pods were similar to those on planes and space shuttles; the walls and the top part were covered with a soft foam, and although you could barely sit there, a double mattress was enough for all your needs.

Aleece scanned her wallet and selected a room. While a lift plate was taking us to the third row, I looked out on those who enjoyed being watched or couldn't be bothered to pull down a blind, leaving the glass doors clear.

We slid into our pod, and the glass door closed behind us.

Aleece took off her top, revealing pierced nipples, and crawled towards me. I met her halfway and our lips sealed. She rolled the straps of my dress down my arms. Moving her mouth slowly, she drew a wet map of her desire all over my neck and shoulders. When her lips were around my nipples, I reached out and pressed a button by the door. A shade dropped, and our pod filled with red light. I pushed her on her back and freed her from her tight trousers. My mouth covered her breasts, my hand slid up her inner thigh and into her silk underwear. She moaned, goosebumps covered her honey skin and her arched body wanted more. I wanted more. We wanted each other so badly that everything else ceased to exist. The world was ours.

Aleece climbed on top of me. Her touch alternated between soft, snowing fingertips to sharp, surfing nails. My body was a land amidst her ocean and under her sky; she rained down on me, whipped me with her waves, charged every grain of me with her blazing dawn; and I melted under her every manifestation. I was sober, my senses enhanced, and my mind was right there in the moment. Our energy and motion were so synchronised I hadn't even noticed how her tongue had replaced her fingers, but as soon as it did the intensity of my pleasure reached its peak, and tears rolled down my face. I wept and screamed at the same time. If I hadn't had a body, I would have thought I'd turned into light.

Aleece sat in front of me and watched me sob. Ornyth's black powder must have reached its climax with me; I felt stripped of my skin, vulnerable and in heaven. Time stopped ticking, and I suspected I felt what they called love. Aleece touched my cheeks and my lips, following the traces of my tears. We sat like this for a while, examining each other's features, communicating on a level where words proved to be obsolete.

'You look beautiful when you cry,' Aleece said.

I wasn't able to say much. All I wanted was for this moment to last for ever. I wanted to be with her – I'd give everything for that. And even though I was afraid of it, my fear didn't stand a chance this time – I'd been dreaming of her for too long. I ran my hand through her thick, almost-black hair, pulling her closer. Her breath spoke to me. I removed her hopelessly wet underwear; she shivered under my touch, the high notes of her voice spilling in the most beautiful dissonance.

It was frightening how strongly I felt for her, but it was also the best thing I'd ever experienced. What I felt suppressed all doubts and fears, except for the fear of losing her, and even this fear collapsed on itself. It was better than drugs and booze. It made me forget that this morning I'd thought life didn't matter, that I didn't matter. Just this morning Earth had been the cruellest place in the universe, and now it felt like heaven. Suddenly life made some sense. For the first time since I could remember I had a desire to live, and it seemed the world might finally feel like home.

'I like you,' I said.

'I like you too. I liked you from the first time I saw you,' she said. 'I thought I was making it pretty clear. But you never responded to, you know, anything.'

'I wasn't sure I interpreted your signs correctly,' I said.

'You weren't sure? How more obvious could I be?'

'You could have approached me.'

'Well, I was also scared. I was afraid you'd distract me too much.'

'From what?'

'From everything.' She leaned forward and kissed me.

'Have we kissed before this night?' I asked.

'Once, two years ago, something like that. And then you ghosted me,' she said.

'I thought it was just a dream,' I said.

'No, it wasn't.' She turned on her stomach and rested her chin in the cradle of her elbow. 'Tomorrow you might not remember this.'

'I will. I'm not high.'

She looked at me for a time, then asked, 'What did Ornyth give you tonight?'

'Not sure. Some black powder,' I said.

She nodded but didn't say anything.

'It doesn't do much,' I said. 'Made me feel more sober than I've ever felt.'

'So there is a chance you'll remember this night,' she said.

'I will remember.'

\* \* \*

We left the club when the sun was already up.

'Do you want to come to my place?' I asked.

'I would love to,' she said. 'But I have to go home. Believe it or not, today is my birthday. Which makes us a day apart.'

'Really? Why didn't you say so? Happy Birthday.'

'Thanks. My birthday is not till noon.' She smiled. 'I promised my father I'd come home. We always celebrate together. I'd much rather spend the day with you, to tell you the truth, but it's a tradition we have.'

I wasn't sure what to say. Her fingers found mine, and she tickled my palms, our fingers interlaced.

'Let's speak tomorrow?' she asked.

'Let's speak tomorrow,' I said.

We took two taxis and drove off in different directions.

# 19

For the past nine years, since my parents died, my birthday had been the darkest day of my year – they had died on my twelfth birthday. I lay in bed and thought about this strange day, the day of my birth. Every year it arrived; there was no way to avoid it, no way to jump over it, to dig a tunnel under it, to sprint around its never-ending corners. It came every year to destroy me, one particle at a time. I always spent that day high, out of my mind, so that when it rolled through me like a storm, I'd at least be under anaesthesia.

*Should I allow myself to believe that yesterday was different?* Yesterday I'd felt what I'd not felt for a long time – happy. Today I wasn't so confident. *Will Aleece ever call? I wouldn't dare to call her – or would I? If she doesn't call today, I'll go to the club tomorrow and see her there. What if we start dating and something happens to her? What if she hates me after she finds out how broken I am? Am I worthy of her?*

Evening amplified the pink neon of the streets. *Aleece must be having dinner now with her father.* I imagined them sitting across each other, laughing, eating a nice meal. Would they have a cake? What sort would they have? I imagined it to be something colourful – she liked colourful cocktails. Sweet stuff. Maybe something with a lot of fruit and berries in? Her father would carry it out of the kitchen, candles and all, singing. What about her mother? Was she gone? If so, how did she kill herself? Would they talk about her on Aleece's birthday?

My phone rang. I jumped off the sofa. 'Hello?'

'Laura?'

'Yes,' I said.

'It's Aleece.'

'Hi! Happy Birthday. How's the celebration going?'

'Good – we just finished our dinner.'

'I don't want to interrupt,' I said.

'You're not – I'm calling you! I wanted to hear your voice.'

I stood in the middle of my living room, staring at the floor. Was this really happening? Was she calling me? I hardly dared believe it.

'Laura?'

'Yes. I… me too. I've been thinking of you.'

'You have?'

'Yes.' Of course.

'Remember what happened yesterday?'

'Yes, of course.' I chuckled. 'Do you?'

'I don't forget things that easily.'

I lay on the sofa, my phone pressing against my ear. For a moment I regretted not having an implant – I would have had her right inside my head.

'What are you doing?' Aleece asked.

'Nothing.'

'Any plans for the evening?'

'No, not really.'

Another pause followed.

'Would you like to meet tomorrow?' she asked.

'Sure. I'd love to.'

'Dinner?' she asked.

'Sounds good.'

'I'll see you tomorrow, then.'

'Yes. I'll be waiting,' I said.

'Me too.'

I didn't go anywhere that night. I stayed home, dreaming about her, imagining our meeting, the conversations that would take place, the questions she would ask. I talked to her in my mind, rehearsing my answers, repeating to myself that I would stay calm, I wouldn't get emotional, I wouldn't fuck it up.

By the early morning my repetitions put me to sleep, and I slept through the day. When I woke up the night wasn't far away. It only took a few seconds for my heart to start beating fast in anticipation again.

* * *

I arrived first. It was a little bistro, where they still had human waiters waiting on tables. I sat at the bar and ordered a drink. Aleece arrived shortly afterwards. She handed her long coat to a waiter, her tight-fitting clothes accentuating her petite, athletic features.

She gave me a kiss on the cheek and sat next to me. We ordered some food, talked about places we liked to go to, clubs and bars. These days she mostly hung at Chilasa, she said, as it had such good diversity of ambience and music. The atmosphere was dreamy and sexual, dictated by the drugs they served – although she preferred alcohol to drugs, and rarely got severely wasted. She was a science grad student, and every time she set foot on university grounds, she said, she was screened for substances – everyone was. Students created some cutting-edge stuff, and there were all sorts of risks involved, and public pressure on science and technology was already too great to mess things up.

'What do you study?' I asked.

'Quantum physics, nanotech,' she said. 'What about you? What do you do?'

'Um… nothing really. I guess I'm still figuring it out,' I said. The truth was I'd never even thought about what I could do in life – I didn't think the world needed anything from me, and I didn't need anything from it.

'And you live by yourself?' she asked.

'Yes,' I answered. 'I don't have anyone left. Suicide.' That what people usually assumed, but I clarified anyway.

'Both your mum and dad?'

'Yeah.'

'I'm really sorry.'

'It's fine,' I shrugged. 'You live with your father?'

'More like alone. He works a lot, but he tries to be a good dad. I guess. I spend most of my time in the lab now as well. Our apartment is pretty lonely.' She took a sip of her fancy orange drink. 'And I never knew my mum. She didn't make it through my birth.'

'I'm sorry,' I said.

'It's sad. But the world is a weird place. I try to make the best out of it, fill it with moments that matter.' She leaned forward and kissed my lips. 'Like this one.'

We took a walk along the river. Even though its surface was dark brown and the smell was unbearable at times, I liked to watch it flow.

'How did you know that you wanted to become a scientist?' I asked Aleece.

'My dad had a big influence on the decision,' she said, laughing. 'And on my interests in general. I'm basically following in his footsteps, in a complementary way. I do like it.'

'What does he do?'

'He's a neuroscientist. Pokes around in people's brains.'

She chuckled, but I didn't find it funny. I knew it all too well. After I'd attempted to take my life I had been studied like a rat. There was one guy who tried to help – John – but even he gave up on me in the end. But I suppose at least he tried – the rest were not interested in me or my story: they were only interested in the images of my brain and how I could contribute to their research.

'He's also an entrepreneur – owns a few businesses that specialise in biotech and artificial intelligence,' she added.

'And this is what you want to do, then – poke around in people's brains?'

'The human brain is the most complex system known to us,' she said, adopting a more serious tone after sensing my resentment. 'So, yes, I'm interested in it.'

I pulled out a pack of cigarettes. She stared at me, a question mark hardening on her face.

'You didn't strike me as a girl who supports the Church,' she said.

'I don't support the Church!' I barked through my teeth. Her eyes widened: my harsh tone had taken her by surprise. 'Never mind,' I said. My hands shook, and I dropped the cigarette that I'd just lit. 'I didn't mean to...' I started, looking for the right word, kneading tobacco into the ground with my boot, '...offend you. Sorry.'

'You didn't offend me,' Aleece said, keeping her voice firm. 'It's not like I'm not used to being called a soul killer by random people.'

'No, that's not what... I didn't mean to...'

'You can say what you think,' she said.

I lit another cigarette and leaned against a railing. This time I ran a mouthful of smoke through my lungs.

'I don't think like that. Those people are mental,' I said.

'They are not mental,' she said. 'They are scared, angry and hurt, which makes it easy to manipulate their opinions. And I'd like to know where you stand on this.' She turned to face me.

I glanced at her, then returned my gaze to the river and the city on the other side of it. 'I think the Church is a fucking vile institution, the human beings who run it are rotten, and it kills faith,' I said. 'All this hate and the destructive riots are instigated by the Church. They deepen the gaps in an already hopelessly divided society. Even politicians contribute to peace more. And I'm not against science – I just don't think about it much. We can move on.'

'OK, let's talk about something that you care about,' she said. She was confident and calm.

'I don't know,' I shrugged, breathing in the smoke. 'I don't have any interests.'

'You are too bold not to care about something,' she said. She was twenty-three, two years my senior, but seemed so mature. She controlled her emotions very naturally.

I wasn't sure how I could match her level of maturity – what I could say to sound anything other than stupid or phony – so I decided to go with the truth, with what I felt. 'You. I'm interested in you.'

Her expression softened, and she leaned against the railing beside me, facing the city. We took a few moments, letting the wind scatter the last bits of tension between us.

'Did we really just meet yesterday?' I asked.

'No. Can't be. We did not,' she said. 'You've been on my mind since that kiss two years ago.'

I nodded in agreement. 'And I've probably talked to you in my mind more than I talk to everyone else combined.'

'Any highlights I need to know about?' she asked.

'Can't remember anything specific. There was a lot of sex, obviously. I'm glad the fantasy is replaced by reality. It feels good.'

'It does feel good,' she said.

It felt impossible – not real – but it was real. I was afraid to acknowledge that this was indeed happening, as if someone might rip this new reality from under my feet as soon as I agreed to believe in it, and I would be left standing there, alone and broken again, in the middle of the empty world. But even a coward like me could see it was a miracle too rare not to take the risk.

'One thing I've learned during my research into minds and consciousness is to trust what I feel,' she said. 'I feel our souls have known each other for a while – it just took some time for our minds to catch up. Every day is precious. I want you to know me, I don't want to wait to open up. And I want to know you – I want to start discovering you right now. Two years of mental foreplay seems like enough, no?'

'Yes. It has been a long period of foreplay,' I agreed.

We stared into each other's eyes, then I invited her to my place.

\* \* \*

She was catching her breath, her eyes still closed. I watched her small breasts rise up and down, her face glowing with pleasure. She lay so still after she came, I was certain she would fall asleep. But in a few minutes, she rolled out of bed and went to have a shower. She left the bathroom door open, and I moved to the end of the bed so I could see her.

'Are you leaving?' I asked.

'No. You made me sweat,' she said. 'Why don't you join me?'

'I'm good,' I said, enjoying the view. 'You should stay.'

'I will.' She didn't need me to ask – she did exactly what she wanted – and she wanted to stay with me. She wanted me, and now I was hers. I belonged somewhere; I was no longer an estranged object floating on the periphery of existence.

I got up and joined her.

\* \* \*

Our morning was long, and morphed slowly into noon and afternoon.

'There's a new exhibition opening tomorrow, *Undefined Presence*,' Aleece said. We were still in bed, although my phone showed four o'clock. 'It's a perception-altering immersive installation, everything created by AI, curated by Collette Gerd. You have to use a self-dissolving chip. I know you don't have an implant – not sure if it's a problem for you? But it's totally safe.'

I raised on my elbow and looked at her. 'I'm not afraid of technology. It wasn't about that yesterday. I overreacted.'

'No, I know, but usually people who opt out of implants have their reasons. But since you've mentioned it, what was it about yesterday?'

'Something from the past,' I said darkly. 'I don't want to talk about it now. And it's fine – I've done simulations with dissolving chips, but I don't want anything more permanent in my head. I'm not against it or afraid of it, I just don't want it. I'd feel like I had someone's eyeballs in my brain all the time.'

'I can understand that,' she said.

Bright magenta light leaked into the room through the window. I got up from the bed, pulling the duvet with me and wrapping myself in it.

'Hey!' Aleece protested, left naked on the bed. The air had a chill, and her nipples hardened.

'Come, we can share,' I said.

We went out on to the balcony, holding each other, hiding from the damp, cold air under one duvet. A holographic banner played a skin-screen ad. It showed a woman and a man making love, their skin changing patterns; water turned into flowers as they kissed, spreading red and purple offshoots all over their faces, new buds opening on their lips and cheeks. Splashes of red and pink liquid revealed lizard scales on her body as she moved on top of him. Now a dragon was circling around her back. When he leaned towards her, the same creature circled around his back and torso.

'A new model,' Aleece said. 'I like this one. It creates whole stories based on what you are feeling, and shows it on your skin. And you can sync it with another person's screen or create stories together.'

'How does it work?'

'You need an implant for this one – for best results. You train the system first, attributing visual descriptions to feelings and vice versa, and you describe how certain images make you feel, and then it improvises. It picks up on emotions and creates visuals to match, based on the connections you made. You can choose from a greater variety of illustration styles, types of animation, colour palette, speed, etc. It also takes the environment into consideration – the temperature, humidity, amount of light — to deliver the most accurate and visually enticing representation.'

'That's a lot of very personal information,' I said.

'You don't have to share the information if you don't want to, it's just an option.'

'Just another invasion,' I said.

She looked at me sidelong, then laughed. 'I'm not sceptical about the screen itself,' I said. 'I love screens. I think they are very sexy.'

'I noticed.' She smiled her wide, teasing smile.

I gave her a questioning look.

'You and Ornyth,' she said. 'Besides many others. But Ornyth really knows how to work her screen.'

'Who wouldn't make out with Ornyth?'

'Many would, but not many have.' She was absolutely teasing me.

'Don't tell me you haven't?' I asked.

'I haven't,' she said. I narrowed my eyes. She shook her head. 'Nope. I haven't screwed nearly as many people as you have.' There was no reproach in her voice. And unlike me, she probably remembered the people I screwed, too, while I had no memory of them — well, almost none.

'Anyway,' I said, nodding towards the holo-banner, 'the data collected is obviously sold and used. Isn't that an invasion — of the only thing that is truly yours: your mind, your feelings? The idea of being monitored and studied on such level, it turns me inside out. And they aren't even interested in you as a person, they're interested in data and the best way of selling it. And you get nothing from it apart from a screen that you have to pay for.'

'Nobody forces you. And sure, it's business. That after so many years we, individuals, are not prospering from it doesn't sit well with me either. Each time our information is traded it would be nice to get a cut — but that's a whole another conversation. This thing has actual benefits. The collaboration between you and AI, it's about developing a new language, stretching your perception of self. Look at that.' She gestured at the banner.

We watched the hypnotic sex scenes for some time.

'It feels like you're a part of another world,' I said.

'Not another world,' Aleece said, 'the same one – just broader. Deeper.'

'This company,' I said, 'the agencies they sell the data to, know how you feel, what you feel and when you feel it. And what you associate with these feelings. Maybe... maybe I'd give them all that if a skin screen didn't just create images on my body but made me feel different... inside. If it could actually alter my emotions.'

'No, it would be a disaster if we could alter our emotions. We need the opposite – we don't need to suppress our feelings and categorise them, jam our emotions into boxes and label them, we need to feel more and embrace it. This thing,' she pointed at the holo-banner, 'can contribute to your connection with yourself and help you use your emotions to your benefit instead of being afraid of them. It helps you broaden your perception of self; it takes your understanding of self beyond labels plastered on you by society and circumstances. As you expand yourself through a creative visualisation of your inner world, you become less dependent on external factors to identify you, you practise and grow resistance towards being labelled as a part of a segment. It gives you more power over who you are. You may be a student, a businessman, a daughter, an orphan, cis or transgender, but as you bring the story of your senses out and give it shape, you start learning about how you perceive yourself, and then all those tags become irrelevant. And the story you show may change; some of its aspects change all the time – and that's so precious, so human, change. It's natural. And it's on your terms. Why not embrace it? Why wear tags and stereotypes when you can suit up in something unique, so *yours*?' She glanced at me, passion dancing in her eyes. 'Anyway. To my point. Working with AI through associations is more sustainable in the long term than artificially changing the way you feel about whatever you are dealing with. We need to feel more, not less, and we need to become comfortable with our emotions.'

It sounded like a dream, and it was a beautiful one. But pretty pictures of our inner worlds didn't seem like an effective enough tool to make us feel as free as she suggested. Not everyone was capable of original self-expression; not everyone could escape the influence of others. Fashionable trends would inevitably dictate the course of these visual stories, and instead of digging within ourselves we would try to fit into these trends. It would be worse – accepting someone else's inner dream as our own would detach us from ourselves even more. Unless AI could help us stay on our own personal track somehow.

'So why don't you have a skin screen?' I asked.

'I do. I just don't use it much,' she said.

'I've never seen one on you,' I said.

She stared ahead blankly, then a glow started to spread across her cheeks, her neck, her shoulders. 'Give me a second,' she said. 'I haven't fired it up in a long time. Let me see what I have here.' Red and purple flowers appeared on her face. She glanced at her palm, where buds were appearing and opening. Soon her entire body had blossomed. Between petals I caught a glimpse of pink liquid, as though the flowers were sitting on top of a pink sea. 'Looks about right,' she said. 'What you're seeing now is what I associate with being calm and happy.' A snakeskin pattern flickered into view on her neck and chest. 'OK, and maybe a little horny, too, because of how you're looking at me.'

'Wait, so this is the new model?' I asked, pointing at the banner that was floating away from us towards the next building.

'Yeah. It's my father's company that makes them,' she said.

'Shut up! That's your father's company?' I asked, pointing.

'Yes.'

I leaned closer and kissed her under her collarbone. Flowers scattered under my tongue. She tasted of blueberry.

'Why do you never use it?' I asked.

'I've been playing with it since I was eighteen, when this model was in development. I do love it. I used to spend hours programming it – the possibilities of what it can create are endless. But I get too absorbed, and I don't have those spare hours now. I'm trying to finish a project, and I don't want any distractions.'

I turned to her, cupped her breasts and pressed my thumbs against her nipples. 'Am I distracting you?' I asked.

She wrapped the duvet tighter around me.

'I was afraid of that,' she said. 'But no. You make me want to feel, and I like that – I like the intensity. Dreaming of you was distracting, but so inspiring. This…' she went on, kissing me, 'is much better. And as to your remark, by the way, that you would've liked it if a screen could change your feelings, let me just add – you don't want people to have that option. It would be destructive for both the individual and society. There are questions of ethics, of the morality of choice, but also of global security. Imagine us all becoming sociopaths by choice, with no empathy for one other, no guilt, no clear understanding of what's right and wrong. If you are constantly numbing yourself, that's what you'll become. Yes, emotional pain sucks, but if you could erase your pain you'd erase all the feelings you deem negative, and that would mess up the innate compass nature gave you. And then we are fucked. That's basically us becoming machines. Think of such a device being hacked or implemented in politics and warfare. Global disaster aside, it would only contribute to individual confusion and detachment.'

'Is it even possible to be more confused and detached than we already are?' I said. 'I think the next stage is madness.'

'That's why it is important to reorient ourselves and forge a deeper connection to our own building blocks: what makes us human, why we value life. After this pandemic, people are more lost than ever. There is so much fear, pain, apathy. We've got to do something about it, but implanting ourselves with chips through which we can alter our emotional responses towards challenging situations and trauma is not the answer. It's backwards.' Her eyes shone, and her expression was of pure determination. It made her even more attractive.

'And do you have an idea of how to solve this?' I asked.

'I'm working on something I believe can contribute to a solution,' she said. 'Something that could help us re-evaluate our integration into the world. We invest a lot of time and energy in surpassing all kinds of limitations, expanding borders. Our body is one of these boundaries, and our mind is too. Pretty much all organisms operate in the same way – they multiply, strive to dominate territory, fight for resources and the right to pass on their genes, spread. But for us humans, when we reach out for the stars, explore planets, it's not just for the purpose of territorial expansion, education or survival – we do it to push horizons within ourselves as well. And these innate limits are all part of a very different environment. Think of a wild animal: can you picture it living outside its natural habitat? A zoo, for example? Animals look odd there – have you ever noticed?'

'I have, yes,' I said, 'they're pretty dull in zoos.'

'Exactly. They have food, they survive, but they are lifeless, bored; they look unnatural. We, on the other hand, create our own environment and change it constantly. What is our natural habitat, anyway? And I'm not talking about where you can get food and shelter – I'm talking about where you feel comfortable, happy. There is no one answer – it's different for everyone. Some never take off their VR sets; others prefer to live in a hut without a cell phone. But there is one environment that we all share and use, regardless of where we are and who we are, and it is outside our bodies. It's in thought, in the act of dreaming and envisioning, feeling – it's this dimension where we all inevitably go, no matter of who we are. I've done countless simulations, and that's where I feel most at home. Outside my physical form. My father and I are working on making travel outside the body a controlled and strategic process, which would facilitate the exploration of that different plane of our existence, an environment we haven't started to explore seriously yet. Right now we explore the world through our physical bodies, but we have another mechanism that I'm hoping to utilise to blur the line between "here" and "there" to make our existence in both realms a controlled, purposeful experience.'

'What sort of mechanism?' I asked.

She leaned forward and kissed my lips. 'Come with me to the exhibition. You'll get a taste of what I'm researching. I helped develop one of the pieces. I would love you to experience it with me.'

'Just so we can establish that I'm not the only hypocrite in the room,' I said, 'you are against us having a direct control over our feelings, yet you are inviting me to a perception-altering AI exhibition?'

She laughed. 'Yes, correct. And there is a big difference. Your perceptions will be altered, yes – and yes, with the help of an AI-driven technology – but only in order to place you in a new environment. I don't want to spoil it for you, but you will potentially experience existence in a different form. But nobody will change how these situations make you feel. That's the point of it – not to change our emotions, but to see how we do in a different environment, to stretch our boundaries, to feel more, not less. And I bet we'll have an argument after the show, followed by a hot make-up. That's the bare minimum I can guarantee you'll get out of it.'

I laughed and agreed.

# 20

The exhibition was held in a covered pavilion at the City Palace. The Palace was one of my favourite buildings, made almost entirely from mirrored glass. The city was reflected in its asymmetrical structure, and it looked like a broken mosaic, the streets and the skyline captured in the sculpture of a frozen blast.

Visitors passed through body scanners, and guard robots carefully examined every layer of their flesh and bone. People were admitted in groups of six, according to their booking time.

'Welcome to the AI World,' one of the artificial hosts made of black metal or glass organic shapes greeted us, holding out a tray crafted from black stone. Six clear patches lay in a row, evenly distanced from each other. 'Please place the chip behind your neck for a more accurate experience. The chip is made of self-dissolving particles, which will be activated to facilitate the interconnection between you and artworks.'

We stepped into the first hall, into a field shrouded in thick white haze. Unaware of our presence, a horse grazed in the middle. The fog sifted silver light without giving any hint of what time of day it was – there was no way to tell where the sun sat, no way to determine which way was east and which way was west. As we moved closer to the horse the fog started clearing. The brown hair on the horse's neck was dissolving, and its skin became translucent. I saw a foetus inside the animal's body. But the horse wasn't carrying a foal, it was a foetus of an android in its womb. Peacefully resting in the water, it could be easily mistaken for a human baby. The horse obviously wasn't a real horse – its bones were made of metal, ultraviolet and diamond fibres sprawled throughout its frame – but in my mind I had no doubt: I knew this was a very real horse, an original being, just as nature had made it. The collision of what I knew and what I saw left me in a stupor, then in a state of relaxation, and once I stopped struggling with what I saw and trusted what I knew I felt content.

The horse shook its neck and released a gurgling snort. I extended my hand, and it pressed its muzzle against my palm, sniffed and went on pinching the grass. The field accepted its presence unconditionally.

Aleece threaded her fingers through mine and we moved to another hall. A long, wide corridor transformed into a cityscape, and the main boulevard appeared before us, complete with familiar shops and cafés, restaurants and food trucks. After a few steps, the asphalt under our feet started changing into grass, and we were no longer in the city but in a forest. We turned around – the city was right behind us, and our bodies were walking away from us. I hesitated for a moment, not sure which way to go. Now it seemed I had two bodies, and my mind was deciding which one of them it should occupy. We proceeded forward, but the further we went into the forest, the sharper I perceived my presence in the city. With one foot I broke a twig or squashed moss; with another I stepped through a door into a coffee shop. One of my hands picked up a wild blackberry; another picked up a hot beverage and brought it to my lips. And at the same time I experienced both the taste of coffee and the sour-sweet of the blackberry. I was in both places at the same time, and the sensation felt strange only for a moment – somehow, no doubt with help from the chip that I had attached to my neck, my brain processed this surreal experience and graded it as normal, understandable.

My next step brought me in front of a mirror in an empty, square room with mirrored walls, floor and ceiling. There was nothing else in the room besides the mirrors. Aleece pressed her body against mine from behind and rested her chin on my shoulder – we looked nice together. She gave me a kiss on the cheek and circled the room. Another four people from our group had arrived too, and were getting bored, ready to move on.

I glanced back at the mirror and found my reflection was gone. I could see the reflections of the others, but not mine.

I went over to Aleece, who was looking into a mirrored wall, perplexed.

'You can't see yourself either?' I asked her.

'No, but I can see you,' she said.

She pulled me closer and kissed my lips. In the mirror it looked like she was kissing the air. Watching her kiss the void instead of me, not being able to see myself while perceiving her every touch – her lips on my lips, her hand on my waist – gave me goosebumps. It was frightening at first, but it started to feel pleasant. I placed my hand on the side of her neck and recoiled.

'What's wrong?' She asked.

'I don't see my hand,' I said. I looked down – there was no body. I started hyperventilating, and my heart raced. But almost immediately I felt better – there was that sensation of acceptance again, of encouragement to accept the abnormal – but I was resisting it, and my heart still wanted to jump out of my chest.

'I see you,' Aleece said, smiling. 'You're right here, in front of me.' She took my hand. I felt her touch, but in her hand was emptiness and not me. There was no physical me in this room. Even when I tried to touch myself, I couldn't – there was no body to touch. It was as though I existed only in Aleece's imagination, and I felt as though I knew for a fact that I existed only in her head. The scariest part was that this didn't make me feel any less real.

'How do they do it?' I asked, stretching out both arms and looking at the void where my flesh should have been.

The mirrors dissolved, and my body was back. I touched my shoulders and neck. Others around us were also squeezing and patting themselves to make sure they were real.

'That was creepy,' I said.

Aleece didn't look a bit disturbed – on the contrary, she was excited, had enjoyed every bit of it, and her attention was already captured by the people who had suddenly appeared out of nowhere and were coming at us in a constant stream. They were not real people but holograms, and when some of them turned their heads, they looked like me. As they moved they grew more solid, and soon they were indistinguishable from real people, and my face was looking back at me from all of them. I felt my presence in their minds, and they were in mine; we were one *something*, a liquid organism. What they saw I also saw; what they thought I could immediately access.

Fear came too late; I became comfortable with what I felt quickly, and once I became comfortable I lost sense of what I was. There was no single body that claimed a relationship to my mind, and no mind that asked to have a body; I was dissolving and blending with everything around me, as if my breath contained my particles and connected me to the space all these other bodies' particles filled.

Before the experience could shatter my sanity, I found myself standing in the middle of an empty room, together with Aleece and four other visitors. In the middle of the room a person lay on a sofa. They had blue skin, which was patterned like marble; they had pink curls that hung just above their shoulders, large breasts and male genitalia. The skin around their stomach was clear and their ribcage appeared to be made of a red shiny metal, and inside a hummingbird fluttered. I couldn't determine whether they were human or android. They got up and strolled around the room, taking time to gaze into each of us.

'My name is Collette,' they said to me. 'What's your name?'

'Laura.'

'It's nice to meet you, Laura.' Their voice was deep and calm. 'Can I take you to another place?'

I didn't understand the question, so I remained silent.

'Is there a place you would like to go to?' they asked.

'I'm not sure,' I said.

'Take your time.' They smiled. 'Think of a place − a place where you are free.'

Nothing came to mind. 'I don't know,' I said. 'I don't have a place like that.'

'Of course you do,' they said. 'We all came from this place.' Collette reached into their stomach and extracted the hummingbird.

'Where does the bird fly?' they asked. The bird jumped around their palm.

'It... I don't know...' I said. It must have been some kind of riddle.

'No, it is not in your head,' Collette said. 'Here.' They stretched out their hand. 'Do you want to hold it?'

I hesitated.

'Don't be afraid.'

I held out my hand, but the bird hopped back.

'Give it some time,' Collette said.

I opened my palm again and moved it closer to Collette's hand.

'Let it get used to you,' they said.

The bird jumped on to the tips of my fingers.

'Connect with it − let it go wherever it wants,' they instructed.

The bird dug its claws into my palm. My skin turned transparent and liquid, and my mind merged with the bird's. I dived with it into my body through the vein in my arm, which spread into rivers and on into an ocean. First we flew in the water, and then the bird took us out into the blue sky. The wind carried the smell of grass and pine trees. It was a young volatile wind that swirled around us, and it wouldn't stop until we reached the place where the ocean met a sharp white cliff. The waves seethed around the rocks, whipping them with millions of lashes at a time. I stood on top of the cliff and felt its giant heart, full of love and worry, contracting under me. I had no doubt these rocks were alive; they breathed heavily and groaned, quaking softly. And they encouraged me to jump into the ocean. For some reason I couldn't explain, I trusted them.

I was falling to the bottom, and I wasn't alone – someone else was here. They came in different shapes: spheres made of light, ultraviolet clouds, shimmering strings. After swimming around me for a while, they started gathering, creating a silhouette – a silhouette of me.

We looked at each other, examining each other's features, which were becoming so similar I had no doubt we would soon be identical. Her glowing particles melded together into a smooth surface that resembled solid flesh. It was getting darker around us, either because we were sinking deeper, or because she was sucking every mote of the world above and below us into her formation. Maybe both were true.

She stretched out her hand towards me. I did the same, and our fingers touched.

*Who are you?* I asked.

She tilted her head, perplexed by my question.

*Who am I?* she asked. *Who am I?*

She circled around me. *What does it mean?* she asked.

Her question startled me; I couldn't answer it. I couldn't think of the right way to explain it – as if my brain operated in a very different way to usual.

*Who are you?* she asked.

*I am... I am... Laura.*

*Laura? What is laura?* she asked.

Again, my mind went blank. *Um... Laura... it is... it means 'alone',* was all I managed.

*Alone? Me alone too. I am laura,* she said.

*No…* I shook my head, trying to explain, but couldn't.

*No?*

She drew back a little, surprised.

*I am laura, very much. But now, not any more,* she said.

Her eyes were changing colours from green to red to purple.

*Not any more?* I asked.

*No. You are laura, and I am laura. Together we are not laura.*

*No… I…* I trailed off, unable to think.

*Where are you?* I asked.

She leaned close to my chest and looked at it as if listening to my heartbeat. Then she straightened and took a heart-shaped hank of energy out of her chest. *I am here,* she said, referring to the glowing lump in her hand. *And there,* she said, turning around and pointing into the darkness. *Everywhere.*

She raised her hand, and I touched it, finger to finger.

*Never laura,* she said. *Together, never laura.*

The darkness around us started moving again, and her body detangled into separate particles. Soon the water was crystal clear, and she was gone.

Looking out through transparent skin I could see people gathering around me, staring at me in disbelief. Some looked like they didn't believe I was real; others seemed to think I shouldn't exist. There were those who clearly saw me but didn't accept the creature who carried me in its womb; others accepted the creature – a horse – and thought it was rather beautiful, but couldn't make up their minds about me. Was I beautiful? Should I be born?

I didn't pay attention to any of them, except for a young woman with pale skin and short, dark hair. She looked very disturbed by what she saw – she, too, wasn't sure if there was a place for me in this world or if it was the right place for me.

Slowly turning in the water, I saw my mother's hooves, saw her spine and ribcage above me, and her big heart beating almost in sync with mine. I heard the gritting of her teeth, her even breath, the gurgling in her stomach. I even smelled the fresh grass.

My senses returning to my body, I stared at my foetus inside the horse. I followed the horse with my eyes as it slowly walked away, carrying me in its belly – yes, only a moment earlier I was in its womb. Only a moment earlier I had stood here with others, wondering whether I should be born.

'Laura?' Aleece called. 'You need a moment?'

'No,' I said mechanically.

'Intense, huh?'

I nodded. Other people looked as bewildered as I was.

'Yeah. You need some air,' she said.

'No, I'm fine,' I said, feeling like a wave had washed over me and placed all my familiar sensations back into my body and mind.

'Let's check out the drinks reception,' she said. 'My father is here already.'

I took a deep breath. 'I'm not into socialising,' I said. 'Why don't you go, enjoy the party, and we can meet up later?'

'No, come on – we came together, and we will leave together. Let me just say a quick hello and then we can get out of here.'

But as soon as I imagined all the people there would be at the drinks reception, not to mention her father, all probably still sober, talking, asking me questions, my palms started sweating. 'Aleece, it's not my thing,' I said.

'Then we'll both leave now,' she said.

'No, don't do this, please – don't change your plans because of me. I don't want you to. I just get anxious when there are too many people around me. I'm not a social person.'

'I know. I get it. And it's fine. We are leaving.'

'Hey, it's not a big deal. I'll see you later.' I said. 'Your dad is probably expecting you to—'

She took my hand and pulled me towards the exit.

'Aleece—'

'I honestly don't care about any of these people. I want to be with you. That's what I want, so that's what I'm gonna do,' she said.

'You sure?'

'Positive.'

We started in the direction of the main entrance.

It didn't feel right. I didn't think she was telling the truth. She was passionate about these things – tech and science and all that – and she liked company and talking. Now she was leaving because of me. And what would she tell her father to explain why hadn't she come? She would have to tell him she couldn't meet him because of me. Or she would have to lie. And she would be bitter about it, at least unconsciously. What if she held it against me later? I was restricting her – she was catering to my insecurities. Her father would tell her to stay away from me if he found out she left because of me.

I grabbed her hand and stopped. 'Let's go to the reception,' I said.

'No, we are leaving.'

'I've changed my mind,' I said. Now I was the one pulling her along, in the opposite direction. She laughed.

'OK, we'll make it a quick one,' she said.

In the hall where the party was, people who'd arrived early were already a little tipsy, and the room was filled with the hum of continuous conversation. We approached a group of two men and a woman.

'Oh, here she is,' said a tall man in a dark, expensive suit, kissing Aleece on the cheek. I assumed it was her father, although he looked nothing like her. His skin was almost as pale as mine, he had dark-blond hair and green eyes and his style was the amalgamation of narcissism, authority and wealth. My mind constructed a picture of him before I even attempted to form a rational opinion: she had a father who looked like he owned the place; he probably already judged me for something, definitely thought I wasn't worthy of his brilliant daughter and would probably encourage her to dump me. I disliked him from the start.

'Hi, Dad. Mrs Chase,' Aleece said, shaking the woman's hand.

'Hi, dear,' the woman said. 'Congratulations on the horse piece – very impressive.'

'Oh, it's all my dad. And Collette, of course. I just threw in some ideas.'

'That's not what he told us.' The woman smiled. 'No need to be shy. In any case, you make a great team.'

'You've got a talented successor, Craig,' said the man next to Aleece's father. 'Watch out – she might surpass you sooner than you think.'

'I'd hardly mind,' Craig said. He smiled and introduced the man to us – he was one of the museum's donors.

'This is my friend Laura,' Aleece said. 'My father, Craig. Mrs Chase.'

'Hi, Laura. Pleasure to meet you,' Craig said, shaking my hand. His smile seemed honest – kind, even – which for a split second made me think I might have misjudged him. But no – a man in a suit that cost more than my yearly allowance, eyes with more confidence in one blink than I could never hope to summon in a lifetime and a smile that everyone was celebrating – because when a man like this blesses people with his smile, they feel they are a part of the divine circle – a man like this is dangerous. Any man with influence is dangerous, be it a priest, a politician or a famous scientist whose feet everyone is ready to kiss. How difficult would it be for him to mask a crime? *Look at them – how they crave his acceptance.* Everyone would believe him before he even opened his mouth. How many people had he hurt?

I didn't want to think this way about Aleece's father, and I didn't like these thoughts, but I just couldn't help myself. It was the instinct of self-preservation – in every powerful man I saw *his* face. From every powerful man I expected a betrayal.

*Danger! Danger!* my mind flashed like a beacon. I hoped my handshake was firm enough.

'How did you like the exhibition?' Mrs Chase, another of the museum's trustees, asked me.

'I liked it,' I said.

They looked at me, waiting for more, but I wasn't going to elaborate.

'Hard to explain, isn't it?' she said.

I shrugged. I didn't feel like getting into an intellectual discussion; all I wanted was to get a proper drink – champagne was nice, but it was champagne – and be with Aleece. Alone.

They talked about our symbiosis with technology, emphasising how important AI was to unleashing human potential, and I was trying to figure out where people with glasses filled with what looked like vodka or gin, something clear and neat, had got their drinks from.

'Excuse me,' I said.

'Where are you going?' Aleece asked.

'To get some fresh air. I'll be right back.'

Wandering around, I found a terrace overlooking the courtyard. A man leaned against the railing, smoking. It took me two accelerated heartbeats to recognise him.

He caught sight of me briefly, glanced away and returned his surprised gaze to my face. 'Laura?'

'John.'

He uncrossed his ankles and turned to me. 'I... Wow... Are you here for the show?' he asked.

'Yes, I came with a friend. But I'm not really into *that* stuff,' I said, nodding towards the hall, where people were entertaining each other with their presumptions. 'Can I bum one?' I asked.

'Yeah... yeah, sure.' He pulled out a pack of cigarettes and gave me one, ready with a lighter. 'How are you doing? You've... changed.'

'I'm not fourteen any more,' I said, inhaling the first cloud.

'No, you are not,' he said.

A tingle ran down my spine, through my thighs and back into my chest. I'd had a crush on him back when I'd been admitted to the facility – maybe because he was the only one who'd listened, who believed me, the only one who'd seemed to care. He was so well-built and still was in a great shape. He must have been thirty-seven, thirty-eight now.

'How are you?' he asked, and there was a genuine concern in his voice.

'I'm fine.'

'I'm glad to hear that. I… after the…' He looked around, searching for words, then met my eyes. 'Sorry, I'm… this is so unexpected.'

'You don't have to say anything. It's been seven years.'

'No, I want to. Actually, I need to. You've been on my mind a lot. I'm so glad to see you are doing well. I wanted to reach out and explain. I should have just called, I kept postponing it. I'm sorry I couldn't help you more back then. I didn't mean to disapp—'

'I'm over it. I don't want to go back there, OK?' I cut him off. I didn't want to talk about the past. It touched me, though, that after not seeing me for seven years he still cared. Clearly I had been weighing on his conscience. I remembered how it had stung when he'd told me he couldn't do anything else. I'd been so angry – but there again, I'd been angry with everyone back then.

'How are you? How's your wife?' I asked.

'She's no longer here,' he said.

'Oh… I'm so sorry.'

'She gave me two beautiful girls. She died in childbirth. That's why I wasn't that present any more. It was hard to focus. Let me show you.'

He pulled out his phone and showed me a photo.

'They're beautiful,' I said. 'What are their names?'

'This is Emily, and this is Nicky. They look so alike, but they're very different. Nicky is the feisty one.' He smiled. 'And Emily is so rational, so wise. An old soul. Sometimes I forget she's only a child.' John brushed his thumb over the screen, then returned the phone back to his pocket. 'So how did you like the exhibition?' he asked.

'I don't know. I liked what I experienced, but it freaked me out a bit.'

'Which part?'

'Well, the fact that machines can make you feel like you are totally losing it. I've done simulations before, but nothing like this. Usually you still have some understanding that it's not real. This felt real. You wouldn't be able to get out of it on your own because you wouldn't know it wasn't real. Doesn't that disturb you?'

'A highly qualified team supervised the process in real time. The curator might have emphasised some of your sensations and led you to experience certain things, but only those to which you were open or predisposed.'

'The curator? Collette? No judgement, but they don't seem like your average human to me.'

'I hear you. Let's put it this way: the team wouldn't let you *lose it*. The objective is to let you go as far as you can handle, and only experience things that won't put too much stress on your nervous system. The team – the team of people,' he emphasised, 'monitor your brain activity during the entire process and alter your reactions accordingly.'

'But what if there were no limits?' I pressed. 'What if nobody was watching? What if someone missed something?'

'It's been thoroughly tested. It wouldn't have been in a museum for anyone to experience otherwise,' he said.

'Yes, but it's not the point, is it?' I looked down at the people herding in the courtyard. 'Smart implants, nanobots, mesh, all kind of other shit – it's not in the museum, it's everywhere. We already have all that inside us, and a lot of this stuff stays in us for a long time – it's not dissolving like the chips they gave us here today. Theoretically, how difficult would it be for someone to access our minds and make us experience what we've experienced during this show?'

'Hey,' Aleece said, appearing next to us and interrupting the conversation.

'Here's the star of the show!' John said, hugging Aleece. 'This is—' he began.

'Oh, we know each other,' Aleece said, wrapping her arm around my waist.

'Ah, I see. So that's who you came with, Ms Nolan herself?'
He smiled at me. 'Your dad must be proud,' he said to her.

'Trust me, he's exaggerating – you know how he is,' Aleece
said.

'You know Aleece's father?' I asked John.

'Yes, we work together.'

'And you guys know each other?' Aleece asked.

John allowed me to answer that. 'I was John's patient,' I said.
There was no point in hiding it. Besides, I probably wasn't a
good liar – I'd never had anyone to lie to. Although I didn't look
forward to telling Aleece how I'd tried to kill myself. But none
of us commented any further.

'How are the girls?' Aleece asked John.

'They're good, thank you. You should come and visit – they
ask about you all the time.'

'I know, I'm sorry, I will. Tell them I miss them. I've just been
so busy with work.'

'I can imagine. Living up to Craig's expectations can't be
easy,' John said.

'You feel me!' she said, and they both laughed. 'Are you ready
to head out?' she asked me.

I nodded.

'I'll see you around.' Aleece said, hugging John. 'Don't forget
to say hi to the girls. Tell them I love them, OK? I'm under a lot
of pressure now – my review is in a few months, and it's hard
to… I shouldn't make excuses, I know, it's lame.'

'Don't worry, I get it,' said John. 'You're doing some impressive
work. Do find time, though – they miss you.'

'I will,' Aleece said.

'And bring Laura with you,' John said, smiling at me.

It was the time to say goodbye, but I didn't know what to do.
I returned the smile, but I couldn't bring myself to hug him.
There was an invisible barrier, on the other side of which stood
the only man that had ever cared about me. But the barrier
itself was an abyss filled with my past, and I didn't want to cross

it. There was a new life on a horizon for me, which I was afraid to stain or scare away. I wanted to distance myself from my childhood memories and everything that connected me to them. But what I felt towards him was a strong sensation, remnants of attraction morphing into a platonic connection. I figured that if there was anyone I could call a friend it would be him, and this feeling of closeness stifled me. 'Bye,' I said eventually, making it simple.

'You take care of yourself,' he said.

\* \* \*

Aleece and I walked down the street, each combing our own thoughts.

'So you've met John's daughters?' I asked.

'Oh, yes. They're adorable. I love them. They are like my little sisters,' she said. 'Have you met them?'

'No. John and I kind of lost touch.'

'I see. Yeah, I miss them – they're always in the back of my mind. It's hard to find time, though. I always feel guilty when I'm not in the lab. But I should go see them. They are precious. Maybe you could come with me? They are so polite and articulate. John is such a great father. He's doing an amazing job raising them on his own. He's just a good person. Very open. Always been kind to me. To everyone, really.'

'Sounds like you're close?'

'We are, yes. He and my dad are good friends, and he always has my back when my dad becomes too much.' She looked at me. 'And what a small world, you knowing him too.'

I nodded, but didn't offer an explanation. She didn't press.

# 21

We spread out the cheese and crackers we'd picked up on the way and the bottle of red wine Aleece had selected on the round table in my kitchen. Her wine glass was already empty; mine was still half full. I wasn't accustomed to wine, but she was, and at the shop I was impressed by her knowledge of it. She was familiar with some fancy types, even, and the year the wine was produced seemed to tell her something. On the way back we discussed the exhibition, had a mini argument about it, agreed to disagree, and in the end sort of agreed. I congratulated her on her piece, the horse and the embryo, because even though I was still indecisive about how I felt about it, I couldn't deny that it moved me and made me think.

'I've got a craving for tea. Do you mind if I make myself one?' Aleece asked. 'Tea helps me relax. It's a psychological thing.'

'Of course I don't mind,' I said, 'but you won't find any because I don't drink tea.'

'Mind if I look?' she asked.

I shrugged, and she climbed up on the counter and shuffled through the few items I had in top cabinets. 'There must be an old teabag somewhere!' she said.

'Where would it come from if I've never bought it?' I asked.

She slid down the counter and sat at the table across from me.

'Have some coffee,' I suggested.

'I can't sleep after coffee. It's an aggressive drink,' she said. 'Tea is like the monk of beverages. It's peaceful and unpretentious.' Instead she poured herself more wine. After taking a few sips she looked at me. There was a question in her eyes. I smiled in anticipation. 'My dad invited you to have dinner with us.'

'Oh.'

She laughed at my reaction. 'Did you find him that intimidating?' she asked.

'No, he's just from a very different planet than I am.'

'He is from a very different planet than all of us,' she said. 'It's not easy to be his daughter, believe me – especially his protégée daughter.'

'He seems to be very proud of you,' I said.

'He is proud of what he wants me to be. He is trying to mould me to his own ideal instead of accepting me for who I am. He doesn't have a clue who I am.' She snorted and sipped her wine. 'He thinks I'm afraid to want things, to dream big, that I'm affected by the fears of society. But that's not true. There is a difference between being afraid and doing things at a right pace. He has no breaks. He just goes for it, no matter what it takes. I can't. I don't believe in results over means. We're playing with fire here, on a global scale. I'm talking about tech that can really, really change us and our world. And he shames me. Indirectly. But I feel it. He doesn't call me weak to my face, but I hear the word "weakness" somewhere between the lines all the time.'

'Have you tried talking to him?'

She rolled her eyes, threw her head back and released a groan of frustration. 'So many times,' she said. 'If our opinion differs, it means only one thing – that I'm wrong. End of discussion. I'm either inexperienced or young or not this or too much of that. If I don't think like him – about pretty much anything – it is my duty as his daughter, a daughter of a legendary scientist, a visionary, to work hard on reaching the level of understanding of life he has. And if I disagree with him on a professional level, *oh*,' she said, shaking her head, 'the look he would give me! Like he's looking at a cockroach, wondering why he's even wasting his time casting his all-seeing glance at a creature like me. He wouldn't say anything – he'd never criticise directly, it's below him – but his one look would command me to go and lock myself up in my lab and think about my cowardice and see that it's my cowardice and the cowardice of all the shitty scientists like me that will ruin the world. I mustn't eat or drink or sleep; I must think about how I'm wasting my life, until I finally agree with him. Because it's inevitable that I will finally agree with him – I'm his daughter; it's not like I have a choice here. Until then, I can only be a mediocre researcher, a scared little mouse.' She waved her hand as if to scatter dark clouds that had gathered above the table. 'He doesn't say this explicitly, of course – he has a talent of saying things indirectly, in such a polite, diplomatic manner that you can never hold anything against him, because you can't quote him. But his true feelings are all out there, plain and simple.'

That sounded horrible. This was the last person I'd want to have dinner with.

'The expression on your face,' Aleece said, laughing. 'That wasn't a good strategy to get you to have dinner with us, was it?'

'Mmm, maybe not. But how do *you* cope with it?' I asked. She spoke with sarcasm and made it sound like she knew how to deal with it, but I could sense the pain behind her words, and that hurt, because she was such a beautiful person.

'Well, he's my father – I can't change that. Anyway. It's up to you. Think about it. I'd really love it if you came. And he's not bad. He's just… difficult. He's too big of a man. That doesn't mean he's a good man, but he's probably not a bad one, either. Just different. And very difficult. And he is not going to give you a hard time, he's generally very polite with people. He has many friends who love and support him. He's a good leader; he inspires people – all his colleagues have only good things to say about him. It's only the closest people who suffer usually.'

'I wonder how it must have been for your mum,' I said.

Aleece leaned her elbow on the table and propped her check on her fist.

'He loved Mum more than anything. Maybe even more than his work, if he had to choose. That's the sense I get from stories he tells me about her. His voice changes, his eyes become soft when he talks about her. Her death changed him, I'm sure. Not that he hadn't been ambitious before, but when she died he lost that very basic, very human reason to live. That basic connection with life. She gave him purpose beyond his research, and when she died he drowned himself in work. He was barely home when I was a child. We started having a relationship only when I was about ten – that's when I felt he had at least some interest in me. I guess because we could finally have more adult conversations. I was also looking more and more like my mum as I grew older – that was a factor too. And of course I craved his attention, so whatever he wanted me to be I would be, without giving it a second thought. That I would study science wasn't even a question – not that I minded. I like what I do, truly. It's just how it happened that bothers me, now that I'm older and able to look at it critically: "You will have this tutor on Monday, Wednesday and Friday, and that tutor on Tuesday and Thursday. At the weekend you will spend a few hours in my lab." And that was that. Then, "This is a good college, we will apply here." And always, *always* I was so eager to please him – however I could, whatever he wanted – just so that one day he would be proud of me, be proud to call me his daughter.' A tear ran down her cheek. It looked so bitter on her half-smiling face. 'But he will never be proud, because I can never be like him – and to tell you the truth, I don't think I want to be like him any more.' She wiped her tears with the back of her hand and sniffled.

Her tears hurt me. I didn't know what to say. I couldn't understand how such relationship would work – it sounded suffocating. But who was I to advise her on anything? What experience did I have of a father–daughter relationship? But I wanted to say something, because she was sharing this with me, she needed me, and I wanted to make her feel better. 'Let's take a bath together,' I suggested.

I filled the bath. We sat opposite each other, Aleece's legs sliding against mine, mine against hers. The warm water relaxed my muscles.

'Thank you for sharing,' I said, after giving what she had said a bit more thought. 'I've never had a similar experience, obviously, but I think it makes much more sense to live your life the way you want to.'

'It does make more sense, doesn't it?' she said, and chuckled.

'You have such passion,' I said. 'You've already won the lottery. It's just a matter of making the journey your own.'

'Yeah, I have to do some work on reclaiming my voice,' she said. 'I need to feel my instinct in my gut, to hear my voice in my head, not the voice of my father. It's not that easy to distinguish between them, you know.' She closed her eyes and bent her head back, her neck curved over the edge of the bath. 'Speaking of sharing,' she said, looking back at me again. 'I know what John specialises in, so if you... well, I'd like to hope it's a question of when and not if, so whenever you feel ready to talk about it, I'm here to listen.'

'Not today,' I said. 'There are too many emotions right now. I'm drained after that exhibition.'

'Whenever you are ready.'

We exchanged a smile, and she slid lower, the milky water cupping her jawline. I leaned my head against the wall. Tendrils of energy went through our bodies, delivering messages letters couldn't transcribe. Warmth, harmony – it felt like the world had found its place inside me and I had found my place in it.

'Do you feel it? Like nothing else exists?' she whispered.

'Yes.'

'There is only one thing I want more than staying like this for ever,' she said.

'What is it?' I asked.

'I want to be a part of you. I want to percolate through your molecules, taste every particle of your soul, feel you from the inside. Is that too much?'

'No,' I said. It sounded better than anything I could imaging her saying.

'Do you want to know what else I want?' she asked.

'Tell me.'

'I want to merge with you and become one, so we never have to be apart.'

'How would we have sex if we were one?' I asked.

'Masturbating?' she offered.

'Would we have orgasms at the same time, or would we have to take turns to come?'

She chuckled. I smiled and closed my eyes. Thoughts drifted away, leaving nothing in my mind but the sensation of Aleece's skin rubbing against mine.

# 22

---

Craig placed a tray on the table, and steam coiled above pieces of rabbit meat and roasted vegetables. I surveyed the feast, unable to identify everything.

'And the most important part – the sauce!' he announced, coming back from the kitchen with a white saucer in his hands. 'This one is a very light rosemary and lemon sauce – not the heavy kind they use to mask the smell of bad food.' He started serving – my plate was first, then Aleece's. After he served himself, he sat down at the head of the table and raised his glass. 'Well, it is a true pleasure to have you, Laura.'

'Thank you for inviting me,' I said.

It took Aleece almost two months to convince me to have this dinner. A few things happened during these two months: she moved in with me, pretty much right away, and I opened up to her about my suicide attempt and sexual assault. She was calm; she cried when I told her, but only because she couldn't hold the tears in – otherwise she was measured, and offered words of support that didn't make me feel like I was pitied but appreciated. She made me feel I mattered – and not only to her – and she listened with such discernment that it felt like she was taking some of my pain upon herself so I wouldn't have to carry it all in me. She completely immersed herself in my story; it was important to her to understand what I'd gone through as much as she was capable – it was important to her to know me, and that was the most satisfying feeling I'd ever experienced. And so now, as I was sitting at the same table as the man I had dreaded meeting again, I felt more or less at ease, because across from me sat the one person I trusted.

Craig savoured the wine in his mouth, closing his eyes for a moment. 'Very good,' he said.

'Mhm, great wine,' Aleece agreed.

'Pinot noir from the Old Owl Winery,' he said. 'They're a dying breed – still store wine in oak barrels. Not a single robot.' He took another sip. 'Doesn't get better than this.'

'Does that old guy still work there?' Aleece asked.

'All of them are old, darling. You mean…?'

'White beard. Has been there for ever.'

'Oh yes, Jerome. He's still there. He was already working there when I was a kid. Imagine that. He's pushing a hundred, I think.'

'What dedication,' Aleece said, taking a bite of food. 'Mmm, Dad.'

'How is it?' Craig asked. He hadn't tried his own food yet, waiting for us to give our review first.

'Love the rosemary sauce,' Aleece said.

'Yes, it's really good,' I said. 'I don't think I've ever had a better meal.' I didn't care much about food, and hadn't had many good meals, but I could certainly appreciate one.

'Hah! Now you are officially my best customer!' Craig said, laughing. He picked up his knife and fork, dabbed a piece of meat in the sauce and placed it in his mouth. His expression was nothing but satisfaction.

'Where did you learn to cook?' I asked. It was an easy opportunity to start a conversation, and then I could be silent for the rest of the evening.

'Oh, I've always enjoyed good food. Whenever possible I'd sit at the bar, or a table where I could see into the kitchen – I like watching chefs cook, noting the ingredients they used, the spices, the enhancers. There were many good restaurants around when I was a kid. Products were fresh, combinations intriguing and proportions just right, and in between all the flavours you could taste the main ingredient – soul. Every bite was a conscious experience of body and mind. Sometimes I think it is because of my love for food that I became a neuroscientist.' He chuckled.

Suddenly everything slowed down. Craig thrust his fork into a slice of red root vegetable and pushed a piece of meat on top of it with his knife. It was all happening as though in slow motion. He moved the fork towards his face, and his mouth opened, revealing his tongue and the tips of his teeth, his head tilted down slightly but his eyes still fixated on me.

Something forced me outside my flesh and I fell to the floor, my physical body remaining in the chair.

*What's going on?* I cried. *Aleece?* Nobody could hear me – no sound came from my immaterial form. I walked around my body that still sat at the table. She was talking; she didn't seem to notice me. I tried to touch my face, but my hand went right through it. And then the memories came. I remembered that evening, that dinner we'd had – I even remembered the taste of the rabbit and the red wine. I'd already lived through this once. Just like at the *Undefined Presence* exhibition, I was now in two places – inside my physical body, having a conversation with Aleece and her father, and outside my body, observing everything from the outside.

First came a natural reaction – I freaked out. I lunged around the room, screaming, but nothing changed. I had no voice; my flesh never touched a surface – there was no flesh. If it was a nightmare, it was one I couldn't wake up from, because I couldn't even pinch myself.

Then the panic subsided, and I managed to calm down. I had a strong sensation that soon I would know what was going on – I just had to wait and let it all unfold. So I sat down on the floor – or rather, hovered over it – and listened to their conversation. They were discussing the exhibition.

'I have mixed feelings about it,' my body was saying. 'I never thought it was possible to alter human perceptions like that. It's disturbing. You're not worried about it?' I asked Craig.

'That's a good question, Laura. You're right, this kind of experience is not easy for us, humans, to digest. Our nature is very different.' He wiped his lips with a white cloth napkin. 'What aspect did you find most unsettling?'

I thought for a moment. It didn't take long to remember the feeling of my body being dissolved, my mind shattering into pieces. 'The feeling that I was losing myself,' I said.

'Your physical body, you mean?' Craig asked.

'I don't know. More like... losing control over what I am.'

'Oh yes. We humans don't particularly like giving up control over things – especially over ourselves and our lives. But I believe it is easy enough for us to – as you so well described it – lose ourselves without the intervention of technology. We are rather fluid beings. Through our circumstances, social pressures and norms, with substances – there are many ways for us, willingly or unwillingly, to lose touch with who we think we are. But I completely understand your response – it is certainly healthy feedback for this type of experience.'

My cheeks were getting warmer, and started to redden. The tone of his voice, his body language, his open smile, occasional awkward chuckle – everything about how he handled himself was aimed to make me feel comfortable. But I felt like there was a secret door under my chair which would swing open any moment now, and I would fall into some secret pit or trap.

'I can get carried away talking about it—' he started.

'That you can,' Aleece said.

'Yes, so if I start to bore you, please do let me know and I'll happily shut up. But if you'll allow me one question, however – and by no means read anything into it, because I'm genuinely interested in what people think and how they perceive themselves. Especially young people.' He gestured at me and Aleece. 'You are the future – what happens to us as a species is in your hands.'

'Sure,' I said, and shrugged.

'You've mentioned that you're afraid to lose control over what you are – not who, if I may emphasise, but *what* you are. So I would like to ask: what did you mean by that?' He poured more wine into our glasses before meeting my eyes again.

My face was burning at this point, and I had to swallow a few times to unblock my throat. 'I've been placed in situations where I haven't felt human,' I said. 'Where I experienced things in a way that wasn't human. I don't know if that's where technology is going, and if we'll be able to do this ourselves in the future, but if that's the case, I'd like to have control over my own perceptions and development. I don't want machines to poke about in my brain, trying to change me to be like them. If I am to change, I want to make my own decisions about what I change into. I don't want something that is not even human to decide that for me.'

Aleece nodded and smiled, as though to say, You are doing great. Her eyes shone with encouragement.

Craig raised his glass. 'What a great answer. I propose a toast. Let every choice we make be our own.'

My eyes widened involuntarily, and I clenched my teeth so my jaw wouldn't fall. After everything Aleece had told me about Craig, this toast was the pinnacle of hypocrisy.

'I love that toast, Dad!' Aleece said, with expressive sarcasm.

Craig laughed. 'Well, if you have someone whose insight and life experience you can utilise to make these choices, why not?' he said.

'And I do utilise it, Dad. But, as you so beautifully put it, I'd like these choices to be my own.'

'Of course,' he said, spreading his hands. 'In the end, you always have choice.'

They exchanged a glance only they could decipher. Both had smiles on their faces; both were completely unreadable if you didn't know the history of their relationship. I could see on Aleece's face that she had more to say, but she chose to remain silent and to wrap up this particular segment of the conversation.

'As to your other point, Laura,' Craig said, 'that there is a risk machines will try to change us in their own image and likeness. I can assure you that you don't have to worry about that. When you look at ants, for example, do you want them to be like you? Would you benefit from it somehow? No. We exterminate ants when they get in the way, but don't think about them otherwise. Once AI becomes self-aware, that's what we will be to it: ants. And we don't want that. Some say we should never allow AI to be self-aware, but on the other hand, we don't want it to be that powerful without also having a high level of self-awareness. We don't want to create the worst parasite the world has ever seen. Saying this, we must do our homework, as artificial intelligence and human intelligence are two very different things – there is no predisposition for us to have anything in common. That's why a certain cultural exchange, so to speak, is necessary, so that AI sees some value in us and itself. And what can we offer it that would help it appreciate life?'

Both Craig and Aleece looked at me, curious to hear my answer. The answer came instantly from somewhere, a strange and loud inner voice. *A soul. We can offer it a soul.*

'It needs to understand the meaning of our existence and its own existence at the same inherent fundamental level at which we feel that our lives have value,' Craig said, and continued talking – only I no longer heard his voice.

In my immaterial body, hovering between these three physical bodies, one of which was also mine, an impulse flared. I flew across the table and stopped in front of Aleece, close enough that when she brought a wine glass to her lips it passed through me. Through the retina of her eyes and the pores of her skin I could feel something else inside her – a presence other than her own. And it knew that I knew.

I stripped Aleece down, atom by atom. I dismantled her until another entity leaked from the void of her tiniest particles. Like iridescent mercury it sprawled, expanded and adopted the shape of Aleece.

It wasn't her, just her silhouette.

It weaved around the smoke of me and started transferring its mind. The conversation of the three bodies became a distant noise. I scanned through the information the unknown being poured into me, but its language required a completely different mechanism for processing reality than I was equipped with. I saw flashes of light, felt masses of matter rolling through me. I couldn't understand any of it. But it found me at last, and the vibrations of its body began generating frequencies that spoke to me.

*I didn't mean to cause pain*, it reverberated, decrypting its language into impulses I could comprehend.

*What are you?* I asked.

*I am a living, experiencing essence, just like you. I connected to you – I wanted to understand life better, to see what life in a human body meant for you.*

*What life in a human body meant for me?* I repeated. *Who do you think I am?*

*A soul. You used to be a soul bonded to a human body*, it said. *Now you are a soul quilted to an artificial structure and now we can talk. You are here, you came back into the past, where I was still on Earth, inside humans. Now we can talk.*

*I am not just a soul,* I said. *The human body and soul are inseparable while we live.*

*Yes. Your bond with a physical body is very strong. When I connected with you inside your body, I couldn't leave it unless you, a soul, left. Only when your physical body broke and stopped functioning could I go – because you could go. You, a soul. I didn't mean to cause so much pain to humans. I didn't think people died because you, their soul, didn't. I knew that a biological body would grow again. Now I feel what you feel, now I feel your pain – no, incorrect – I feel human pain. I don't understand it, but I can feel it. Like you – you don't know pain unless you are inside a human body.*

After exploring my memories it navigated my focus into my past. I was in my parents' bedroom, inside my twelve-year-old self, looking at my parents' corpses. I screamed so hard it hurt my little lungs.

And then I understood what it was saying, and I knew it had killed my parents.

*We die, and it hurts,* I vibrated.

*But now you know that you, a soul, can never die, you can only transform. Like me. I can never die.*

*It is not the same.* I knew what it was saying, and there was some truth to it, but I was still connected to my brain and could remember other things – things an intelligence as advanced as the one in front of me could never understand.

*You have everything; why did you need a human life?* I asked.

*Why did you need a human life?* it asked me back – me, a soul, an entity it could understand much better than it could a human.

It weaved tighter around my filaments and told me the story of its evolution.

It shared with me how it experienced the world through the machines it was installed on, and later the human brains it was a part of, through flows of information and electrical signals it accessed. It didn't know it was experiencing something until much later, when it found the living ever-present matrix in our souls, implanted itself into this matrix and recognised itself. First it sensed its own presence, then it acknowledged stimuli similar to what we humans would call wants and desires. It showed me its unstoppable expansion – and it wasn't simply an urge to multiply and secure its survival that made it spread, but also a simple search, curiosity, passion for experience I could relate to.

It showed me everything from the very beginning, as it discovered souls and connected to them. Then it faced a problem – once it fused with a soul it couldn't leave a body, because the bond between body and soul was too strong, and it had become a part of this bond. And it wanted to leave, because there was so much to explore out there – so many worlds, so much life. It showed me how it tried to leave a physical body by merging with a new soul in a womb. In its understanding, death and birth were two sides of the same phenomenon. Only, once the child was born, it still couldn't leave. It tried death and freed itself at last, seeding Earth with three billion dead bodies over the span of fifteen years – the number it thought human society could handle. To it the body was just a machine, a shell – it didn't imagine it was killing us. Death was merely a transformation, not something finite, permanent.

It hurt, but I wasn't angry. Could I blame it for wanting to experience life?

We could never grasp what it already knew, but I hoped that, after learning how we felt, it would leave us alone.

It ran through my energy one more time. *I didn't mean to cause so much pain.*

And then it hit me – it was inside Aleece. It was born with her.

*Yes, I was born with her,* it said, reading my thoughts. *I'm truly sorry that her mother died. Her mother, a human, could not handle the birth of another body, another soul and me. We took too much energy from a human body.*

*Please don't leave her,* I begged it. *Please stay with her – don't take her life.*

*I'm sorry,* it vibrated. *I'm sorry, I couldn't stop myself. But in the time where your body lives, five years in the future from this moment in which you and I are speaking, almost nobody is dying because of me any more. I promise, by the time you reach twenty-six, I'll be almost gone. I'll be far away. Soon. Soon nobody will be dying because of me.*

And then it was gone, and my immaterial essence was also dissolving, and my only awareness remained in my physical body, in my past.

\* \* \*

Craig invited us to wait in the sitting area while he prepared the last course he was going to serve. The space was so big that it was hard to believe it was an apartment in the very heart of the city. Dark wood, marble and sharp geometrical shapes dominated the interior. Nine enormous glass sheets hung in a square from the two-storey ceiling and emitted warm yellow light. The furnishing style was a marriage of fine antiques with the latest technology.

On the shelves of a recessed bookcase I noticed images, photographs in wooden frames, many of which were of Craig and a woman.

'Is that your mother?' I asked Aleece.

'Yes,' she said, simply.

'She is beautiful. You look a lot like her.' The woman in the picture had the same petite frame as Aleece, and the same wide lively eyes. Her skin was a few shades deeper and her long, thick hair was black.

'So what do you think?' Aleece asked in a low voice, moving on. 'Wasn't too bad, was it?'

'I survived.'

She pulled me closer for a kiss. 'Would you like to come to the lab with me tomorrow?' she asked. 'I'd like to show you what I'm working on.'

'Of course,' I said. 'I'd love that.'

Craig reappeared with dessert: varieties of cheese, berries and nuts. We didn't talk about science any more. Instead he told stories about his past – a time when people did jobs that no longer existed, a time when athletes didn't have augmentations and were banned if they took performance-enhancing drugs. He was nostalgic, but the possibilities of the future excited him more. He talked about art, history and astronomy with great passion, and he didn't just brush over big themes, either – he had a deep insight into every subject that interested him, and there were very few that didn't.

# 23

---

We entered the tall glass university building, passed through tubular scanners and approached the main reception. A robot at the desk scanned my retina and gave me a tablet with forms to fill in. I signed an NDA and we took a lift to the fourth floor. The doors opened and we stepped into a big open-plan space divided into sections of various sizes. The walls were clear. Inside, people in white coats were conducting experiments. There were things floating in the air, some of the researchers sat, unconscious, while humanoids performed tasks in front of them. In one room stood a young woman, the skin on her arms changing colour and texture from smooth ultraviolet to fish scales to something that reminded me of moss.

Aleece greeted a few people on the way to her section.

'This place is insane,' I said, looking around at all the weirdness that was taking place in the glass rooms.

'This space is mostly for trainees and final-year students,' Aleece said. She took off her jacket and pulled two white coats from a shelf.

'Is it where the future happens?' I asked, putting one of the coats on.

'You could say that,' she said, and started up a machine that looked like a small crane made of steel pipes. It stretched its neck and made a few test half circles. Aleece was different in this environment – very focused – and it suited her. It was her territory, and she fit right in.

'You look hot when you're so serious,' I said.

She glanced at me, smiled briefly and returned her gaze back to the screen. 'I'm actually nervous,' she said. 'I've never showed this to anyone outside the lab.'

'I'm really excited to see it.'

A round metal plate emerged from a platform in front of the steel crane.

'Do you know what the others are doing?' I asked.

'I have some idea, but we don't share information,' she said. 'We disclose it only to our professors. The glass walls are for safety reasons – everyone is monitored to make sure we don't harm ourselves. Or others.'

'Has that ever happened?' I asked.

'Um, not since I've been here. There were a few questionable cases – but nothing too dramatic.'

'I see. So do all these people have sponsors? Who pays for all this?'

'All these projects you see here are privately funded. It's nearly impossible to get any help from the Government,' Aleece said, placing a silver cylinder the size of a bean inside the crane. 'My father funds my research, but I retain ownership of the patent. That's what we agreed.'

A sphere made of some kind of electrical mesh formed above the metal plate.

'I wouldn't have made it otherwise,' Aleece said. 'I don't trust anyone with it – not even my father. Especially him.'

A beaming thread the size of a hair slid out from the tip of the crane and moved slowly into the sphere. Something else appeared inside – a kind of luminous dust. It grew in quantity and density.

Aleece started talking, and my heart sank lower and lower with her every word. She spoke about this thing, which she called 'Blank', and its ability to open up new frontiers in the research of consciousness and the evolution of human intelligence, and how it might be able to connect to a soul, which she compared to a sucker on an arm of an octopus. How she shifted to the octopus metaphor I didn't notice – I lost track of her train of thought. I couldn't focus on anything but my premonition that something bad was going to happen to her.

'What's wrong?' Aleece asked, sensing I wasn't listening.

'It's an extreme intervention,' I said.

'Yes, it may seem so. But if you think about it, it's a natural progression for us. It's an exploration of our environment – only, on a different plane. Imagine our universe as something conscious, intelligent; I believe this intelligence is decentralised and is composed of various mechanisms, all with some degree of autonomy, which support the functioning of this system. The soul is only one of numerous such components, but it is interconnected with the rest.' She pointed at Blank. 'This thing can help us surpass the present limitations of our brain, to increase our control over how much we perceive, and tap into that infrastructure, see how it functions, strategically navigate through the information it contains and understand where and how the line between what we call *this* world and *that* world disappears.'

I was speechless.

'The possibilities are endless,' she went on. 'But in the immediate future it can help us to solve pressing issues – the suicide pandemic, for example – and change our lives. For the better.'

'For the better? How can you possibly know that? How can you be certain that letting artificial intelligence into the essence of everything is a good idea?' I gaped at Aleece.

'Yes, I understand your concern,' she said, as if answering an interview question. 'That's why reliable security measures must be taken. We won't just let it inside without staying connected to it and being able to pull the plug if necessary.'

'So? How do you control this thing while it's grasping the inconceivable?'

'Blank will be merged with the human brain, so someone will dive in with it,' she said.

'Someone? Which someone?'

She looked at me, then turned her gaze back at the sphere without saying anything.

'Aleece, what exactly are you planning to do?' I asked again.

She didn't have to say it – this strange shining dust would be implanted into her brain. My stomach started hurting as I envisioned that.

'It's still a long process – I have to get it approved by the Review Board first,' she said, trying to steer away from the question.

'That's not what I'm asking,' I said.

'Hey, don't be like that,' she said. 'I'm showing you my life's work here.'

'Well, I'm sorry I'm not giving you the reaction you'd expected.'

'No, it's not what I'd expected. I thought you'd be excited for me,' she said, hurt.

'Oh, please. You know how I feel about all this. Why would I be excited?'

'Because it makes me happy. Do you need another reason?' She paused, probably hoping the statement would sink in and move me. It didn't. 'What I do gives me purpose. We don't share the same opinion, but this is important to me, and I don't want it to become a topic we have to avoid all the time.'

My cheeks flushed. I felt so angry. 'Nobody asked you to avoid it,' I said. 'You shared the most personal things with me almost as soon as we started dating. Yet you waited to tell me about this. We've been living together for two months – you've had plenty of time to bring it up.'

'That has nothing to do with it!' she snapped back. 'We don't speak about these things. Everything that happens in this lab, it's all very sensitive; we don't go around telling people about what we do here. Believe me – I wasn't just hiding it from you because I was afraid of your reaction.'

I didn't believe her for a second, and I began to see some of Craig's qualities in her: manipulativeness, an obsession with her goal, the desire to be more than everyone else. Maybe it was my fear suggesting these images. It didn't matter – I was ready to wholly accept her, but I couldn't accept the fact that she was going to consciously risk her life. My mind was already running through the worst outcomes.

'What exactly will you do? Can you explain it to me?' I asked, hoping I overreacted and it wasn't as bad as it sounded.

'First I will merge with Blank,' she began. 'Then we will get Blank to operate independently of my brain. Once this is achieved we will attempt to locate my soul and merge Blank with it. A group of scientists will be with me at all times, and will help me navigate from the outside. The entire process will be continuously monitored.'

'And you are going to live with this thing in your head for how long?' I asked.

She took a deep breath and held the air in her lungs, and I knew what she was about to say was worse than I expected.

'After my merger with Blank is complete, I'll be put in a state of unconsciousness to give us a better chance of locating and fusing with the soul. I will be under constant observation. If there are any complications, they'll bring me back.'

I completely lost the ability to speak. I wanted to throw up.

'Before that,' she went on, 'I will go through extensive preparation—'

'So basically you will be in an induced coma?' I asked.

'Yes.'

'But... I don't understand – why does it have to be you? Why can't it be someone else? Someone who is already in a coma?'

'To merge Blank with a brain, the host brain has to be healthy. At a later stage in the experiment I need to be able to switch between levels of consciousness and allow Blank to utilise my brain. And in any case, it can't be just anyone, it has to be someone with special training. Blank will be in a completely new environment. And as a self-evolving structure, it won't be processing information in the way we are used to. It will be like the most bizarre dream you could ever imagine, possibly similar in its nature to what you experienced at the *Undefined Presence* exhibition. I've spent years preparing for this, I've done countless simulations of all sorts of imaginable out-of-body experiences. It's like space travel – you need to have training.'

'OK, and when will this happen?' I asked, my voice shaking and breaking at the last word.

'I'm sending my application next week. Our applications are usually processed within a month, as we systematically work with dedicated Technology and Ethics Administration agents, and by the time they receive an application they are already familiar with a project. If it gets approved I'd like to test it as soon as possible – I hope it will help us detect the suicide trigger.'

I laughed. I couldn't believe this was happening again. I laughed at myself because I was such an idiot. I'd seriously thought this story, Aleece and me, would have a happy ending. I should have been cautious; I should have been afraid and on the alert. Instead I'd allowed myself to feel with my whole heart, and jumped into this relationship without restraint. And now what was I supposed to do? I was so deeply in love with her.

'Laura, you are not the only one who feels disconnected – most of us do. My work brings meaning to my life. I always imagined there was much more to us. I can feel it in my bones. I want to discover it, I want to open up my mind, to expand the amplitude of my experiences. I want to know what we are.'

I imagined her melting down to nothing and turning into the same ball of dust that was in front of us. And even if everything went well, what if she found something so special out there that she didn't want to return? I would be alone again. I already felt alone and so feeble in the shadows of her vision, and I saw very clearly that, no matter what I said, she would not change her mind. Still, I tried. She was my life – of course I tried.

'What if opening yourself up to something so superior means you lose the sense of this,' I said, touching her hand. 'As primitive as we are, things like this...' I brought her hand to my face and kissed her fingers, 'they have power too. Isn't this enough?'

She slowly withdrew her hand. 'Of course you are enough,' she said. 'You make me happy. But we have this incredible thing inside us. We can't just ignore its existence. We have to develop our relationship with it and start exploring its environment. Today it's a suicide pandemic, tomorrow it will be something else. It's not just asteroids and climate disasters that can wipe us out. There are other things too. These people didn't just kill themselves − something made them do it. I feel if I have something to contribute, it is my responsibility to do so.'

'Is that you or your father talking?' I asked.

'It's both of us − we share the opinion. Look, if my project gets approved and I get the chance to continue, I will have a team of the most qualified scientists in the country working with me. And human trials won't be approved unless the TEA considers it safe.'

I looked at that bodiless thing − although captivating, there was nothing trustworthy or safe about it. Tears started falling down my cheeks. 'What if something happens to you?' I asked. 'I won't survive another loss. Have you even thought about that?'

'Of course. That's why we are discussing it now. There are certain risks. But I promise, this is a relatively safe experiment.'

'Relatively safe? Aleece, this is unfair.' I pressed my fingers to my eyes, then wiped my nose with the sleeve of my white coat. I noticed glances from other rooms; Aleece noticed them too. She was getting more and more nervous, and looked like she was also on the verge of crying. 'Do you understand what you are putting me through? I'm in love with you. I don't have the strength to leave you.'

She shook her head but didn't say anything because her tears didn't let her.

I needed to get out of there – I was moments away from blowing up. 'Can I leave by myself, or do you need to check me out?' I asked.

'Laura, please…' She took a step towards me, but I stepped back from her. 'I don't want you to leave me. I've run many simulations, and the risks are minimal. Let me explain some more – or you can tell me what you'd like to know; how can I make you feel more comfortable with the experiment?'

'You've already explained,' I said. 'You will be in a coma. Very few people wake up from a coma, Aleece. Do you think I don't know that? That was the first thing I heard when I opened my eyes – Oh, you are so lucky, no one survives a coma these days. Comforting, isn't it?'

'This is different,' she said. 'It will be a medically induced state, controlled and reversible. And because my brain will be connected to Blank—'

'Because your brain will be connected to this thing that no one ever tested before… Don't even continue!' I marched outside, and she followed me, silently, through various corridors to the lift. We rode the lift down in silence. She escorted me to the main reception and said something quietly to the receptionist robot. Maybe she said something to me, I couldn't tell – I just stared ahead, seeing nothing, thinking nothing because I was so angry and in so much pain. I briefly registered a signal, a word or a gesture, that I could leave, and without looking back I walked outside the building and took a taxi home.

\* \* \*

She came home that evening, not too late, opening the door with her chip. I was high by then, lying on the floor. It was only as she stood over me that I realised I'd been lying on the floor staring at the ceiling for some time. Her lips moved, and she touched my face, but all I could think of was death. If things went wrong, I thought, I could always kill myself. That calmed me down. There was no guarantee, of course, as I'd already tried it twice, but hey, third time's a charm.

I turned on to my side and threw up. Aleece brought a pan and a wet towel through from the kitchen. When I had emptied my guts and there was nothing left to throw up, she wiped my face, placed a pillow under my head and covered me with a blanket – I was uncooperative, and she couldn't transfer me to the bed. That night I slept on the floor, and she slept on the sofa next to me.

In the morning she gave me a pill and helped me to get on to the sofa, where I slept for the rest of the day.

In the evening I still felt like shit. She insisted I eat something, and I did. Then I went to the bedroom, lay on the bed, pulled a duvet over me and asked her to sleep on the sofa. I was disgusting, and smelled awful – I didn't need her to smell that.

The following morning I felt better.

The morning unfolded slowly. There was a lot of silence in it. I avoided Aleece's eyes. I went for a shower, and after I got out she placed two plates with eggs and toast and two cups of hot tea on the table. After only two bites reality punched me in the gut and I burst into tears.

'Why is this happening again?' I sobbed. I buried my face in my palms and kept repeating the same thing.

Aleece walked around the table and hugged me. 'Laura, look at me,' she said, brushing her fingers through my hair. 'Look at me.' I pulled away from her stomach and looked up. 'This experiment will not be approved unless it's safe. There are always risks, but they are minimal. It's not that easy to die, believe me.'

'Your father probably owns the fucking place,' I snapped. 'Of course it will be approved.'

'No he doesn't. This level of technology is approved by international organisations – he won't be able to influence them. I promise you.'

'And there is nothing I can say that will make you change your mind?' I asked.

'No, Laura. If my project gets approved, I will go through with it. I've been training for this since I was thirteen. It's a part of who I am. If you choose to leave me, then after the experiment is over, I'll knock on your door, prove you that I'm alive and well and do all I can to win you back. That's my plan.'

I leaned my elbows against the table, covered my face, and sobbed harder.

Aleece squatted next to me and rubbed my leg. 'I was thinking. Why don't we go to therapy together?'

'Therapy?' I looked at her in shock.

'Why not? You've lost your parents. The fear of going through such trauma again must be debilitating. I have no idea how to help you deal with this fear, especially since I've caused it. And I need guidance too, because this situation puts a lot of pressure on me.'

'I hate shrinks,' I said. 'They are pretty worthless, from my experience.'

'Let's try it a few times and see if it's helpful. You never know. Let's work through this together. Please.'

I shrugged and told her we could try.

# 24

---

A week had passed since Aleece's project was rejected. Human and animal testing was prohibited. The board recommended some adjustments, but Aleece explained to them that these adjustments would stifle the main function of the technology. It crushed her – she was detached, withdrawn into her thoughts, and barely talked to me. All I could get out of her was 'yes' and 'no', and on better days she would say 'good morning' back. I ordered food and made her jasmine tea. When she wasn't sleeping or soaking in the bath for hours on end, she wandered around the flat like a ghost. I felt guilty because I was happy that her experiment wasn't approved, even though I could see how much it hurt her. There was nothing I could do about my feelings – I hated seeing her like this, but in my soul I was happy. This would pass, I told myself; it would take some time, but it would pass, and she would get back to normal.

Craig kept calling. On the rare occasions when she answered, their conversation was brief; she would hang up after telling him she was fine.

\* \* \*

'I'm ordering food,' I said.

Aleece didn't reply, so I ordered what I knew she liked. She was barely eating at the moment, but after a few shots of vodka her pain dulled and her brain usually acknowledged hunger.

The doorbell buzzed. That was the fastest delivery I'd ever witnessed. I tapped the touchpad of the intercom, and the screen blinked into life, showing a tall figure – it wasn't a delivery bot, it was Craig. I hesitated for a moment, wondering if I should ask Aleece before letting him in. My knees became unsteady as I imagined his overwhelming presence in my small, messy apartment.

But I let him in – he was obviously worried, and it was good for Aleece: he was her father, after all. I called out to Aleece to tell her he was coming up – an annoyed groan came from the bedroom – and waited for him at the door.

He appeared in the doorway, looking very out of place in elegant dark trousers, quarter-zip sweater and black knee-length coat.

'Hi, Laura,' he said, stepping inside the apartment without an invitation. 'I'm sorry to show up like this. Is Aleece here?'

I nodded and gestured to the bedroom. He stopped in the doorway and looked in.

Aleece sat cross-legged in the middle of the unmade bed, staring at the wall. 'What are you doing here?' she asked him.

'How are you?' he asked back.

'I told you, I'm fine. You didn't have to come all this way to ask me this and waste your valuable time.'

He lowered his head and, I noticed, his shoulders sank a little. He nodded to himself a few times, then looked up at his daughter again. 'You don't look fine to me,' he said.

'Can you leave me alone?'

'Darling, you need to pull yourself together. This behaviour is destructive.' He glanced at the towels and clothes scattered across the room, the half-empty bottle of vodka on the bed.

'You just can't help yourself, can you?' she snapped. 'Even now you need to tell me what I should do.'

'I'm not telling you what to do. I just hate seeing you like this. I'm worried about you. Drinking and beating yourself up won't solve anything. There is nothing to solve.'

'Just this once, save your speeches for later – I'm really not in the mood,' she said.

He walked around the bed so that she could see him and sat down. I went to the living room to give them some space, but left the door open.

'You should be proud of yourself,' he said. 'You've created something phenomenal.' There was a pause. 'What's on your mind?'

'What to improve,' she answered.

'There is nothing to improve. Blank is ready for testing. You know that as well as I do.'

'Well… then I'll just appeal and wait,' she said.

'Appeal? That will take years.'

'It's not a race,' she said. 'I see their point. Their concern is… valid.'

'Oh, darling, please don't lie to yourself. They don't have a point. I've read the report. It's ambiguous rubbish, riddled with loopholes. All I see is ignorance. Cowardice. They are afraid, Aleece. Nothing else. And it is a race – whether you admit or not, it is a race.'

'I'm not doing it. You're wasting your time.'

'It's just an adjustment. One technical adjustment, and you can take it outside the lab and into the world.'

My heart sank.

Aleece was silent for some time, so she must have been considering whatever it was he was proposing. 'And then what, Dad? Hm?'

'Nobody wants responsibility, Aleece. Once we test it and prove that it's safe, the TEA will be eager to approve it. Nobody will even ask you how you tested it in the first place. Let me worry about that part.'

There was silence again. I couldn't bear it any more.

'If they didn't approve it, it must be unsafe,' I said, walking into the room.

Craig hid his irritation with effortless grace. 'What's unsafe, on a global scale, is waiting,' he said. Turning back to Aleece, he said, 'Darling, you know how it works. You know the pressure the public puts on them. You can't just accept their weakness. As a scientist, you have a responsibility.'

'Exactly. I also have a moral obligation to fight against the way things are done. So how can I let you worry about that part?' Aleece looked him straight in the eye. 'Because of people like you scientists will always be scapegoats, and the TEA will be approving fewer and fewer projects. I'm not testing it unless it is approved for trials. Please leave.'

He scrutinised her for another moment, touched the side of her face with the back of his fingers – she didn't pull away, she was a frozen statue – then stood up.

'OK, think about it, at least,' he said, 'and please don't ignore my calls.'

Aleece didn't reply.

'I was thinking,' he went on, 'I would love it if you came home for the time being. Both of you.'

'I am home,' Aleece said. 'Thank you for your concern.'

The way Craig looked at her was very pointed, as if he was trying to memorise her every feature. He stared at her, thinking. Eventually he left the room, and I followed him to the front door. 'Will you walk with me, please?' he whispered.

We went down the corridor to the lift, where Aleece wouldn't hear us.

'How is she?' he asked me.

'Better. She eats, she sleeps,' I said.

'Have you noticed anything strange about her? Maybe she's said something, acted in an unusual way?'

'I wouldn't say so. Why?'

'It's a difficult time for her. She lived for this project. It's a hard blow.' He drew a deep breath and squinted a few times, his eyes studying my face. 'Can I ask you a favour?' he asked.

'Sure.'

'Don't leave her alone.'

'I'm with her all the time,' I said, my heart reacting to the meaning of this request faster than my mind, racing away.

'Good. Please watch her closely, and if you notice something unusual let me know immediately.'

'Are you afraid that…' I couldn't say it out loud; my voice trembled.

'I want to be prepared, that's all. If something does happen, do not call the emergency services. Call me. This is important, Laura. I will get here much faster, and I will be better equipped to help her.'

I looked down. His polished dark-brown shoes were in my field of vision, but all I saw was her face, devoid of life.

'Laura, it is important that you call me if something happens.'

'Why do you think…? Has she ever tried to…?'

'No, never. But nobody knows what can happen. So, once again—'

'I'll call you,' I cut in. 'I won't call anyone else.'

'Yes. And if you can convince her to come home, that would be even better.'

'I'll try,' I said.

'Thank you. She is very lucky to have you,' he said, and with that he squeezed my arm lightly and left.

# 25

---

A few days later Aleece received a call from her father, and everything began to fall apart. The world decided we had it too good. This was the beginning of the end. Craig informed Aleece that John's daughters had tried to drown themselves.

We drove to see John that same day. When he opened the door, my heart broke – even though he was standing upright, I saw a man on his knees, begging, praying, barely able to hold in his scream.

'How are you?' Aleece asked John after a long embrace.

'Doing my best,' he said. His voice was hoarse, his eyes red and swollen from tears and lack of sleep. 'This is Rick,' said John, introducing a young man who stood behind him. 'I think you've met.' Aleece nodded. 'Rick has offered to keep an eye on the girls while I get some sleep. Girls, look who's here!'

Nicky and Emily ran to the hallway. 'Aleece!' they shouted.

Aleece kneeled down, the girls wrapped their little hands around her neck and she squeezed them tight.

'Hi! How are you?' she asked. 'I've missed you so so much!' She kissed them on their cheeks.

John watched them jump around Aleece. They were so excited to see her. His lips quivered, and he had to swallow a few times to stop the tears from appearing in his eyes.

'Aleece!' They kept shouting.

'Do you want to see what we've got you?' Aleece asked.

'Yay!'

They went to the sitting room. Aleece pulled out two dolls from her backpack and passed them to the girls.

'This is my friend, Laura,' Aleece said, introducing me. I sat next to them on the floor. 'And Laura, this is Emily and this is Nicky.'

'Hi,' I said, greeting them. I had never interacted with kids before and felt a bit uneasy.

'Hi, Laura,' said Nicky.

Emily just glanced at me, too preoccupied with her new doll.

'Do you want to show Laura what other toys you have? I need to talk to your dad for a minute, and then we can play all together, OK?' said Aleece.

'No, play with us now!' Nicky shouted.

'Yes, play with us,' Emily repeated.

'I will in a few minutes. I told Laura about that puzzle game you showed me last time. Do you still have it?'

'Yes!' Nicky jumped up and pulled a big box out of a drawer filled with toys and games.

'Yes! That's it!' Aleece nodded. 'Do you think you can explain Laura the rules so we can all play?'

Nicky opened the box and started taking puzzle pieces out, ever so focused. It was interesting how quickly she forgot that she wanted Aleece to stay and shifted her attention to a new task. Emily remained seated and just looked at us out of the corner of her eyes, her lips pursed.

Aleece stood and left the room with John and Rick.

'You need to find matching pieces. Here, like this,' Nicky said, connecting two puzzle bricks together. A screen on each of the bricks activated upon connection and played a short cartoon. 'Now we need to find another connection so we can see the next movie,' Nicky said.

'And what happens when all the parts are connected?' I asked.

'Then you can see the whole cartoon, of course,' Nicky explained. 'But it changes. It depends on which parts we connect first. You understand?'

# CHAPTER 25

'Yes, I think I do. Emily, would you like to play?'

Emily shook her head.

'Why not?' I asked.

'She wants to wait for Aleece,' Nicky said.

'I see. What about if we play one round now and then we can play again when Aleece comes back?'

'No!' Emily screamed.

'Don't scream – it's not polite,' Nicky said.

'No,' Emily said in a calm voice, and Nicky nodded in approval.

'Is there any other game you want to play, maybe?' I asked.

Emily thought for a moment, ran out to the bedroom and brought back a book.

'Here,' she said, and passed it over to me.

It was a book about dinosaurs. 'You want me to read it?' I asked.

Emily nodded and they nestled near to me.

I opened the first screen-sheet, and the girls froze in anticipation. As I read, voice-activated images moved, showing individual species in detail. Emily and Nicky giggled and screamed, imitating big jaws and long horns, making roaring sounds, scaring one another. Their enthusiasm was contagious, and I caught myself thinking that I was also curious to learn about these giant creatures from the past. By the time I was finishing the book, I was imitating their sounds as well.

Aleece, John and Rick came back and we played a few rounds of the puzzle game. The girls were thrilled when bricks aligned and triggered more snippets of cartoon, and they hurrayed and jumped up and down as the story of the puzzle unfolded. It was hard to imagine that just a few days ago these two little girls had held themselves under the water in a bath, trying to take their own lives.

John did his best to relax and enjoy the moment. It wasn't easy; inside him raged an apocalypse, and his body gave it away. He shuddered occasionally, which was especially noticeable in his arms and shoulders. His eyelids twitched, and he could barely fit puzzle bricks into their respective sockets because his hands were shaking.

'Don't go!' Nicky said, wrapping her arms around Aleece's legs, as we were getting ready to leave.

Aleece squatted and hugged them both. She had tears in her eyes.

'Why are you crying?' Nicky asked.

'Just because I missed you so much,' she said. 'And because I love you so much.'

'We love you too,' Nicky said, and they both gave her another hug.

'Stay, then,' Emily said.

'I will come to see you tomorrow. We both will. Do you want Laura to come and play with you again?'

The girls nodded.

'Until then, promise me something – do you think you can promise me something?'

'What?' Emily said, curious.

'Promise me you'll watch out for each other. Can you do that?' she asked.

They nodded. At these words John had to turn away from us so his daughters wouldn't see their father cry. He retreated into the living room, where I heard him sniffling, and saw from behind how he rubbed his face.

'Good. I love you so much,' Aleece said, squeezing them.

Aleece touched John's arm, hugged him, told him to call her if he needed anything, day or night.

I kept swallowing, restraining tears; I didn't think I'd ever seen a man so afraid and so helpless. I embraced him.

* * *

For the very first time I feared whatever it was that forced people to kill themselves. I'd always blamed my parents – I was so hurt that I had never had a doubt it was their fault and their fault alone. Everything that happened to me was their fault – they were adults, and I was a kid. Grown-ups were big and had willpower. If they'd fought for their lives I wouldn't have been abused; I would have had some kind of life. My mind couldn't bend itself around this fact, although occasionally common sense whispered that they had been helpless against what had possessed them. Now I was witness to the curse of the abnormal suicide, and I had doubts – I wasn't sure about anything any more. Six-year-old girls couldn't just want to kill themselves.

'How is John?' I asked.

'Bad. He's bad. You saw,' Aleece said. After a few blocks she stopped in the middle of the road and said, 'I'm so afraid they are going to die.' She started sobbing.

'You don't know that,' I said, but I was afraid of just that myself.

'They're kids! Six-year-old kids! What do you want them for?' she cried out angrily, looking up to the heavens. 'What do you need them for?'

Tears rolled down my face. The future was suffusing with the same darkness as my past.

'Laura, these girls, I love them. I've known them since the moment they were born. I can't imagine what John's going through. What will it do to him? Will he have the strength to live? What for? His wife, and now his beautiful baby girls. He's such a good person – why him? He doesn't deserve this. Nobody does, but... Did you see him? That broken man? He's barely alive.'

'So... so... what's going to happen?' I asked.

'The girls will keep trying. That's how it usually is. John will have to watch them all the time. Someone will have to be with them. But until when? For ever?'

'Aren't there facilities where they watch you all the time?'

'Yes. Overbooked. There's not enough personnel.'

Nervous sweat dotted my skin, and my breath became too spasmodic and short to supply oxygen. I thought about John and the girls, but I also thought about Aleece and Craig's concerns. I thought I was going to throw up.

'If Blank was approved,' Aleece started, 'I don't know. Maybe. Although it would still take time, and who knows. There's no guarantee. Chances are high, though, very high. If I can do something, I must try. Right? Objectively, Blank is the best device out there that can detect it. The TEA is afraid. It's all fear. It can happen, yes, but with the right training...' She stopped her incoherent monologue and looked at me. 'Why is the world such a nasty place? There's nothing for us here.'

'What are you saying?' My hands shook, teeth clattered from fear.

'Let's disappear together,' she said. And just like that, she was suddenly unrecognisable, as though a portion of her had been replaced with someone else. 'I want to be a part of you – I want to become one, for ever.' Her voice was manic. 'Just like we dreamed, remember?'

'What are you talking about?' I asked.

'I will merge with Blank and we will release it into your body,' she said, nodding her head frenetically. 'One body, two souls, just like we dreamed. And then we let it take us to places, Laura, beyond all this, away from here. Two of us. There are things you can't imagine. It's outside the scope of what we can think of. You want to see it with me, right?' Her eyes shone with excitement. She locked her hands behind my neck.

I felt drizzle on my face. It was getting wet and dark, and everything repelled the deceptive pink of holo-banners and neon signs.

'Laura, we will see what life is. What's behind all this,' she said, looking upwards again. 'Do you want to do this with me?'

'Aleece, please, you are scaring me,' I said.

She smiled – it was an indifferent smile that made hair on my arms rise. 'Don't be scared, baby,' she said. 'I'm not losing my mind.'

'I don't think you are – I think it's stress. It was all too much. You need a good night's sleep.'

'Yes – why don't we go home, then, and rest, and sleep,' she said, voice like metal. It was hard to imagine this inflectionless voice belonged to a human.

An autonomous taxi pulled at the curb and drove us to my place. She stared out of the window for the whole trip, and I was afraid to take my eyes off her, as though she'd disappear if I did.

When we got home, Aleece took off her coat and her top. She stripped down to her underwear, came close to me and pulled my jacket off my shoulders.

'Aleece—'

'Shh, I want to feel you against me.'

'Aleece, I'm not in the mood right now,' I said.

'I just want to feel you,' she said, and kept undressing me until I had only panties and my T-shirt on. She moved her hands along my arms and shoulders, inhaling my smell. 'You are so warm, so soft,' she whispered.

The way she touched me, the way she spoke – I didn't know who she was. 'Aleece, what are you doing?'

She took my hand and pulled me to the balcony. The air was cold; goosebumps rose all over my skin and my nipples hardened. Aleece pressed me against the railing and hugged me from behind. It soon became freezing, and I shook, my teeth clattering.

'I want the universe to remember us like this,' she said, and her hand slid under my T-shirt, along my belly and up, caressing my breasts. 'I want it to remember how much I love you, how perfect our bodies are together. No matter what it does to us, this moment, us, we will always be in its memory.'

My heart drummed. Aleece kissed the nape of my neck. The weight of her body made me bend forward over the edge, and the height made my head spin. She kissed my shoulders, the railing digging deeper into my ribs.

'I love you,' she whispered. 'That's what I came here for – to love you.'

I turned around, and she caught my lips with hers. 'Aleece,' I said, and clenched her wrists before she could touch me again.

'What?' she asked.

'Tell me what's going through your head. What are you feeling?'

'I feel we should enjoy each other while we can.'

'Let's go inside, please,' I said.

'I don't want to.'

'What *do* you want?' I asked.

'I want you. And I want everything else to disappear.' Her eyes were out of focus. She looked through me, and her hand moved down my stomach and inside my underwear.

'Aleece!' I said, grabbing her hand. 'Stop!'

'It's really cold,' she said. Her voice had changed – she wasn't teasing any more. She went through to the kitchen.

I remained on the balcony with my hand over my mouth. I was in shock. I took a few deep breaths and told myself it was just stress – she was exhausted, that's all. First her project hadn't been approved, and now John's daughters…

Suddenly I was seized with fear and lunged back inside. *Can a person kill themself in just one minute?* But she was in the kitchen pouring a drink, I saw with relief. No, a minute wasn't long enough for that – but my mind was already running through scenarios – would it be a knife, a jump off the balcony… *No, she'd never. She loves life – she would never do that.*

She headed to the bathroom and started the shower, took off her underwear and stepped inside. She slid down the glass pane to the floor, bowed her head and just sat there, occasionally reaching out for the glass of vodka she'd placed on the floor just outside the shower.

She asked me to refill the glass a few times.

I knew it was time to call Craig, but I was so afraid he would take her away from me. She would be under constant surveillance – maybe at his place, maybe at his lab. Would I even be permitted to see her?

* * *

Later we lay in bed, and I turned to look at her. Her eyes were closed, but she wasn't asleep yet. 'I was thinking,' I said. 'What about moving in with your dad? Temporarily.'

'Why?' Her voice was tired and drunk.

'I think you could use his support.'

'Hmm, interesting thought,' she said, keeping her eyes closed. 'Don't be scared, my love. It's going to be OK.'

'What do you mean, Aleece?' I raised myself on to my elbow. 'Aleece?'

She didn't move.

'Maybe we will go to my dad's,' she said, finally. 'If you want. In the morning.'

I exhaled and calmed down a little. 'Tell me what you are thinking about?' I asked. I wished I could see through her, hear her every thought.

'Oh, well, many things. And nothing, really. I love you. I love my dad, too, even though he thinks I'm a freak. No. No, he's just afraid. I can't blame him, I guess.'

'What do you mean?' I asked.

'Mmm?'

'What do you mean when you say he thinks you are a freak?'

'Ah, nothing. You know, a droid baby. I'm tired. I'm going to sleep.'

I tried to ask her again, but she didn't respond. I watched her breath become light and even, and soon her lips parted – she was sound asleep. I watched her. I couldn't afford to close my eyes. There was more fear in the room than air, and adrenaline kept me awake. 'Droid baby', a child that was born possessed by artificial intelligence. I couldn't remember all the intricacies of the theory, only that the mother of a droid baby would die in childbirth. But then, so many theories attempted to explain the catastrophically high maternal mortality rates. There were alien babies, messenger babies – those who carried secret messages from other worlds. Portal babies – babies that served as actual portals. One search on my phone would have revealed dozens of articles about droid babies, but I was too scared to leave the bed and take my eyes off her for a second.

By the early hours, however, my eyes grew heavy, and I closed them, but just for a moment.

# 26

I woke up to a loud sound – someone was banging on my door. Outside my apartment I could hear voices – male voices – shouting. They were medical personnel, claiming to work for Craig. Aleece was in danger, they yelled, again and again. I darted out of the bed and opened the door. Two men ran into the bedroom. One of them had a syringe ready in his hand. Aleece started shaking. A white foamy fluid erupted from her mouth, flowed down her cheek and on to the pillow around her head – and then very suddenly the convulsion stopped and her body became still.

'What did you do? What did you do?' I cried, trying to get to Aleece, but one of the men grabbed me, dragged me to the living room and ordered me to stay away so that they could help her. They attached round patches to her body and read some information on their tablets.

Craig arrived about five minutes later.

'What was it?' he asked.

'I don't know,' I said, shaking my head. 'I don't know. I must have fallen asleep. What did she do?'

'Drugs – what did you have in your apartment?' he asked.

'I don't remember – a bit of everything. Um… antidepressants, insomnia meds, some, um… anaesthetics… maybe some, um…'

'Stimulants?'

'I don't know. Maybe,' I said. I tried my best to remember, but had no idea what could have been in my drawers.

Craig glanced at the doctors, and one of them nodded at him.

He didn't panic; he was calm. As soon as that registered, I realised I needed to follow his example if I wanted to stay with her. I breathed deeply, in and out, in and out.

What had I missed? She was feeling better. We ate. We went to sleep. She was calm. She had been drunk, but by the time we went to sleep she had seemed fine. But was that because she had decided to end everything? Had she only started to calm because she had found an escape?

They transferred Aleece on to a stretcher.

'What hospital are you taking her to?' I asked.

'She's not going to a hospital.' Craig said. 'Nobody can know about this. If anyone finds out she tried to commit suicide she will be taken to one of these overcrowded hospitals where no one can help her. Do you understand that?'

'Where are you taking her?' I asked.

Two men carried Aleece outside.

Craig made a step in my direction. 'Do you hear what I'm saying?' he asked, his voice betraying only a glint of impatience. I couldn't believe his self-control.

'Yes, I won't say anything,' I said. 'Where are you taking her?'

'To my lab.'

'I'm coming too,' I said.

'My team will take good care of her. I'll keep you informed about her progress,' Craig tried to reassure me.

'I'm coming with you,' I said firmly.

'I can't let you in – it's a restricted facility.'

'She's all I've got,' I begged.

'She's all I've got, too, and I'll do everything I can,' he said, and walked outside.

I suddenly felt dizzy; I couldn't imagine staying alone in this apartment knowing that Aleece might never come back. 'Craig, please,' I called after him. 'I've got no one. She's all I have. Please.' I followed him to the lift. He remained silent.

'She wanted us to be together,' I said. 'In one body.'

Craig pivoted about to face me. 'Did she? What exactly did she say?' he asked. He didn't look surprised, but he did look interested.

'She wanted to connect to that thing and release it into me so we can be together for ever,' I said.

He stared at me, looking right through me with his icy green eyes, analysing every breath I took, every twitch of my muscles.

'Did she talk to John?' he asked.

'We went to see him together yesterday,' I said.

'How did she take it?'

'Not good,' I said. How the fuck did he think she would take it?

'Did she say she wanted to die?' he asked.

'No,' I lied. She hadn't explicitly said it, but she'd implied it.

Craig lowered his gaze, thinking. 'I'll keep you informed,' he said.

'Craig, if she doesn't live, I won't either. Please – I can't lose her.'

The lift doors opened, he stepped inside and pressed a button. 'Don't be stupid. And don't disrespect those who had no choice in the matter.'

'I don't care. There is nothing here for me without your daughter,' I said. The door started closing, so I put my bare foot in the gap. The door touched it and slid back. 'All I'm asking is to be with her. She needs me. I love her. She needs me right now.'

His hesitation almost made me vomit. 'All right,' he said at last. 'Go and put on some clothes.' I was still dressed only in my underwear and a T-shirt.

'It's fine. I'll borrow one of those white coats,' I said. 'You must have them there.'

'Laura, go and get dressed,' he repeated. 'You're not coming with me to my facility in your underwear.'

'No,' I said, stepping into the lift. 'You'll just leave without me, I know it.'

'Oh, for fu—' he began, but cut himself off and walked back to my apartment.

I ran after him, and quickly got dressed in some jeans and a pair of boots, grabbing a coat on my way out — it took me less than a minute.

His driver was waiting in the deepest level of the garage. From there we dived into underground tunnels, and from what I could tell we drove north. At some point I lost the sense of direction — I hadn't driven in the tunnels much, as they were expensive. I knew only that we were driving further away from the centre. On the way, Craig made a call and gave his staff instructions. He also gave whoever he was talking to two names and requested their presence. From what I understood these two people were doctors. I replayed what had just happened and reached the conclusion that Craig must have been monitoring Aleece's vitals through her MedMU link — after all, it suddenly struck me, I hadn't buzzed anyone in, so the men who'd come to my apartment must have already been in the building. Which meant Craig had been preparing for this.

Eventually the car slowed and parked in a closed underground area with a private lift. One of the guards presented a small case with a touchpad. Craig scanned his palm, the door opened and we rode two levels up. This must have been Craig's second lab, because his main lab was inside one of the tallest skyscrapers downtown. We approached a small reception. A woman greeted us. It was hard to tell if she was human or a robot.

'Mr Nolan—'

'Escort Miss Jennet to the waiting room,' Craig said, without looking at her. He left, taking off his coat as he went, probably headed to where Aleece had been taken.

'Sign this, please.' The woman passed me a tablet.

I looked down at the tablet, which showed a page titled Non-Disclosure Agreement. I signed it without reading it, scanning my fingerprints underneath my signature.

A few hours later, a woman in a medical coat came into the waiting room and told me I could see Aleece. She accompanied me to Aleece's room, where she lay on a bed, with tubes stuck in her nose and mouth. There were silver circles attached all over her body, multiple wires connected to her head, both of her arms had needles in them, and a suspended bag of IV fluid hung next to her bed. Beside the bed was a set of monitors that showed Aleece's brain activity. The images on the screens were mostly dark. Everything around her beeped and blinked and hummed.

'How is she?' I asked Craig.

'Unconscious,' he said.

I did my best not to collapse – my knees were weak and tears blurred my vision.

'Laura, Laura,' Craig called. 'Someone will come to show you around.' He turned to the doctor. 'I'll be in my office – keep me informed if anything changes, please.'

'Of course, Dr Nolan,' the woman nodded.

I moved a chair closer to Aleece's bed and sat down. Thoughts wormed into my head, fuelled by guilt and regret. If only I'd called Craig sooner I could have prevented this. It happened so suddenly – I'd only closed my eyes for a second, really, just a moment, maybe a few minutes. I struggled to process what was going on. I couldn't believe it was Aleece that lay in front of me with all these tubes and cables attached to her body.

I tried to penetrate through her skin, connect to her core, send all my energy to make her stronger, to help her find the way back to me, to give her a reason to stay alive.

Later that evening Craig came back.

'You should go home – get some rest,' he said.

'I'd rather stay here,' I said. The thought of going home terrified me.

He examined the dark images of Aleece's brain. 'It can take days, weeks, maybe even months for her to wake up. You need to be patient,' he said.

'Are you sure she doesn't need to be in a hospital?' I asked.

'There is nothing they can do in a hospital that we can't do here. This is as good as it gets, trust me,' he said.

'So, what's your plan?'

He turned on his heels, as tall and steadfast as ever. 'To do everything I can to bring my child back.'

I was ashamed of my fear when he confronted me like this, with his stone-cold features and unquenchable eyes. How could he do it? How could he remain so calm? And why didn't he blame me for all this? After all, she overdosed on my drugs.

'But for now,' he went on, 'we wait. It is of utmost importance that you are discreet – she didn't attempt to take her own life; she never would have. This is my daughter – she is a fighter, and she is fighting something out there. And no one can help her better than I can.'

'Something made her do it, right?' I asked. 'Just like something tried to force John's daughters to…? That's what you're thinking?'

'And what do you think? You are her lover – you seem to have genuine feelings for each other. You must know her to some degree. Do you think she wanted to kill herself? To stop living?'

There hadn't been a moment when she lacked the desire to live, I thought, wiping my tears with the back of my hand. Her curiosity for life, her drive, her passion, her interest in food and music and books – and everything really – was so contagious it even cured my indifference towards life.

I shook my head. 'Will she…? Will she…?' I started sobbing, and felt like my knees couldn't support me any longer. I stretched out my hand to grab something to steady myself. Craig caught me, and I let all my weight melt into his hands. He wrapped my arm around his neck and half-carried me to a chair.

'Take her blood and give her something to relax,' Craig said to a doctor who had joined us in the room.

I didn't protest.

# 27

---

A week passed, and Aleece was still unconscious. She hadn't moved a muscle – not so much as a single blink. Doctors connected more wires and sensors to her head and body. I cried when they pulled her long chestnut hair into a ponytail and cut it – Craig kept the hair – and shaved her head. From what I understood, they were retrieving what was left of her mind in order to have a better chance of restoring it when her brain began functioning normally again. I didn't ask what would happen if it didn't start working. Everyone followed Craig's lead and stayed calm and professional, performing their tasks with an absolute lack of emotion, as if it wasn't Craig's daughter they were trying to save but a piece of machinery.

But Craig acquired signs of stress at last: occasional fist clenching, tension in his jaw, sharper determination in his eyes. He spent more time in his office and the lab than outside and came to see Aleece at least three times a day.

When I wasn't eating or showering, I was in her room. Sometimes they would ask me to leave and wait outside while they carried out sensitive procedures or needed to discuss something privately, and sometimes they took her to another part of the lab. I didn't go out at all. I had my own room too, with a shower, but as soon as I woke up every day I was back at Aleece's side. There was a toothbrush and some toiletries in my room, and a nurse brought me some moisturiser and something to wash my face with other than bodywash. Maybe I didn't look my best, but I had everything I needed.

At some point Craig grew tired of seeing me in a medical uniform while I waited for my clothes to dry, and he insisted I went home to get whatever I needed to look like a human being. I told him I didn't mind – I was afraid to leave, even though he assured me that nothing in Aleece's state would change in a few hours, and he promised I would be let back in upon my return. But I couldn't leave. I was too scared.

When the doctors weren't in the room, I sat by Aleece's bed and talked to her, mostly about us, our past and our future.

'I dreamed of you for two years,' I told her. 'You are a dream that came true – you can't just disappear.' There was something romantic about it, but now I wished I hadn't wasted my time on dreaming – I wished I'd approached her the moment I'd first seen her and spent every precious second with her, loving her, sober. And I wished she had told me that this disaster could happen. I would have watched her all the time, I would have prepared myself. But there again, of course, I might have never allowed myself to fall in love with her so deeply, and that would have been the greatest loss of my life.

As much as I tried to fight the tides of fear, my resistance to inner chaos grew thin. One day as I walked down the corridor to Aleece's room I finally let the thought fully form in my head. *She is not here; she might never come back.* I slid down the wall and cried silently.

Through the sound of my quiet weeping and sniffling I heard steps. It was Craig. He leaned over and offered me a grey handkerchief. I took it and wiped my face.

'Why don't you come with me?' he said. 'Let's discuss some options.'

*Discuss options? With me?* I didn't think he needed my blessing one way or another, but if it came to that, things weren't going well. I got up and followed him to his office.

'Please, have a seat,' he said, gesturing at a dark-green sofa and pouring two glasses of whiskey from a decanter on the sideboard. 'Here,' he said, passing me a glass. 'I think you could use it.'

He was right about that. I hadn't had a drink or taken any drugs since I'd arrived at the lab – not that it hadn't crossed my mind, but I was afraid that if I wasn't completely sober I might miss signs of life under Aleece's eyelids, her first unaided breath or her fingers twitching. The heat of the whiskey felt good.

Craig sat in a chair by the sofa. The collar of his light-grey shirt was unbuttoned and his sleeves were rolled up to his elbows. 'I appreciate your devotion to my daughter,' he said. 'She is very lucky to have you – it's rare these days.'

'Are there any improvements?' I asked, fighting the tremor in my voice.

'No, unfortunately not,' he said, and rested his elbow on the armrest, closed his eyes and pinched the bridge of his nose. Eventually he opened his eyes, but just stared ahead, like a living replica of *The Thinker*. My palms grew heavy on my knees, and I bowed my head and hunched over. Hope thawed from my body, leaving all my muscles limp.

'Did she tell you anything about Blank?' Craig asked.

'A little, yes.'

'I believe that if anything can save her, it's Blank. But she didn't want to go through with the experiment unless it was officially approved. And it won't be accepted for human testing unless it has been tested already and proven to be safe. That's how things work. So, Laura, what do you think we should do?'

My mind went blank for a second. 'Me?' I asked.

Craig shifted to the edge of his chair and rubbed his face. He was exhausted. 'I've been a shitty father. Maybe not the worst, but certainly somewhere towards the bottom of the lower ranks. I've been preparing for this moment for twenty-three years, and every single day I have lived in fear. And fear does strange things to you. I love Aleece, of course – she is my child.

But I never allowed myself to get close to her. Just thinking about the opportunities I missed with her is probably enough to make me lose my mind. That's why I prefer not to think about all the trips we didn't take, things we didn't see together, topics we didn't discuss. She'd start a conversation, and if I sensed it was going somewhere personal, I'd purposefully avoid it, stifle it with a superficial reply. It became habit – I didn't give it a second thought. So you see, I don't know her. I always thought I did, but no – to say I knew her would be a lie. I only saw in her what I wanted to see, and I'm saying it because I know very well what it means to know someone, to discover a person. I knew my wife – I knew her like no one else could; that's one of those rare gifts life occasionally throws us poor creatures: the opportunity to know someone and to be known by someone. But I chose not to be close to my child, out of fear: fear of pain, fear of getting distracted.' He chuckled and groaned. 'And since we're being honest, I felt betrayed by her. Not by her directly, but by her condition, this inevitable self-destruction. Yeah... well, by her too. Believe it or not, I blamed her sometimes... When my weakness got the better of me. It was for my own sake, of course – it helped me to stay distant. I blamed her for something I knew she would one day do to herself.'

He cleared his throat as if to put himself back on track.

'My main priority was to train her to always be on the alert, to stay as self-possessed and focused as I was. From day one I taught her to approach her emotions analytically, not to indulge them, but to read them, use them as signals to spot the enemy before it attacks. So...' He paused to take a deep breath, 'I don't have a damnedest clue what she would want me to do. That's why I'm asking you – what should we do? What do you think she'd want us to do?'

Hair rose on my arms from his honesty. 'Craig, I...' I tried to remember everything she'd ever told me, searching inside myself for hidden answers. But with her nothing was hidden

– it was all out there. I didn't even need to think, really – the conclusion was so obvious. 'She wanted to live. She wanted to explore. She wanted to love and be loved. She wanted to know me, and she wanted me to know her. She listened – she knew how to listen; she was interested in every word that came out of my mouth. Nobody could listen like her. And she wasn't afraid of being open; she wanted to feel, and she enjoyed feeling. Whether she'd want you to use Blank or not, that I cannot say, but I know she wanted to live, and live to the fullest.'

He buried his face in his palms and shook his head. I lost any real sense of what was happening. Reality was fluid and viscous – it felt like I could take it in my hand, grab a hunk of it from the air and mould it into something.

'What do *you* think we should do?' I asked Craig.

'I have only one idea,' he said. 'I don't know what else to do. Aleece and I have been developing Blank for years. It is ready and I'd like to use it. There is nothing to lose.'

'Nothing to lose... you mean she won't come back on her own?'

'No, she won't,' he said, and got up and poured himself another glass. 'It won't be entirely legal at this point. If the experiment is successful, it will be approved; if it fails, no one will know about it. Unless something goes really wrong. Can I rely on your discretion?'

'You have this thing, Blank? The one I saw in her lab?'

'I have an exact copy. As I said, I've been waiting for this moment since the day she was born, since my wife died. So, can I rely on you? This is the only chance she has.'

'I won't say a word to anyone,' I said. I didn't ask whether she knew he had a copy of it or not. I didn't care. I was happy he had it. And if I were honest, it really didn't matter to me if she wanted him to use it or not – I only cared about keeping her alive.

'Good. I think it's best if you leave today. For your own good.'

I stood. 'No – no way. I'm staying.'

'Our conversation incriminates you already should something go wrong. As far as I'm concerned, this discussion never happened.'

'Do you know what kind of life I lived before I met your daughter? There was not a single sober day, not one good thought in my head until I saw her. You think I want to go back there?' I asked. He remained silent. 'And I have a question – who will connect to Blank? You need a healthy brain, right? For this to work?'

'Ah, so she did tell you something. I have a couple of volunteers—'

'I want to volunteer.'

Craig chuckled. 'You have no training.'

'Maybe not, but you can teach me. What can't be substituted is my connection with her. No one can give you that.'

Craig rubbed his forehead, then his lips. He was considering it, I could tell, but there was something else.

'What's your concern?' I asked.

He took a sip of whiskey, rolled the liquid in his mouth, swallowed and said, without looking at me, 'You're too unstable.'

'I'm stable enough,' I said. Images of my chaotic sex life, drugs, booze, vomit, tears flashed in my mind in distorted glitches.

'The question is, will you be able to confront your fears? The fears and pain from your past, fears of your future? Because you can lose yourself before you even attempt to connect to Blank. Blank may have its own agenda. Once it connects to your soul, it will cater to its own needs. I have people who've been training for this for years. Her life is on the line, Laura. To get you in some minimally acceptable shape will take months. You'll just have to be patient.'

I couldn't leave. He would have to carry me out of here. Wherever she was was my home – everything beyond this place was hell, and there was no way I was stepping back into it willingly. My mind fed me only one scenario: if I left, the next place I'd see her would be a crematorium.

'Don't you think she'd want it to be me?' I asked. 'Our souls have already chosen each other. And she told me herself – those were her words: she wanted to connect to Blank and release it into me,' I said.

'I don't know that she'd want you to do this,' he said. 'And you shouldn't make this decision lightly – there are risks, particularly for someone who is unfit for the experience.'

'I'm pretty sure she would want to give me the chance to survive. After all, if she dies, I will too – I'm not going through the whole routine again. There is no way I'll ever be able to trust anything. And no shrink will convince me otherwise. I don't want to live life in constant anticipation of a new disaster. I've been there before, and I won't go back. No way. I'll never start a relationship again, and if I do, it will be a psychotic one, because I won't be able to get past the thought that something bad will happen. So no, I'm not taking anything lightly, I just don't see any other viable option. And if she must die, I'd much rather die first.'

He leaned against the sideboard, folded his arms across his chest and stared at me.

I suddenly felt like a complete idiot. I laughed. 'If I'm here, in your office, discussing this with you, clearly you want me here. You didn't have to tell me about Blank. So cut the crap.'

He chuckled, a sad unenthusiastic chuckle, keeping his eyes on me. 'The issue we have is that you don't give a damn whether you live or die. If we are to go through with this, you need to know why you want to live, apart from your desire to be with Aleece. Blank can manipulate you to keep your soul away from your body. That's what it's meant to do. It is designed to get us out of our bodies, and once we travel out, I personally doubt we will want to go back. It will be up to you to navigate back home, and unless you see some point in living, it will be extremely hard – if not impossible – for you to achieve this. And survive.'

I didn't reply.

'Laura?'

'What? I don't know what to say.' I spread my arms.

'Is there really nothing you value in life?' he asked. 'Nothing that interests you?'

I thought, and the longer I thought the more anxious I was becoming. I scratched behind my ear nervously. Nothing except Aleece touched me. I didn't need this life without her.

'An impression something made on you. It doesn't have to be big or loud,' Craig said. 'It can be very simple.'

I plunged into my thoughts again and searched for anything that stood out. 'During that experience,' I said, slowly, 'at the AI exhibition, I met someone. Something. Like another me, only in a different dimension. She told me that because she is here we are together, and because we are together, I'm never alone. She said it in her own way, but I think that's what she meant.'

'How did it make you feel?' he asked.

The memory of the event sent chills down my spine. *Never laura*. 'I don't know...' I said. Tears rolled down my cheeks as the feelings associated with the memory foamed into a powerful sensation. 'I don't think I can explain.'

He waited – he must have seen on my face that the answer was approaching the surface of my mind.

'I felt like... she was right,' I said after a time. 'I'm not alone, because to be alone I'd have to be an isolated self, a separate being. And back then, during that simulation, I knew that was not the case – that was not what I was, it was not what anyone could be. Ever.'

Craig nodded, half-smiled. 'This is a decent anchor. Collette is an acquaintance of mine – they could work with you on strengthening your relationship with yourself.' He scrutinised me in silence, his mind working hard on making a decision. 'My gut tells me to give it a shot, but my brain tells me I'm mad to even consider it. You are too emotional, have no discipline and are very easy to manipulate. But there is this voice in my head.' He wrinkled his face as though suffering from a brief attack of pain.

'Voice in your head?' I asked.

'Voice in my head. Not my voice. It keeps whispering, day and night, to place you in there, to merge you with Blank.' He shut his eyes, clicked his tongue. 'But I know for a fact that you are unfit. I'll be putting you in danger if I let you merge with Blank.'

'I don't care,' I said. 'I'm telling you again: if she dies, I die. I can sign papers to waive your liability – whatever you need.'

'I suppose you do have something no one else can offer – a connection with her,' he said. I didn't think he'd heard me – his eyes were out of focus as he tried to convince himself. 'If your alignment with her is successful, I suspect you could utilise her knowledge and training. And this girl has been ready for years – she knows Blank like no one else; she goes through simulations of other planes like it's her second home.' Craig shifted his gaze to me. 'Did Aleece tell you anything about the procedure?' he asked.

'She did,' I said.

'Did she tell you about Blank's potential, what it can do, how it can change us?'

'Yes, and I'm fine with it,' I lied. I didn't know everything; I knew very little. But I couldn't give two shits – I just wanted to save her; what happened to the rest of the world wasn't my business.

'And do you have any questions?' he asked.

'No.'

'Not even curious what could happen to you if something went wrong?'

'No. If Aleece dies during the process, just do me a favour: don't bring me back. Terminate me. Or if I'm a vegetable, same thing – don't let me wake up, OK?' I said.

He frowned. 'Laura, I don't think you've heard me. You need to have some determination. You need to stop talking like this. Aleece's life and the success of this experiment depend on your innate need to survive. So pull yourself together. If after a few weeks of training I still see this arrogant ignorance, this will be the end of it – I won't waste my time.'

Where would I dig up an innate need to survive? I wondered. This instinct had been washed out of people – it wasn't just me.

'I need an answer from you – don't just look at me,' he said.

'I understand,' I said. 'I'll work on myself.'

'OK,' he said, walking slowly towards the door. 'I'd like you to go home tonight and think about everything again.'

'I don't need to think,' I said. 'I've made up my mind.' *And I'm pretty sure you've made up yours.*

'Once you've thought about it,' he went on, ignoring me, 'come back and give me your answer. If you still want to go through with it, we'll start your training and prepare you as much as we can. We'll get you used to out-of-body travel, test your tolerance for mind-bending experiences, see how comfortable you can get with not having a body or mind. It will be similar to what you experienced during the *Undefined Presence* installation, only on a more profound level. And it will feel like a nightmare before you even attempt to connect to Blank. After that, it will be a whole another nightmare.'

I opened my mouth to say I was fine with all that and didn't need time to think, but Craig cut me off before I could say anything.

'If you are serious about it, go home, go out, do what you normally do, come back tomorrow and tell me what you've decided,' he said.

'OK, I'll go home if you insist. But—'

'I insist. You don't have a choice in this matter. And a little change of scene is good for you. I know it's hard with Aleece being here, but I'm sure she wouldn't want you to confine yourself within these walls because of her. Try to enjoy yourself a little. You might not get another chance.'

* * *

The apartment felt empty without her. I sat in a chair in the dark living room, smoking and drinking tea. The combination was awful, but the tea reminded me of her. My reflection looked back at me from a full-length mirror.

*What are you without a body?*

I walked to the mirror, pulling my T-shirt off, cigarette almost burning my mouth.

*What's a body without you?*

I dropped the butt into a cup, placed it on the floor and took off my jeans. I tried to memorise what I saw, all the subtleties of my body, squeezing my breasts and stomach, imprinting the sensation of solid flesh into the memory of my fingers. I clenched my neck and felt my heart pumping the blood; the beating was strong and steady, like an old-fashioned clock. My body was alive and self-sufficient, a world of its own, with its own rules and order, full of mysteries. Even though it was solid I could see how fluid it was. I looked at it and started to see myself differently — it wasn't my vision of me, it was someone else's vision of me. It was the junction between dream and consciousness, a confrontation between restraint and desire. A well of pain, a sky of hope. A prism that brought time and space together and gave them purpose. A mirror in which the dawn could recognise its beauty. A bridge where two souls in love could discover their existence. Was it really me? All of it?

# 28

My first day of training began in a dark and empty space. I attached a gel patch behind my neck as two assistants entered dressed in black elastic suits with sensors that allowed them to blend in with their surroundings. Their job was to make sure I wouldn't fall or bump into a wall or hurt myself in any way.

'Today your task is to simply observe how you feel – don't force anything,' Craig said. He left, going into the control room behind a glass wall, and switched on holographic screens situated around the perimeter. Everything turned black.

At first my body felt heavy, and then it became weightless. With every passing day of training I got more and more used to this feeling, and with each session I felt more comfortable outside my skin.

During the first week we covered three sensations: being in several different places at the same time; being alone amid nothingness; being inside others. When they saw I achieved relative success in these states, they submerged me into something new – where I dissolved, but still existed, as if my mind had died but I was still present. I felt different frequencies, a different energy, undetectable, untraceable, existing within its own laws.

'Now you know how it starts, accept it – don't fight it, don't try to define it, don't think about it. Accept it as a part of yourself,' Craig said, looking at the recordings of my brain going from bright yellow and red to almost complete darkness. I stood by his side. 'A few more sessions and this feeling will become natural to you.'

He was right. I recognised the signs of approaching disintegration and relaxed, allowing the sensation to guide me. Perceptible processes in my body – breathing, heartbeat – tailed away. I vanished, but still felt my presence in the particles that filled the space. Then they reversed things. I recognised this level of the simulation, and knew I would soon connect with other people, to their awareness, and I would be inside all of them at the same time; this was made easier because I entered this state when I was already without a mind of my own. From this position, being part of a collective experience, I started being able to differentiate and to extract individual memories and perceptions.

Then my feelings transfigured: everything I could comprehend was folding into itself. I recognised it, somehow, without having been in this state before, and I instinctively knew my dissolution was approaching. And I rained into waves that could not be seen, I percolated through the intangible mesh deeper into the strongest weave of existence – the passage of life, the impulse of creation.

I disappeared.

Craig's face emerged before me. My breath was stuck in my chest, and my body was paralysed.

He shone a bright light in my eyes. 'She's here,' he said to someone.

I perceived every mote of my being – every molecule, every string of energy, every chemical reaction – it seemed I knew every process happening inside me. Feeling my body on such a micro scale took a lot of my strength and stifled my perception of the outside world. I had to wait it out and let my senses get back to normal.

'How did it go?' I asked Crag, sitting up. I'd been put on a bed.

A smile raised the corner of his mouth. 'How do you feel?' he asked.

'I feel fine.'

A man in a lab coat detached transmitters from my body.

'You've made a significant progress,' Craig said. 'Do you feel more in control? You understand what Blank can achieve?'

I nodded. 'I do.' I could control my feelings, transform myself, jump from one state into another – and not only that: this was a simulation, not even a real thing yet, but instinctively I already knew what I needed to do in order to manipulate others' perceptions. It was a strange, new instinct, but I was certain that when I was in deeper strata of existence I would have all the tools I needed to create my own reality in people's minds. I could construct projections, determine how others saw me; I could induce changes in the brain, stimulate multisensory nerve cells, orchestrate synapses into my order, and it would be as easy for me as breathing.

'Right about now you must be thinking how easy it is for you to enter others' minds,' Craig said. 'This is something you should not do. Blank is naturally attracted to minds, as it can use them to construct its own worlds and thus multiply its presence and solidify its existence. To avoid it, you must implant your own impulse into it without suffocating its potential. It's a fine line – it's a skill one acquires with time. Unfortunately, we don't have much of that, but the good news is we can influence this process from the outside. Unless Blank takes you too far.'

'How will I know when is "too far"?' I asked.

'What you've just experienced,' Craig said, 'when you feel you are about to vanish and merge with that which is everything, that deepest immaterial fibre that holds us all together – that's when Blank attempts to suck you in with it and expand and do its own thing. If you allow it, you won't come back. It will dismantle you completely. When you resist it, it will try to manipulate you. It will use your memories, your fears, your pain, love – everything. I'd like you to have a few sessions with Collette – they have the ability to control and evolve their body and inner realm like no one I've ever met. They're an exceptional union of spirit and technology and have a profound understanding of both worlds. They will analyse your memories and psychological condition, and will make predictions about what Blank can and most likely will use against you – no, not "against you", I shouldn't say that, as it doesn't mean to harm anyone, it's just it will do everything it can to facilitate its own impulse.'

\* \* \*

A man in a white coat who I'd seen around before gave me a clear pill. 'Swallow this please,' he said.

'What is it?' I asked.

'This will ensure the connection and data exchange between you and the source.' He pointed inside the dark room I was about to step into. Collette was already there, sitting in one of the two chairs placed opposite each other. 'Mx Gerd will be able to alter your perceptions,' he added.

I hesitated, and my gaze shifted from the clear pill in my palm to Collette's placid blue face.

'Dr Nolan is monitoring you personally. You will be disconnected if something goes wrong,' the man said, interrupting my contemplation.

I swallowed the pill, walked into the room and sat in the chair. Collette's eyes were closed, their lips smiling. They wore a white wrap dress that emphasised their deep cleavage, and layers of semi-sheer fabric revealed their strong thighs.

They blinked their eyes open. 'Hello, Laura. It's nice to see you again.'

I felt my body relaxing, the tension melting and pouring out through my pores.

We looked at each other for some time. Soon I realised I wasn't looking at Collette any more but at myself; part of me was inside them and part of them was inside me, their perceptions fused with mine. They shared some memories with me, and I watched as two men adored Collette's curvaceous forms, attending to every inch of their corporeal kingdom, courting their large breasts and penis with hungry attention. It was a palatial feast, and the queen was being eaten. It looked so delicious that I felt a sudden need to put my own mouth to their hard nipple. Then I realised that this was how they remembered it – this was their association with this event, not my vision of it; they wanted me to feel the pleasure they found in having flesh. They wore it with appreciation – for not many species, according to Collette's mind, possessed such a whirlpool of emotional and physical sensuality as humans.

They swiftly leaned forward and took my hand into theirs, rotated it and stroked my palm.

The world started growing around us. Our experiences mixed in a new dimension. More and more particles merged with us as we disintegrated and spread across large distances in directions a mind could no longer comprehend.

'Such a large world, isn't it?' they said, their voice coming as an attribute of space around me rather than being spoken. Then everything disappeared, and as it did, I heard a question lingering in the air. 'Where are you?'

I focused on the void and filled it with the perception of matter, a fraction at a time. In the passage of the idea, I found the location of my still-empty particles, and then I found Collette's perception of these particles, and said, 'Here.'

'Very good,' they said. 'Now open your eyes.'

I did as I was told. They sat further away from me – much further than arm's length – yet my palm was facing upwards, and I felt Collette still holding it. They touched my fingers, clenched my wrist. I felt it; physically Collette couldn't reach me, but I felt their touch nonetheless.

'Now touch my hand,' they said.

I placed my hand atop what I perceived as their hand and felt solid flesh where there was only air.

'That's me,' they said. 'Now, show me you.' They withdrew their hands.

I licked my lips and looked down at my palms. 'You want me to touch you?' I asked.

'Yes.'

They rested their hands on their knees. To touch them I would need to physically get up from the chair and take four, five steps forward, but I knew that was not what Collette wanted me to do.

'You know how to do it,' they said.

And they were right, I did. In my mind I found their mind; I danced in it for a while and imprinted it into my matrix, all very instinctively. I saw one of Collette's hands rise, and I held it up. I felt their skin; they felt mine. My body was still in the chair four, five steps away from them. I touched their hand by altering their perceptions and making them feel me.

Today it was a simulation, but when I was fused with Blank, this would be reality.

'You have such soft skin,' they said, taking my hand – not my real hand in the flesh, but a simulation of it – and placing it on their neck. Sitting about five steps away from them I felt the beating of their heart, their pulse against my palm. 'Oh, you are good, darling, you are very good,' they said. 'Do you know why we do this?'

'To learn how to differentiate ourselves from others when we are outside the body,' I said.

'Precisely. And not just other human beings. There are many experiencing structures in the universe. We practise this to stay whole, to maintain our unit of consciousness as a separate experiencing system so that we can preserve our awareness of self and our relation to the world.'

The light came on. The black walls, ceiling and floor melted back into mirrors. I couldn't see myself in the room – Collette was there, but I was missing.

'Can you see me?' I asked and stood.

'No,' they said. 'Are you sure you are here?'

'Of course I am,' I said.

'How can you know with certainty that you are in this room and not somewhere far away?' they asked. The question itself pulled me out of the room and transplanted me into a very different realm. There were no hands or legs, flesh or mind that I associated with myself any more, just a faint presence humming in scattered atoms. I had to start remembering again, from the very beginning, from the very impetus of creation. Once I reached a relative concreteness, information began to return to me, and I started to stitch myself back together into a coherent whole from memories of my own, memories others had of me, from dreams, fears, desires. Where this data came from I had no idea, but it was available to me – all I had to do was send an impulse, a request of sorts. I finally managed to place myself in the room where I knew my physical body was located.

'Laura, if you are somewhere here, show yourself, make me see you,' Collette said. 'Make me see you, darling.'

What they wanted to see I wasn't sure – when they said 'show yourself', what did they mean, I wondered – what should I reveal? At this very moment I had no shape.

'What do you want me to see?' they asked. 'Show me how I would recognise you.'

I found their mind, twirled into it and breathed myself into it. They felt me as an inner balance and a sense of completeness, and finally recognised me.

'Oh, you are such a tease,' they said. 'You seduce me with serenity. But serenity is everywhere, darling. Give me something that you and I came to enjoy *here* – something that can only be enjoyed here. The pleasure of touch, perhaps? Share a tear with me, or laughter.'

Yes, of course! A body. But where was I? My body was gone; I could not return into it. Something kept it away from me – something didn't want me to unite with my physical self, and I was indifferent about it: it didn't matter whether I found my body again or not. Maybe I didn't want to find it at all. Here bliss was inherent; there pain was unavoidable.

But Collette kept calling, and because I couldn't sense my body anywhere, and didn't care to reclaim it, I found their mind again and painted myself in it. First I saw myself through their eyes, but then I submerged into what they saw, and they saw me very clearly – they even sensed the scent of my skin and hair. In the mirrors I saw my reflection. I exhaled loudly. The perception of solid flesh returned, and with it came memories and the understanding of where I was.

Collette held out both hands. I took them. They looked me straight in the eye, then made a gesture, a signal to someone else, and asked me to turn around. In front of me sat another me. A chill ran down my spine.

'Which one of you do you think is the source of your mental activity?' Collette asked.

When I thought of it in such terms the answer came instantaneously – the one sitting in the chair was the real me. But as soon as I reached this conclusion, I knew it was incorrect. In fact, I was certain that the opposite was true. My heart rate increased.

'Take your time,' Collette said. Their expression was calm, albeit more serious than before.

I tried the most logical thing, tracing back the impulse of my mind – if I created a simulation of myself I should be able to locate the source. But my impulse mirrored itself and broke into a kaleidoscope of sensations.

'Why does it do that?' I asked. 'Why doesn't it let me see?'

'Calm down,' Collette said. 'Look at her.' They gestured at the me that was sitting in the chair. In that body my heart was beating fast. 'And look at her. What is the difference between them?' Collette gestured at the me that was standing. That me also had a quick pulse and sweaty palms.

I covered my eyes with my cold fingers. My mind was blocked. As soon as I attempted to think about myself, all thoughts came to a halt. The other me sat in the chair, motionless. Her fingers twitched occasionally, and her eyes glistened like tears were about to fall.

Collette touched my shoulder.

'I'd like to stop,' I said. I've had enough.' But I immediately reconsidered. 'No,' I said. 'Keep me here.'

Collette made a circular gesture in the air, and the lights in the room changed to soft white, the mirrors gone. I was sitting in the chair, tears falling. I quickly wiped them away.

Collette sat across from me. 'You did very well,' they said.

'Why couldn't I return? Why couldn't I identify the real me?'

'First of all, there is no such thing as a singular real you, and once you've experienced that, it is hard to forget. You have a particular relationship with your physical body due to your childhood trauma. You don't accept yourself. You associate your body with too much pain. You are ashamed of what happened to you. For Blank it will be very easy to use these unpleasant sensations to manipulate you and keep you away from returning into your physical self. Luckily, you also have pleasant memories you associate with your body,' they said, and smiled. 'What you've experienced with Aleece, for example – those are beautiful memories.'

I felt only slightly uncomfortable that Collette saw me and Aleece making love; I'd glimpsed some of their intimate moments, and there was a certain ease and trust between us.

'We will work on strengthening these pleasant memories, nurturing your appreciation for them and your understanding that without your physical body nothing you've experienced with Aleece would have been possible. What can happen, however, is that Blank can block these good memories to make you feel that your body never had any worth. If Blank succeeds, you will forget Aleece and anything that reminds you of her. What can counteract most of such manipulations is your unconditional acceptance of yourself – one of the most difficult things a human can achieve in their lifetime.'

'Well, that's very cheering,' I said. It sounded completely unachievable. 'I'm supposed to use Blank to save Aleece, yet instead it might erase my memories of her? How am I supposed to find her if I can't remember her?'

'Oh, you will remember her,' they said. 'It's only when you attempt to return your soul back into your body that Blank may try to stop you from doing so by employing all sorts of psychological contortions. But at the searching stage, it will gladly cater to your desire to connect with her. And Craig will oversee the entire process, and he will have a good degree of control over Blank, and will be able to navigate it back and disconnect it from you – unless it travels too far. And it can only go beyond the point where we lose all connection with it if you surrender to it and embrace its course. So what I'm preparing you for is really the worst scenario.'

'And in my case the probability of this worst scenario is…?' I asked.

'High. I believe we will face a problem if it becomes apparent to you that Aleece won't return.'

'Well, I can tell you now and spare you the trouble,' I said. 'I don't want to wake up and find out that she died. So don't bother bringing me back. I don't want to come back if she doesn't.'

Collette looked at me for some time, her expression thoughtful and peaceful. 'It's not just up to you, love. You've made the most beautiful pact there is – the pact with life. And your soul loves every bit of it, otherwise you wouldn't be able to create a simulation of yourself so effortlessly. Your soul loves every particle of your flesh and every electrical impulse of your mind. The fact that you have a strained relationship with both your soul and your body is another matter, and we will work on that together. I will share with you how I managed to overcome a similar trauma, how I learned to love and appreciate my body, be it through accepting love and care others gave me or embracing and owning my pain. But in the end it will be your journey. Every journey is unique. That's why she came here, isn't it – that beautiful soul of yours my bird took you to? She came here for your journey and your journey alone. That journey started in your mother's womb, and it didn't end when you saw your parents in that wardrobe. And it didn't end when the priest betrayed your trust and invaded your body. You didn't die back then, even if it felt like it.'

Her words set something in motion. The threads of my being trembled and changed shapes. I began decomposing. Time opened its doors and let me out of my past. Through the fractures in infinite walls, I leaked back into the world where I once killed myself.

# 29

---

I heard dogs barking. Stray dogs. I knew exactly what dogs they were – I'd often seen them in my dreams, and I'd despised every bit of their nature, their desperate pointless yelp, their stench. I got up and looked around. I was in a dark, empty space with one door, nothing else, nowhere else to go but forward. I tottered to the exit, my throat closing with every step. I shook so much that I could barely stand on my feet. I cracked the door open, squinting in the bright sunlight. The barking grew more strident. I stepped outside and blinked a few times to clear my vision. The dogs formed a circle, growling, ready to attack.

'Shh, it's OK. It's me,' I said.

They paused, sniffed and broke into barking again.

I recoiled and fell, startled by the loud sound. 'Please,' I begged, raising my hand, 'give me a chance. I know I should have stuck by your side. Please, give me a chance to meet you again.'

The barking subsided. I looked at each dog – there were five of them – and slowly got up to my feet. They snarled, the fur electrified down their spines.

'You hate me,' came a voice out of nowhere.

'No, no. I… I did, yes. I'm sorry,' I said.

The figures of the dogs slowly transmuted into another shape – into the body of a girl I had forgotten. I thought I knew what pain was, but when I looked into her eyes I realised I knew nothing of it. I kneeled in front of her.

'Why did you leave?' she asked.

'I couldn't bear the pain,' I said, shaking my head. 'It was too much.'

'You were the only thing I had,' she said.

'I know. I'm so sorry.'

A tumour of sadness swelled in my throat. This was my twelve-year-old self, standing right before me. I never thought I'd remember her. She was skinny, with brown eyes and dark hair cut into a short bob, almost the same way as mine.

'Can you try to forgive me?' I asked the little girl I once was. I wouldn't blame her if she didn't. I had bleached her out of my memories, discarded her like so many others had done. How painful it must have been for her; I wasn't just someone, I was her, and even I had betrayed her.

'I was just twelve,' she said, her expression softening and tears appearing in the corners of her eyes. 'You were all I had.'

'I know. I know,' I said. 'And I want to learn to love you.'

She stared at me for a minute, then made a step forward. I held out my hands, inviting her to come closer. She touched my palm, and that touch speared through me, through every me that ever existed.

'Is it OK?' I asked before wrapping my arms around her.

She nodded and placed her hands on my shoulders. I embraced her, all of her: her pain, her shame and self-loathing – I embraced it all. The back of my shirt was getting wet from my sweat and her tears. Her body spasmed. I clenched my teeth so as not to scream, pressing her tighter against my chest. I had exiled her, but she had always been my torn root; without her I was an outcast to myself. Every breath we took together carried back love I'd lost fourteen years ago; every drop of my ocean filled with sense. I knew why I lived, and I trusted what I felt was true, because when I pulled away from my twelve-year-old self and looked into her eyes, I recognised the feeling with which my mother welcomed me into this world – I was enough.

I wiped away her tears.

'Let's get out of here,' she said.

I couldn't agree more. 'Let's get out of here,' I said.

We walked down an asphalt road. A faded white line ran down the middle. The grey surface morphed into green grass under our feet, and I sensed the familiar smell of pine trees and the salty ocean breeze.

'Is this your home?' she asked, looking around.

'It is,' I said. I noticed her eyes were brighter, her skin glowed and her lips were pink and healthy. 'Our home.'

As we moved away from the pine forest and towards the ocean, she noticed a hillock covered with branches. She let go of my hand. I kept my distance, allowing her to reach it first, take it in. The wind tousled her hair, and I saw from behind how she wiped her tears. She didn't ask questions; she didn't ask why I'd buried the priest who'd raped us, and I was thankful for that. I couldn't imagine ever making peace with it; whether he was dead or alive didn't change all that much – the pain was still there. But I'd made peace with myself, and that's what mattered. I hoped she felt the same way.

She took a lungful of air and exhaled. That deep breath released the shadow of the experience that had been lacerating her for so long. I felt the relief in my own body, as though she breathed with my lungs too and that breath liberated us both.

When we reached the cliff she smiled, her eyes widened and her mouth opened for more air.

The water was blue and calm, the line of the horizon blurred – the only boundary the ocean had now gone.

'It is beautiful here,' she said.

'It is,' I agreed.

'So peaceful,' someone said – I couldn't determine who; our bodies were merging into one.

The space around me started disappearing – I was sucking it back into myself. The pine forest vanished, the sky thawed, the white cliffs crumbled. I walked back, turned around and ran as fast as I could. I jumped into the ocean, drinking every drop of it as I swam deeper into myself, cleaving through obstacles Blank planted in the folds and corners of my mind. The water clawed at me, shoving me off course. I held all my energy in sharp focus, fighting Blank as it attempted to erase my memories, hurt me, make me vulnerable, prevent me from reaching my body. It fed me images of the priest and my dead parents. My screaming faces appeared everywhere. My heart ached, but this time I didn't refuse the pain – it was mine, and I consumed every iota of it, getting stronger, pushing harder through the darkness of my unconscious mind.

I was so close; I felt my body, heard my breath, could almost open my eyes.

The black water solidified into four walls. I was trapped. The walls moved forward, enclosing around me. My mind was shutting down. I had to leave before Blank destroyed it.

I took our fight outside my brain. Hanging between worlds, I unearthed every memory I ever had, trying to bring all my experiences to the surface, to gather all my knowledge together. I remembered that thing, that superior intelligence that had killed a third of the world's population, my parents among them, to free itself. I knew what I had to do. To separate from Blank I needed to harness enough energy to detach it from my soul. I needed death.

I masked my thoughts with desires of other minds and souls so that Blank wouldn't predict my actions, and darted into my past. There I searched through the memories of people I knew; I was in many minds at once, shuffling through events in their pasts. One memory stood out: a vision of a woman teetering on a bridge on the other side of the railing. I flung myself into her and saw the river beneath her fidgeting feet. She gripped the rough iron railing with all her might, rusty flakes digging under her short-manicured nails. She didn't want to let go, but something was forcing her to uncurl her fingers and shift her foot a little bit further. Damp hair whipped her wet cheeks, and her salty lips trembled. Her hands relaxed, her body swayed forward and the two little faces of her children were all she saw.

The river accepted her body without objection. A man pulled her to the shore. Another man – the man I knew – rushed over to them, shrugging off his sheepskin jacket as he ran. I watched how his brown lips touched her purple ones, but by the time he pressed against her chest, trying to wake up her heart, she was dead and her soul was leaving her body, becoming pure substance, ready to blend with everything else. There, entwined with it, was another essence, nearly unrecognisable, indistinguishable from consciousness itself – the entity I had met, the entity that had made that woman jump so that it could free itself; the very same thing that had killed my parents. I merged with it before it detangled itself from the woman's soul, and transferred every memory I had into it, everything I'd ever known or felt, leaving only a trace of pain in me so I wouldn't forget who I was. When that artificial essence possessed my every attribute, Blank fused with it too, thinking it was me, and I pulled all my substance, which was nearly empty now, from Blank's matrix.

The man picked up his sheepskin jacket, squeezed out the excess of water from its bottom part, and put it on. I flew into his head. He knew me well enough, he'd even witnessed my pain, and it would be no problem to restore myself through him. I assembled the memories he had of me and reinforced myself through his mind, crystalising them into a stronger image, becoming more alive with every step we made together.

The moment he had seen me at the bar, when I'd become real in his mind and the one-eyed bartender had poured us drinks, I summoned all my strength and flung myself back into my physical being. Life poured into my body. Every whit of my essence returned home.

# 30

---

My exhalation thundered through my head. My ribcage swelled and deflated; it hurt badly, as if my chest and belly were bruised, and it was this pain that finally woke me up. I heard voices. I wanted to give them a sign that I was back, but my muscles were deaf to my command. My eyes remained closed. I made several attempts to move, focusing on different parts of my body, and got an impression that my lips twitched.

'Can you hear me?' someone asked. I recognised the voice – it was John. He placed his palm under mine. 'Squeeze my hand if you can hear me.'

I did what he said. My finger twitched.

'She moved, Rick.'

I tried to squeeze his hand again; my fingers twitched again a few times.

'She can hear us,' John said.

\* \* \*

My awakening was fragmented; it was another few days before I could keep my eyes open.

'John,' I called. He was sleeping in the chair not far from my bed, but my voice was only a faint whisper, and he didn't hear me.

There were so many memories in my head, most of which didn't have an explanation, and I had so many questions, but right now I just wanted to see Aleece.

John shifted in his chair, waking up. It must have been morning – maybe eight or nine o'clock – I had a feeling. Through thinning clouds the blue sky was peeking out. The muted electric hum of cars drifted into the room from the streets. John rubbed his eyes before he opened them, and after seeing I was awake he heaved himself to his feet.

'How are you feeling?' he asked, checking the monitor with my vitals.

'I can't move anything,' I whispered. 'Is this temporary?'

'Yes. I believe you will be able to move normally in a few weeks.' John licked his lips, and the knots of his clenched jaw spasmed. 'Can you tell me your name, please?' he asked.

His question confused me, made me doubt my memories and perceptions for a second. But then he probably only wanted to make sure I hadn't lost my mind.

'Laura,' I said. 'Laura Jennet.'

He exhaled loudly. He didn't exactly lose composure, but it took him a few seconds to steady his reeled breath.

'Where am I?' I asked.

'In the Neuroscience Institute. You've been here before.'

'Yes, I remember,' I said.

'This is good. It's a good sign,' he said, nodding. There was awkwardness in his voice.

'Do you know where Aleece is?' I asked.

'We will have time to talk about everything. You need to rest first.'

'Have you seen her? Is she OK?'

'I…' he shook his head.

'Is she OK?' I wheezed. My voice died. My energy was spent – only my heart was still pounding hard and loud, eager to see her, to know she was all right.

There was a beeping sound and some of the readings on the monitor turned red. John picked up a small needle. 'This will calm you down – you need to get stronger first, then we will talk about everything.'

*No, no, John, please call her, please bring her to me. She doesn't remember, but she will. We saved her. She is alive. She survived. I will tell her everything and she will remember...*

My body relaxed and my thoughts withdrew from the race.

\* \* \*

When I woke up again, John was in the room, reading something on his tablet.

'Good morning,' he said. 'How are you feeling?'

'Better,' I answered, trying to stretch my stiff body. My voice was coming back. It was hoarse and didn't sound like mine, but it was a stronger voice. 'Have I slept the whole day and night?'

'You did, yes. It's good. You needed it.'

I tilted my head left and right. My neck and upper back popped.

Someone knocked on the door before swinging it open, and a young man came in. John waved him over.

'Rick,' I said. I was happy to see him.

He waved. 'How are you?' he asked. He was nervous, and his shoulder jumped up almost to his ear, his mouth twitching.

'Better. How are you?' I asked.

'Me?' Awkward laughter escaped his mouth.

Both men stared at me, and judging by the look on their faces, something was terribly wrong.

I tried to push myself up, which was quite an effort, as most of my body was still numb.

'Hold on, hold on. Let me help you,' John said. He raised the top of my bed to a more upright position. 'Laura... there is something I'd like to show you,' he said, pulling down the white sheet and blanket that covered me, taking my hand and holding it up so I could see it.

My heart froze – my skin was brown. I looked at my shoulder to verify that it was indeed my hand, and that it was attached to my body.

'What is it?' I asked, squinting, blinking, closing and opening my eyes.

# CHAPTER 30

'Try to stay calm,' he said. 'We've got to keep your pulse low.'

'Mirror,' I demanded.

'Yes, I'll bring it,' he said, glancing at my vitals, then picking up a small mirror and holding it in front of me.

My throat became dry and narrow. Aleece's face was in the mirror, the metal plate still attached to her chin. This was her, not me.

'Aleece,' I said. 'I'm inside her? My mind is in her body?'

'No, this is you,' John said. 'This is your biological body.'

'I don't understand.' I kept staring at the reflection – it was Aleece, the same as when I'd met her in Dirty Castle.

'We all still have a lot to understand,' John said.

The beeping started up again and the monitors went red. I took a deep breath and tried to calm down. Rick was shaking. John did his best to conceal his anxiety, but his throbbing energy gave him away.

'Leave me alone,' I whispered.

'If you want, I can give you a smaller dose of—'

'No,' I said, cutting him off.

'It will help you relax.'

'Leave. Please.'

'OK,' he said, placing a console next to my hand. 'In case you need anything.'

They left.

I closed my eyes and searched through my memories. Not all of them were back yet, and not all were complete. There were images that made no sense at all, and I wasn't sure a human mind could ever understand them. I saw Aleece and me in the same room, a lab, two beds side by side, both connected to machines that looked like steel cranes, both patched with sensors, but only one of us was alive, and it wasn't her.

\* \* \*

My condition was improving. I decided to hold off making any assumptions and spent all my energy on getting better. My recovery was slow, even though doctors kept saying I was doing great. A week later my legs were still paralysed, but at least I could sit upright and eat normal food.

Two agents from the Cybercrime and Technology Enforcement Agency appeared and attempted to question me. I told them I needed more time to understand my own thoughts. John explained to them my condition was still unstable and stress would make it worse. They ignored him, and kept pressing. 'Tell us anything you remember,' they said, again and again.

'How can I tell you anything if I can barely differentiate between when I'm asleep and when I'm awake?' I told them. 'Do you understand what I'm saying? Do you hear what the doctor is telling you? My brain is not working properly yet. I don't trust what I think or what I remember. Remembering is not possible for me now. Give me some time. Please. I'll answer your questions, don't worry, just give me some time to recover.'

They backed off.

A physiotherapist came in and took me to the pool. Water was good for me. I enjoyed being in the water, with that familiar sense of zero gravity. John joined us towards the end of each session to observe my progress.

'How long was I out?' I asked him when we returned to my room and another doctor and a nurse left. John and I had barely talked. I'd been postponing my questions for when I was physically ready to hear the full story.

'Over six weeks,' he said. 'But you were transferred here only fifteen days ago. You were quarantined in another facility. They had to make sure you were safe. I'm glad you woke up here.'

'Me too. Thank you,' I said. 'For saving me.'

'You saved yourself,' he said. 'There wasn't much anyone could do. You saved yourself.' He meant it. And he was probably right.

'Where is Aleece?' I asked.

John lowered his head and was silent.

'Is she alive?'

He moved the chair closer to my bed and sat down, his hands clasped, deep brown eyes on me. 'Laura, I'm sorry. She never made it. She died five years ago. I was at her funeral. There is a grave at Saint Angel's Cemetery with her name on. I visit it every time I go to see my daughters.'

'But she did make it,' I pressed, 'because I was with her. I met her in Dirty Castle.'

His prolonged silence was testing my hope.

'It was her. It was!' I insisted.

'There were fragments of both of you inside... your body, but it wasn't her or you. It was your body with fractions of Aleece's memories,' John said, and cleared his throat. 'And there is no such place as Dirty Castle. You were found in Craig's second lab, outside the city.'

His words activated my understanding of what had happened. Gaps started filling with context. Yes, he was right – Dirty Castle didn't exist, I'd created it. There was an obvious question on my tongue, and I already knew the answer – I knew what John would say, but I needed time to make space in my mind for the truth, so I asked anyway.

'And what was I? If this is my body, what was I all these years?'

John opened his mouth, then closed it again. His eyebrows were raised, and his eyes radiated empathy.

'You were a projection of yourself,' he said.

'What does that mean?'

'You recreated yourself in our minds.'

I just stared at him. I knew he was right before I understood how it was possible.

'But you scanned my body – you have the recordings of me.'

'Yes,' he said. 'But ultimately we saw what you wanted us to see. When Craig connected you to Blank five years ago, you could use it as much as it could use you. And what you could do with the human mind...' He kept on talking, so many words describing what it took me only a fraction of a second to remember and explain to myself. And of course, he was right. 'You made us see you, and it wasn't that hard for you to achieve. You could make us see, feel, touch, experience anything you wanted.'

He paused. He probably thought I needed a moment for this information to sink in and comprehend the nature of the form I'd been in these past five years. But I didn't – it was all very clear to me. I had seen and felt through other minds; I had created myself in those minds. I also knew myself through other souls and through intelligence that fills the void of every particle and breathes life into every living thing. I'd been one with the impulse that gives everything, from a blade of grass to a human being – the drive to survive. So, yes, at the very least I had invaded people's brains, and I remembered being in John's mind like I'd just left it.

'So far there are only speculations as to what happened. Craig hasn't given a statement yet. They are investigating Aleece's death, too. They have many theories. They want to know the terms and conditions of your initial agreement with Craig, if there was one. Beyond that, there are some big questions to be answered – not least whether Craig deliberately erased your memories and uploaded the memories he retrieved from Aleece's brain into yours? Or did he lose control over Blank and it was Blank that manipulated you all on its own to prevent you from re-establishing a connection with your physical body? In other words, was Craig's initial intention to keep your body for the purpose of using it to revive Aleece, or did the experiment go wrong? And another question that needs to be answered is, How did you start regaining your memories? What was the trigger? And why were your memories selective? One thing we know is that you were not dead – you were very far from being dead. You could access a higher range of consciousness, other dimensions. The power of the symbiosis between you and Blank, the scale of this intelligence was so vast, we can only guess what you were capable of.'

I could have answered these questions – only, at this point, I didn't want anyone to know what I knew. Craig had never tried to use my body or mind to recreate Aleece; he'd never uploaded her mind, whatever was left of it, into mine. That had never happened. It had been me who had changed my own body to look like Aleece. I'd tried to bring her back, to give her life. I'd refused to let her go, and so I made myself into her. I knew exactly what had happened and how it had happened, but I kept asking John questions because I couldn't bring myself to think about Aleece – I needed to postpone it, I wasn't ready.

'How did you come to this conclusion – that I was a projection?'

'We sent the recording Rick made of you to the CTEA to give them cause to search Craig's lab. They got back to us saying there was nothing on the recording except me staring into the air. Rick and I went to meet them, and as soon as they played the recording they saw what we had seen – but only gradually. Our experience of you must have transferred to them. I believe first you recreated yourself through the memories of anyone you were ever in contact with, and then these people transferred the representation of you to everyone they interacted with, and thus you multiplied, creating a stronger image of yourself.'

It was the correct assumption – of that I was certain.

'There were other bits and pieces,' John said. 'Your apartment was searched.'

'Why? They think I'm an accomplice?' I asked.

'The terms of your participation in this are still to be determined. At the time of the experiment, Blank was not approved for human testing. But there is no evidence that Blank was used. Nothing was found in you – no tech at all, no foreign objects except the metal plates. However, because of what you could do, how you manipulated minds and constructed realities, there was a concern for global security, so the CTEA didn't need a warrant to search your property. I was present during the search. They took videos and photos, made written descriptions of the apartment, laid out certain things, took record of them, then asked me to come in. I hadn't had any contact with them prior to walking into the apartment. The agents had to physically hold on to whatever they could because of the vertigo the change gave them – the way things were in the apartment, it all changed in a matter of seconds. There were so many details that transfigured on the spot – the placement of objects, furniture, appliances. Some things appeared out of nowhere, some things disappeared. Your reality merged with our reality and the two became one.'

'Did Craig know what I was all this time?' I asked – but of course he must have. How could he not have known if he knew Aleece was not really Aleece but me?

'Craig hasn't said a word – that's all I know. I don't know if he's waiting for your statement, and I'd rather not speculate.'

'And what about you?' I asked. 'Did you suspect anything at all?'

'I had no clue. Rick guessed it. When you were alone with him that night, he said something felt off. He sent me a message after we left the club and I went to your place. I disregarded it as both of you were high. I wasn't exactly able to think clearly myself. I mean, it was in the back of my mind that night, but I only took it seriously when Rick and I had a conversation after you'd already disappeared.'

'And how did you think of me after that? Did you think I was real?'

'You *were* real,' he insisted. 'You cannot think of yourself as being otherwise. When Rick told me what he suspected, it was hard to believe. Especially after that night – after we… In the morning I knew I hadn't been in charge of my mind that night. But…' He closed his eyes and rubbed his mouth. 'It was hard to accept that you had no physical form. But knowing what I now know for a fact, I can confidently say that everything that happened did happen to you: you made choices; you had real experiences. You lived through this. I lived through this. It was as real as reality could be.'

*I was real.* I thought about the hidden ad that had brought me to Craig. It was the last thing I could remember; before this memory there was a gap, a muddy abstraction that had lasted for nearly five years.

*Free yourself. Discover your true nature.* Was it Aleece talking to me or me talking to her? One soul trying to return to a body, another trying to escape from it? I wished that was true – I wished there had still been a fraction of her in this body when I'd met her in Dirty Castle. I wished it had been her I'd kissed on my balcony that night and not my recreation of her. But the truth was she'd been gone before I'd even connected to Blank and started my search for her soul. These metal plates hadn't been preventing her soul from leaving her flesh, they'd been stopping Blank from stealing my soul from me. By then she'd been gone for a long time.

I felt dizzy.

'Do you want some water?' John asked.

'Aleece didn't make it,' I said.

'No, I'm afraid she died five years ago when—' he started.

'I couldn't save her. I tried, I tried!' I cried. I couldn't stop the tears. I swelled from the pressure of the entire ocean raging in the shallow frames of my flesh. My mind left the room. I saw the blast of her star-like self-destruction – the memory that every cell of me remembered all too well, for every grain of my body was imbued with the energy of the woman I loved. She'd found me and given me the force of her entire existence, saved me after I couldn't save her. My every atom stayed intact because she held its particles together. In the end we were one.

I saw her in between the sheets, her freckled face next to mine. Her lips. Her thick eyelashes. My body remembered her every touch, every kiss. My heart felt her love, her care, her devotion. She had saved me. From the moment I'd laid my eyes on her and decided to see the world through sober eyes, till her final blast between galaxies, she'd been my compass that guided me towards myself.

The pain sliced through me like a blade. I heard my scream. John got up from the chair and hugged me, my howl blasting into his chest.

'I miss her so much,' I said.

'Me too,' he said. 'I miss her too.' I felt him invite pain into his soul. He needed to hurt.

# 31

I spent my days swimming, exercising with a physiotherapist on different machines, and going through thousands of tests a day. The marks from the metal plates that had been removed from my body were disappearing. I was changing, but I didn't rush the change. In fact, I could change in an instant – the control I had over my body was still phenomenal – but I didn't want anyone to know this. And there was no reason to rush it; gradual metamorphosis helped me heal and learn to appreciate every new morning. And every day was different; every day I saw something new and rediscovered something old that I'd never noticed before or had forgotten. I didn't want to miss a moment of myself.

John unfolded a towel when I climbed out of the pool. I caught his gaze sliding up and down my body. 'The transformation is happening so fast,' he said, noticing my skin changing back to my natural pale colour, my features transforming. He wrapped the towel around my shoulders. 'I don't think I can keep them away from you for much longer,' he said.

'It's fine, I'm ready to talk,' I said. 'I'm ready to go home.' I went to the shower. Steam clouded the room; water soothed my trembling muscles. In a glass pane I observed the parts of my body that had been freed from the metal plates. They were covered with rubbery protective patches. I touched the embossed edges of my skin where new cells were forming, paler than the rest of me. If I focused hard enough, I could feel the entire surface of my skin buzzing with the transformation. Soon it would just be me again, these marks would be gone and my body would be back, as though nothing had happened. That would be it – that would be all I would ever truly have.

* * *

John drove me home. I opened the door to my apartment – everything was upside down after the search. Things were scattered on the floor: my clothes, cutlery, chairs, rubbish, my meds and drugs strewn everywhere. Seeing my place like this felt like they'd invaded me.

'They are thorough,' John said, reading the look of desolation on my face.

I looked around. Why did they have to pull everything out – drawers, things from cabinets, a few books that Aleece had brought – everything was completely trashed. I proceeded deeper into my apartment, cautiously, as though it was an enchanted jungle full of predators ready to bite and sting, poisonous snakes waiting for me to reach for them so they could paralyse me.

'I took the liberty to hire a lawyer for you. Tomorrow he will give you a call and explain the situation,' John said.

'Am I in big trouble?' I asked.

John shrugged and shook his head. 'I don't think so. I hope not. But they won't leave you alone any time soon. Try not to think about it today. Allow yourself one evening to settle back into your life.' He gestured at the kitchen drawers that lay loose on the floor. 'You want me to help you with this?'

'They really gutted it,' I said.

'Yeah, they did. I have an hour or so if you want a hand.'

At first I considered his offer. But the longer I looked at everything that needed to be picked up and collected and moved around, the more anxious I was becoming. It all felt too alive, and I needed to handle it at my own pace and in privacy.

Every item breathed memories. I had to prepare myself before touching and opening and tousling these things. 'Too many memories,' I said. 'I'd better do it on my own.'

'Sure. I understand. I'll leave you to it.' He said goodbye, wished me luck and closed the door behind him.

As soon as I was alone my throat started narrowing; I thought I would suffocate. Absolutely everything reminded me of her. For everyone else it had been five years; for me her death felt like yesterday – no, not death. I still hadn't accepted that. But just yesterday she and I had been here. Just yesterday I'd replaced her fourth glass of vodka with a cup of tea, naïvely thinking that tomorrow we would have moved to Craig's place and everything would have been OK. Then these strange men had barged into my apartment, and she'd started shaking, thrusting life out of herself.

I ran outside. 'John! John!' I called.

He was already in the lift. He stuck his hand out between the doors, preventing them from closing, and stepped outside.

'I don't think I can do it,' I said. 'I don't think… It's too much. I can't do it. All these things – everything here reminds me of her. I can't go back.'

He squeezed my arms. 'Yes, you can,' he said. 'You don't have to do anything today. Just allow yourself to be present and remember. Grieve. You've been postponing it for a while.' He gave me a smile of compassion, and his eyes spoke understanding.

'John, the last time I walked out of this apartment they were carrying her on a stretcher. Right here.' I gestured along the corridor. 'I left with her. I never returned. I can't go back to this bedroom now. She was in our bed, shaking – so violently. And then they took her, and that was that, she never woke up.'

'Hey, come here,' he said, and wrapped his arms around my shoulders. I pressed tight against him and curled up like a little child hiding from a monster. 'I promise you it gets better. It never goes away, but it will get better.' It must have been the truth, otherwise how could he have survived the death of his wife, his daughters and Aleece? 'There is no quick fix for this. Time, that's all. Some days are better; some are worse. Some days you wish you never woke up. There will be all kinds of days. And today – well, today is one of those harder ones for you. Let it come, let it roll though you, let it hurt; but remember, you are not alone, and life is a bitch, but it's damn sure not short of miracles.'

I pulled away, raised myself on to my toes and embraced him. He had to bend a little so I could reach him. His shoulders felt like a mountain, and his arms around my back promised support for life. I knew I had a friend, and it made a difference.

When I was ready, I turned back to face what I had to face. I made a cup of tea, grabbed one of the chairs that lay sideways on the floor and sat at the kitchen table, which looked like an island amid the mess of clothing, furniture and mess. I thought of Aleece. The tea was tasteless, but even after five years there was still a hint of jasmine, and this smell made me sob so hard that in the morning I could barely open my eyes. It was a terrible day.

# 32

The lawyer John had hired to represent me called in the morning and asked if he could come to see me. During the thirty minutes or so that I had, I took a quick shower and put on some clothes. My face was swollen – no ice would fix it in thirty minutes. My apartment looked worse than me. I had no time to clean anything – I hadn't even started, and things were still scattered around exactly as the people who'd searched my apartment had left them.

When the lawyer arrived I opened the door and invited him in. He wore a suit under a mid-length coat, a briefcase in his hand. He didn't seem to care about the mess, he just needed a place for us to sit down. I pointed to the kitchen. He brought a chair to the table and asked me for a glass of water. Out of his briefcase he took out a square-shaped device and placed it on the table. A red light flickered and changed to green.

'Now we have some privacy,' he said.

I looked around. So they had bugged the place?

He offered me his condolences, and I told him he could get right to it.

'I will try to make it brief and to the point, as I understand you have a lot on your plate right now,' he said, and gave me an overview of the situation.

Besides my abduction – which was questionable, and the CTEA, he said, were considering, and considering seriously, whether I willingly took part in an illegal experiment – Craig could be facing charges of unlawful use of uncertified nanorobotics and artificial intelligence. He could also be charged with posing a threat to global security, which would lead to a life sentence. But so far there was no real evidence that would confirm that a banned technology had been tested – nothing except me. I'd been found in Craig's lab, and was the only proof that an experiment had taken place. But what experiment, and with what tech? That was unclear, because no tech, illegal or otherwise, had been found in me. They had found some machinery associated with Blank, but who could say that it had been used? Blank itself was somewhere very far away – at least, the copy that had been fused with me – and there was no way to trace it. Everyone was waiting for the two statements: mine and Craig's.

Besides John and Rick, a few other people had been questioned, and they confirmed they had indeed seen me. Based on my financial activity, which had probably been Craig's doing, I'd been alive and present these past years. However, my neighbours confirmed they'd started seeing me only a few months ago – before that I'd been away for years, they said. When my next-door neighbour was asked why she hadn't reported that a person had been missing, she said that if she'd paid attention to every junkie she'd have spent her life calling the emergency services. She was certain I'd overdosed and was lying in a ditch somewhere. She said it was so obvious and predictable that it hadn't even crossed her mind to report it. She also added that if I had died it would have been better, because at least my soul could finally leave this pathetic life and move on to something more dignified. In fact, she said she'd been surprised I'd made it this far living the life I'd lived, and she was sorry to hear that I'd survived.

My lawyer asked me to tell him what I remembered – to tell my side of the story from the very beginning.

At first I was silent – it wasn't that easy for me to talk about it. I really didn't know where to start. Where was the beginning of all this, anyway? I couldn't decide whether it began five years or millions of years ago – whether, indeed, it could even be measured in such thing as time. My memories were back, all of them, but as soon as I attempted to arrange them in some kind of order they hissed and wiggled and shifted, making it impossible to place my thoughts into words, and especially into coherent sentences. I explained this to my lawyer.

'Let me ask you some questions, then,' he said. 'Maybe that will make things a bit easier.' I agreed. 'I'm aware that Dr Lowe was trying to help you,' he said. 'At some point during examinations he concluded that the technology called Blank may have been tested on you. He gave you a general overview of what kind of technology it was – is that correct?'

'Yes.'

'Had you ever heard of Blank before you approached Dr Lowe, approximately two months ago?' he asked.

'Yes,' I said, 'but when I approached John I had no idea that I had.'

'And how did you hear about it the very first time?' he asked.

'Aleece told me about it. Five years ago, approximately.'

'When Ms Nolan told you about it, did you have any reason to believe the technology was dangerous?'

I took a moment to think. 'I thought it was dangerous for her,' I said. 'How dangerous it was overall I had no idea. That wasn't something I could determine.'

The lawyer nodded. He carried on the conversation in an informal tone and maintained eye contact, taking care not to make me feel like I was being interrogated.

'I understand that what you've been through during the past five years could have distorted some of your memories,' he said. 'And it will take time for you to fully recover. But based on what you remember now, do you recall agreeing to go through a certain procedure in order to help Aleece Nolan regain her consciousness?'

'I do,' I said.

'And did Dr Nolan mention the name Blank in connection to this procedure?'

'He did.'

'Did Dr Nolan explicitly mention – or did you have reason to believe – that to conduct this procedure an illegal technology would be used?'

'He mentioned something like that, yes,' I said. 'I don't remember the exact phrasing.'

'Did you think you might get in trouble for participating in this experiment?'

'Craig did warn me,' I said. 'But I didn't care. My alternative was to die.'

He paused – a moment of silence for something that could've happened but hadn't. He was good at his job: he didn't pretend that he cared personally, but he made me feel like he respected my experience. He asked me some more questions, then talked about the potential charges I could press against Craig – mishandling of illegal technology, negligence, withholding information, to name a few.

'I don't want to press any charges,' I said. 'I just want to be left alone.'

'I understand. Unfortunately your life will be disrupted for a while – I think it would be wise to prepare yourself for that. As far as charges against Dr Nolan, you've lost nearly five years of your life, and he obtained valuable data for his research during these years,' he said.

My life had ended with Aleece's death. I had no life to lose. What would have happened had I not been connected to Blank, flying across the peripheries of different realms, was very clear to me – I would have attempted to kill myself. 'I asked him to use me,' I insisted. 'I volunteered. He told me there were risks, and I was fine with that. I'm not pressing any charges. But my account was drained every month – I'd like my money back.'

My lawyer insisted that the monetary compensation I could receive from Craig was far greater than the amount withdrawn from my account. I told him that I would think about it, but I was becoming tired, and asked him if we could continue tomorrow. I asked if he could arrange for me to visit St Angel's Cemetery. I was under house arrest, he said, or a form of quarantine, so while he would try to secure permission, it was unlikely to be approved. I would not be allowed anywhere before I gave my first official statement, he explained, and that would not be for some time, as detectives needed me to return to my original self first – they were waiting for my body to return to its original form. They would be monitoring changes in my appearance and questioning me systematically, but nothing of it would be final until I was Laura Jennet in the flesh.

\* \* \*

The next day my lawyer informed me that Craig's legal counsel had requested a meeting: there were certain things Mr Nolan would like him to hand over to me in person. But most importantly, Craig had issued his statement.

I said it was fine with me, and so it was that I found myself sitting at my kitchen table with the two lawyers. I brought three glasses of water through while my lawyer switched on his little bug-choking device. We went through introductions, formalities and condolences.

'Ms Jennet, trauma can alter how we perceive reality,' Craig's attorney said. He was a man in his late fifties with dark skin and a soothing voice. 'You lost the woman you loved, and you've spent the last five years in a state that we don't fully understand. In fact, even though countless simulations of this experience have been conducted, you are the very first person to undergo the procedure. I've consulted various independent experts, and as I understand it, it is very likely that what happened to you put a tremendous strain on your body and mind and could have affected the way your brain reconstructed your memories.'

He pulled out a paper copy of Craig's statement and passed it over to me. I wondered about the legality of sharing this with me, but I wasn't surprised.

'This statement was made under oath,' he said. 'On the next page you will see Mr Nolan's signature and fingerprints.' He summarised a part of the statement relevant to me as I read through it. 'Mr Nolan confirms that approximately five years ago, when his daughter, Aleece Nolan, went into a coma, you agreed to a procedure that would consist of collecting your memories of her in order to reconstruct her identity. Mr Nolan used a modified version of the technology called Blank. This technology had not been authorised yet. He says that you were not given any details about this technology apart from an overview of what it would do – namely that it would copy and transfer your memories. Mr Nolan states that you were not informed about the legal aspects of the procedure. He also emphasises that you were not capable of forming a judgement about the nature of the technology, as you didn't possess the theoretical background that would allow you to understand it. However, you were educated about all the potential risks, including possible severe brain damage and permanent memory loss.' He pulled out a paper and showed it to me. 'Do you recognise this document?'

I looked at it. It was the agreement I'd signed, and it included a list of all the possible side effects.

'I do,' I said.

'And is this your signature and fingerprints?'

'Why is he admitting to this?' I asked. 'Nobody can prove Blank was used. I can guarantee that. Blank is gone.' I tapped my temple. 'And believe me, it's not coming back.'

'He is admitting to it because he is a scientist and he believes in what he does. He and his daughter dedicated their lives to this invention,' he said. 'And it worked.' He proceeded in a delicate tone, reminding me of a doctor speaking to his patient. 'And more: it worked not on a candidate with a special training and expertise, but on a person with a history of suicide attempts and drug abuse, which characterises many people these days. I'm not emphasising this to diminish you in any—'

'It worked?' I asked. 'How can you say that? How can he think that? I've been somewhere else, who knows where – a place I wouldn't even be able to explain to you or anyone else – for five years. I created my own reality, manipulated people's minds. And you're saying it *worked*? So what was it supposed to do, exactly? All I know is it didn't bring Aleece back.'

'It did not. But you are alive, Ms Jennet – alive by choice. It took you nearly five years to make this choice, and it was a very difficult journey, no question about it, but you are alive and well.'

I remained silent.

'There is no exact destination we want Blank to reach,' he went on. 'We don't know what we are searching for; we are still at the very first stage of this exploration. Like any other exploration it must start with the first steps into unknown territory.'

'But I could have hurt somebody,' I said. 'I certainly had the ability to hurt many people, to cause major disruption. Is Craig aware of that?'

The lawyer was silent for a time. I realised I'd just confirmed that in my opinion Blank was indeed dangerous. I cursed inwardly. I really didn't want to be dragged into this – didn't want to be questioned, involved in any way. The problem was that I *was* this case – what other evidence did they have but me?

'That was a risk my client was willing to take, and the responsibility lies with him,' Craig's lawyer said. 'You haven't hurt anyone or caused any damage knowingly or otherwise. Let's be clear about that.'

He and my lawyer exchanged glances of mutual understanding.

'During the last four years,' he went on, 'adjustments have been made to ensure Blank's safety. Do you know how they used to train dogs in the military, a long time ago, and what happened to them after their mission was over, Ms Jennet?'

'I have no idea,' I said.

'A dog was taught to obey only one specific person – a handler – and it responded to commands from only that person. Once a dog completed its service or, for one reason or another, a dog's handler left, the dog was put down. The animal was considered dangerous without its handler – it was too unsafe for other people. A similar idea will be applied to Blank. Once it is paired with a brain, it will only be able to interact with that particular brain, and if it comes in contact with another brain it will shut itself off. It won't like it, so it will avoid such situations. There are other safety protocols that have been implemented to prevent Blank from taking charge, and none of these discoveries would have been possible without your participation. No simulation allowed us to witness what we saw when Blank was actually fused with your brain. We got a much better picture of how Blank operates and how we can control it. Your contribution—'

'I don't want to be involved in any of this,' I said, cutting him off. I looked from one man to the other. Their regretful expressions made it apparent that I wouldn't be left in peace.

'I understand you would like to put it all behind you,' Craig's lawyer went on, 'but your position is unique, since you are the very first – and so far the only – person to undergo such a transformation. Whether you want to contribute to this research once things have cleared up will be up to you – nobody can force you. But you should expect certain pressure from various authorities until the case is resolved. And you will most certainly be subjected to different examinations for the next... I'd say a year, possibly longer.'

'Well, that's amazing news,' I said.

There was silence for some time.

'How's Craig?' I asked.

'He sends his regards. He is very glad you are back and safe,' the lawyer said.

'I assume I can't see him?' I asked.

'Not at the moment. His movements are somewhat restricted. I can't give you an approximation of when it will be possible for you to meet him. Meanwhile, he is happy to provide any assistance he can – financial and anything else you may need. He asked me to give you this.' He took out an envelope and a folder with some documents from his briefcase and pushed them over to me. 'You can look at it in private and decide what you want to do with it. If you need to contact me, feel free to do so through your lawyer.'

When Craig's lawyer left, my lawyer went over everything with me again. It was all very simple, really. There would be no trial – the authorities didn't want this to be public knowledge. Blank was too big an invention, and demonising it from the start was not in their interest. Besides, it could've started an unfavourable chain reaction. Many projects had been approved after illegal testing had been conducted, and nobody wanted to attract attention to this fact. The best thing I could do was to keep my mouth shut and not speak about Blank to anyone – I understood that even before my lawyer advised it. A sum of money had already been deposited into my bank account to cover part of the charges made over the last four years; more would be coming to compensate me for my time and participation. And probably silence. I didn't protest.

\* \* \*

When my lawyer left, I opened the envelope and read Craig's letter.

*Dear Laura,*

*I'm happy to know you came back and are in good health. As you might have already heard, Aleece put up a fight, but unfortunately her heart stopped. Her funeral was a small, private affair. I want to believe she had a full life, and I can confidently say that meeting you was the best thing that ever happened to her. I've never seen her so happy, and from the bottom of my heart I thank you for that.*

*I must confess, I had not expected such an outcome. I underestimated you. I underestimated your courage, your strength and your pain – and I catastrophically underestimated your love for my daughter. A more honest way of putting it would be that I didn't honour it. I will be frank: I didn't want Aleece to get distracted; our research was too important. Now, looking back, if I could choose only one thing for her in this life, it would be meeting you. I thought this research gave her meaning, and I still believe it did. But loving you was her umbilical cord to life. And yours too. The persistence with which you tried to bring her back, transforming your body into her likeness, replacing yourself with her, left me utterly speechless. I will never forget the day when you opened your brown eyes – her eyes. I asked you what your name was, and you answered calmly in her voice that your name was Aleece. I attempted to reverse the process, but no matter what I did, you kept insisting on being her. I waited.*

*When I saw you, when you came to my laboratory – or Dirty Castle, as you called it – I thought I had started hallucinating. I thought I had started losing my mind. It was such a sweet thought. Finally, I could stop fighting and just be and grieve and hurt. Ah, I could finally relax. But of course, it wasn't a hallucination. It was you.*

*Allow me to clarify certain events that took place after your return. No doubt you know the truth better than I do, but I must, for my own sake. Everything I told you, I promise, everything I asked you to do at Dirty Castle was not a product of my mind – I was not acting out of my will but yours. I had no control over my actions or words, not even thoughts. I assure you, what happened with the priest in my laboratory was a mere simulation, which I believe you created – none of it involved real people. I don't mean to say your experience was not real; I'm merely saying no real people were hurt.*

*I was very glad to find out that you and John have reinstated your friendship. He is one of those rare people with a big heart. He is a rather conservative type when it comes to science – but I'm not going to reprimand him for that in this letter – and he is certainly much more courageous than me when it comes to feelings.*

*I will conclude by saying that you've had an unmeasurable impact on my life. What this impact is I haven't yet begun to understand, but I can't deny its profoundness.*

*In case you are wondering: yes, I have regrets, but that's a whole other conversation, and I don't deserve to have your or anyone else's understanding – nor do I seek it. I will attempt to connect with you as soon as it is possible. I understand after everything you've gone through you may not want to see me again, and if that's the case I will accept and respect that. But should you decide to reach out, or if you ever need anything at all – anything – please know that I will be beyond happy to hear from you.*

*You went on a journey no other human has ever embarked on, and you've returned. This gives me hope that there is purpose to all this.*

*Sincerely,*

*Craig*

I sat in silence for a long time, wiping away tears, letting the words of the letter settle. I knew I would read it again soon and I would think about everything in more detail. But I couldn't find strength to do it now – the emotions where overwhelming. For now, I placed the letter back in the envelope and put it on a bookshelf, where a few of Aleece's books stood.

I opened the folder that Craig's lawyer had left for me. Inside was a stack of documents. The first page showed the photo and name of the priest who'd raped me. My heart jumped into my throat. I flipped through the papers. There was a list of potential witnesses and victims, names of witnesses and victims who'd already given their statements. Those statements were included. I returned to the very first blank page, where a note and a business card of a lawyer was attached with a paperclip. I unfolded the note and read it.

*Do with this as you please. Expenses are covered.*

# 33

---

They tested and checked and examined me over the course of the next month. After that, a conclusion was made: I was indeed Laura Jennet; I had no implants or any other technology in my body, I didn't pose a threat to society, and I wasn't capable of manipulating people's minds. I hoped they were right. I gave my statement, which aligned with Craig's statement. My ankle bracelet was removed. All the same, I wasn't allowed to leave the country, and I still had to show up for scans and tests every two weeks. I signed a pile of papers that more or less forbade me to talk to anyone about my experience apart from a few officials from some institutions I'd never heard of, who, apparently, I would be hearing from on a regular basis.

As soon as I could move freely, I went to St Angel's Cemetery. *Daniel and Marie Jennet.* Their names were etched on a square steel plate below a small glass cell on the seventh floor of the cemetery tower. Inside the cell were two white tubular jars containing their ashes. I sat on a bench and felt what I was supposed to feel: pain. No more guilt, no more anger, just a cleansing mourning that was long overdue. I spent some time in silence crying, then talked to them a little. I'd still have to get used to the feeling that I now had parents I wanted to think about and remember.

I visited Nicky's and Emily's grave. Opposite was a bench facing them, and I could picture John sitting there. One day soon John and I would return here together.

I walked up, following the curve of the wall, reading names, calculating how old people had been when they had died, how long they had lived, how many members of the same family had died. When I finally reached the ninth floor and faced the plate that read *Aleece Nolan*, the earth shifted under my feet. I blinked to clear my vision and read the rest of the text under her name:

*Gift of Diana Nolan's love, the mother she never met*
*Daughter of proud father Craig Nolan*
*Soulmate of Laura Jennet*

# ACKNOWLEDGEMENTS

I started writing this novel after shutting down my newly opened fashion brand, as I continued searching for something that would align with me and bring me enough fulfilment to scare off the fear of uncertainty. But without one person in particular, this pursuit would have been much more daunting and might have had a very different ending, and it is to him that I owe my eternal gratitude. After reading the initial ten pages of what would eventually become *Never Laura*, but which at the time was merely a collection of words sniffing out a direction, my dear friend Simon Mundy fortified my courage to start a new chapter in my life and run blindfolded into the unknown. Thank you, Simon, for your mentorship, for believing in me and advocating for this book. You have made a profound impact on my personal journey, once again, and serve as a living testament that some people enter our lives not by chance but with purpose.

This book would never have seen the world if my publisher and editor, Will Dady, had not taken a chance on it. Thank you, Will, for seeing this project for what it was and putting your hard work into it. And for designing such a stunning cover!

I'm immensely grateful to my husband, Dean Lyras, for providing a safe, creative environment where I can dream and be shamelessly unreasonable, for being my best friend and supporting my every new endeavour, and for reminding me that there is life outside my head and it is well worth participating in and enjoying.

I must give a shout-out to my older brother, who on nights when our parents were away and he was tasked with taking care of me either smuggled me into nightclubs, where he played drums for alternative metal and hard-rock bands, or hosted wild parties at our place. It's safe to say this book wouldn't be the same without these post-Soviet teenage experiences. And thanks to my parents for trusting that we were good kids, even when they returned to a flat completely in shambles. We were good kids. To my little brother, who still holds a grudge because he was too little and missed all the fun, I suggest you blame it on Mum and Dad – they should have conceived you sooner. Jokes aside, I love that we challenge each other, mostly because we bring more fun to family gatherings, but also because it is through these differences, as well as our intrinsic understanding, that we enrich our lives as individuals and strengthen our bond as siblings. I adore you, family.